Evi Hartmann

B-to-B Electronic Marketplaces

GABLER EDITION WISSENSCHAFT

Business-to-Business-Marketing

Das Business-to-Business-Marketing ist ein noch relativ junger For-
schungszweig, der in Wissenschaft und Praxis ständig an Bedeutung
gewinnt. Die Schriftenreihe möchte dieser Entwicklung Rechnung tra-
gen und ein Forum für wissenschaftliche Beiträge aus dem Business-
to-Business-Bereich schaffen. In der Reihe sollen aktuelle For-
schungsergebnisse präsentiert und zur Diskussion gestellt werden.

Evi Hartmann

B-to-B Electronic Marketplaces

Successful Introduction in the Chemical Industry

Mit einem Geleitwort von Prof. Dr. Hans Georg Gemünden

Springer Fachmedien Wiesbaden GmbH

Bibliografische Information Der Deutschen Bibliothek
Nationalbibliografie; detaillierte bibliografische Daten sind im Internet über
<http://dnb.ddb.de> abrufbar.

1. Auflage Dezember 2002

Alle Rechte vorbehalten

© Springer Fachmedien Wiesbaden 2002
Ursprünglich erschienen bei Deutscher Universitäts-Verlag GmbH, Wiesbaden in 2002

Lektorat: Brigitte Siegel / Nicole Schweitzer

www.duv.de

Umschlaggestaltung: Regine Zimmer, Dipl.-Designerin, Frankfurt/Main

ISBN 978-3-8244-7768-5   ISBN 978-3-663-09446-3 (eBook)
DOI 10.1007/978-3-663-09446-3

Foreword

In the past companies focused on the one hand on rationalizing their supplier base to reduce transaction costs. On the other hand firms tried to take advantage of the research and development potential of their suppliers. Due to these developments buyers put emphasize on the establishment and maintenance of long-term supplier relationships. The primary focus was not the success optimization of single procurement processes, but rather the long-term perspective of supplier relationships has moved into the center of attention. Furthermore, global procurement and joint product development became commonly applied approaches.

Nowadays most firms have been captured by the developments of the E-century. The establishment of electronic networks between business partners promises competitive advantages. Referring to success stories such as General Motors the application of new information technologies (e.g. E-procurement) seems to be necessary. However, past empirical studies do not confirm a relation between corporate success and the application of new information technologies. These studies do not analyze the decision process for using these new tools. They cannot reveal, if and why the IT application in supplier relationships is necessary and which benefits can be realized. Furthermore, it is questionable, which value the classical approach of supplier relationship management has.

Therefore, it seems important to examine the circumstances, which support the application of E-tools. This is the approach of Evi Hartmann. She focuses on B2B E-marketplaces, which can be utilized to support the procurement process of industrial goods. She analyzes the advantages of B2B E-marketplaces from the buyer's perspective. Her results are based on the outcome of an empirical study in the chemical industry, an industry, which has proved - besides the automotive industry – as being highly progressive in adopting the E-environment.

Her basic assumption is: There is not "the" success of "the" B2B E-marketplace. The fit between a given purchase situation and the adapted B2B E-marketplace concept determines the level of success. Depending on the business environment and the status of implementation of the B2B E-marketplace concept the success varies.

This complex background leads to the theoretical and empirical analysis of three areas of impact:

1. The characteristics of the purchase situation
2. The characteristics of the B2B E-marketplace
3. The characteristics of the implementation process of B2B E-marketplaces.

The special value of this study comes from the detailed literature analysis of all three areas of impact, which is the basis for the development of the theoretical framework. Additionally, Evi Hartmann's professional experience as a management consultant in the chemical industry enabled her to select the relevant literature. The operationalization of all constructs of the theoretical framework proved as reliable and valid in her empirical study, so that diagnostic tools could be derived for management and academics. The derived hypotheses have been empirically analyzed by applying various multivariate methods. Therefore, empirically supported recommendations can be drawn.

All in all the study fulfills the criteria "relevance and rigor" and gives directions for management and future research.

Prof. Dr. Hans Georg Gemünden

Acknowledgements

This dissertation could not have been written without the support of several people.

In particular I thank Prof. Dr. Hans Georg Gemünden, my doctoral supervisor, for his outstanding support and personal backing during this study. Especially his pressure in the beginning concerning the delivery of various papers made it possible to stick to a tight time frame.

I also appreciate the exceptional support and help of Prof. Dr. Thomas Ritter. His detailed and honest feedback combined with his special humor enabled me to work efficiently and effectively.

Furthermore, I am grateful to Prof. Dr. Michael Lingenfelder for his fast and positive review.

Especially I would like to thank my employer A.T. Kearney, in particular Dr. Werner Kreuz and Thomas Rings, who enabled my PhD study as part of my career development supported by a financial scholarship.

I am grateful to all the professionals, who participated in my empirical study, for their input and the spare time they spent on answering the questionnaires.

Finally, I would like to say thank you to my husband, my family and all my friends – without their help and understanding this study would not have been possible.

Evi Hartmann

Table of Content

Overview of Figures

Overview of Tables

A   THEORETICAL PART

1   Introduction

1.1   Developments in E-procurement

In the past, the strategic meaning of procurement has increased dramatically. Growing competition, the trend to globalization and internationalization forced the executive management to pay special attention to benefits that can be gained from management of and cooperation with suppliers. Especially since the establishment of electronic marketplaces and internet-supported trading, which builds a new dimension for purchasing with reduced interpersonal contact but transactional focus, the procurement process has gained a new perspective.

Deciding on suppliers' roles and relationships goes far beyond the simple question "make or buy" from a strategic standpoint. Today the question is how to position the firm's manufacturing capability to maximize the benefits that can be derived from combining the strengths of in-house skills and capabilities with the strengths of their suppliers (Lyons et al. 1990). It is essential for both supplier and buyer to understand the costs and benefits of the relationship to be able to accrue any competitive advantage. The supplier's perspective as customer relationship management (CRM) has been traditionally in focus (Zeithaml 1988, Kleinaltenkamp et al. 1996, Stone et al. 1996, Zeithaml & Bitner 2000, Hesse 2001, Mirani et al. 2001), whereas the author focuses on the buyer perspective how to optimize the relationships with the suppliers. Different aspects, such as buyer business impact, supplier market competitiveness and relationship attractiveness, have to be included in the evaluation process before defining the appropriate purchasing strategy (Fiocca 1982). The purchasing concentration impacts the buyer's commitment to specific investments (Stump 1995), similar to the volume contribution of a supply (Dubinsky & Ingram 1984, Burt 1989). Price is not the only issue determining the purchase strategy. "Price takers drive down prices – and get the quality losses that drive up costs" (Burt 1989, p. 127). With a portfolio concept all these various interdependencies can be integrated to develop the appropriate management decision (Turnbull 1989).

Statement 1:   *Determining the purchase situation is the cornerstone of supplier relationship management.*

Electronic commerce is expanding at a phenomenal rate. This is particularly true in the business-to-business sector (Baron et al. 2000, p. 385). Similarly, the procurement department is undergoing a transition from a paper economy to a digital economy. A variety of different opportunities is available enabled by the internet. Although the internet is up to now primarily used as an information tool in the procurement department, innovative purchasers approached further optimization potential and started to use the internet for improving the bottom line.

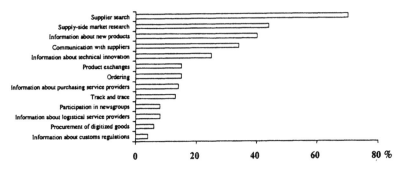

Figure 1.1 Overview of usage of the internet in the procurement department (Portum 2000, p. 5)

The internet provides a transparent means of communication between suppliers and buyers. Many firms have been concerned about obtaining a market advantage by adopting the new B2B E-marketplace solutions.[1] They were afraid about the technical, organizational and market issues and desired a cost/benefit analysis. However, the implementation of the appropriate concept can lead to material cost reduction, process cost reduction, cycle time reduction, transaction cost reduction, reduced error rate, inventory reduction and increased transparency (Baron et al. 2000, p. 403). Apart from these quantifiable savings, intangible improvements can be realized, such as better process integration with existing business processes, reduced number of technological problems and improvements on operational (e.g. integration in legacy system) and strategic issues.

Statement 2:   *The internet opens a variety of new opportunities for optimizing the procurement process.*

---

[1]   For definition refer to chapter 3.

The internet enables different phases of collaboration. Focusing on transactional aspects, purchase orders or invoices can be transmitted computer-to-computer. Furthermore, the trading partners can share and exchange information. They can provide product designs and specifications, which are the basis for product descriptions and prices. The order status can be electronically confirmed, but also critical information such as sales forecasts, production schedules or inventory levels can be exchanged (Fulkerson & Shank 2000, p. 422). The collaborative approach refers to trading partners jointly developing plans, e.g. new product plans or new product designs and technical specifications. Depending on the concept, different objectives can be realized. Various parts of the supply chain can be optimized: inventory, administrative and information flows, production and transportation cost (O'Leary 2000, p. 432). Aspects, such as greater flexibility in choosing partners, or shorter sourcing cycle time, more responsive supply chain network or reduced search costs and errors, can also be in the center of the procurement strategy (Tan et al. 2000, p. 462).

Statement 3:   *The selection of the appropriate B2B E-marketplace concept has to be adapted to the purchase situation.*

From a procurement perspective, various research has been investigated in sourcing strategies (e.g. Dobler & Burt 1996, Piontek 1997, Strub 1998, Hahn & Kaufmann 1999), supplier selection practices (e.g. Ellram 1990, Pearson & Ellram 1995, Bouchard 1998) and supplier relationship management (e.g. Hutzel 1981, Geck & Petry 1983, Freiling 1995, Wildemann 1996, Kiedaisch 1997, Gierke 1998, Hildebrandt & Koppelmann 2000, Wertz 2000). Additionally, detailed analysis has been executed in the area of relationship management (e.g. Gemünden 1990b, Ford 1997, Ritter 1998, Ford 1999, Gummesson 2000, Sheth & Parvatiyar 2000)

On the other hand a variety of reports does exist in literature (e.g. Wichmann & Weitzel 1999, Kafka 2000, Phillips & Meeker 2000, Ploss & Johnson, 2000, Harbin 2001) covering different B2B E-marketplace business concepts by discussing the spread of advantages and disadvantages.

However, prior research does not provide an integrated model for evaluating the purchase situation and selecting the appropriate B2B E-marketplace concept. The author tries to close this research gap, which can be summarized by the following statement.

Statement 4:   *In the literature a satisfying tool for the appropriate management of*
                      purchase situation and B2B E-marketplace concept is missing.

1.2   Objectives and structure of the study

These four starting points mentioned above have built the author's motivation for how to
successfully design new B2B E-marketplaces for given purchase situations. She is interested
in the appropriate fit between purchase situation and B2B E-marketplace concept to optimize
the relationship success. Additionally, the author wants to analyze the effects of the
procurement environment and the project management in introduction projects of B2B E-
marketplaces.

The study details the following questions:

■ *How can the purchase situation be determined?*

For answering this question the author gives a detailed literature overview about the existing
research work for classifying the purchase situation in chapter 2. Based on this literature
review, she derives a new concept by combining various important dimensions for
characterizing the purchase situation.

■ *Which different B2B E-marketplace concepts do exist?*

In chapter 3, new trends due to the internet are reviewed. Based on a literature review various
concepts of E-procurement are discussed. Finally, a new concept for classifying B2B E-
marketplaces from a relationship perspective is derived.

■ *Which factors contribute to the success of B2B E-marketplace introduction projects?*
■ *Which levers guarantee a successful project management of such introduction projects?*

In chapter 4, the introduction project of B2B E-marketplaces within the procurement organizations is discussed. After analyzing the different aspects of the project success, the appropriate components for a successful project management are characterized.

- *What is the appropriate fit between purchase situation and B2B E-marketplace concept for optimizing the relationship success?*
- *Which impact does the procurement environment have on this fit?*
- *Which impact does the project management have on the project success and the relationship success?*

Chapter 5 discusses the author's hypotheses concerning the appropriate fit between a given purchase situation and the appropriate B2B E-marketplace for optimizing the relationship success. The author also includes the effects of the procurement environment in her analysis. Next, she focuses on the project management of such introduction projects of B2B E-marketplaces and their impact on the project success and – consequently - on the relationship success. Finally, the hypotheses, that have been derived, are summarized in a theoretical framework.

For the empirical validation of the theoretical framework, which is detailed in the second part of the study, the author has conducted a study of the chemical industry in Germany with 119 companies. In chapter 6 the process of data gathering and the data sample is introduced. Chapter 7 covers the operationalization of the various constructs, whereas chapter 8 details the statistical approval of the theoretical framework by using the software package SPSS.

- *How can companies improve the management of purchase situation and B2B E-marketplace concept for optimizing the relationship success?*

The results of this study are summarized in chapter 9. Based on the theoretical and empirical findings managerial advices are derived. Finally, future research areas are identified.

Figure 1.2 provides a graphical overview of the structure of the study.

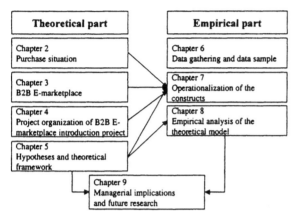

Figure 1.2 Content and structure of the study

2   Determining the purchase situation: Cornerstone of supplier relationship management

Due to the enormous benefits that can be gained from cooperation with suppliers increased strategic attention has been paid to this issue. Accordingly, procurement has moved to the agenda of senior management. Modern procurement approaches are reflecting this changing emphasis towards the importance of quality and innovativeness of suppliers as opposed to pure price negotiations (Hakansson & Eriksson 1993). However, different approaches are suitable for different purchase situations depending on the specific circumstances the buying firm embraces. Detailed evaluation and analysis of the purchase situation are even more crucial to a company's sustainable success, since new ways of interacting, such as electronic marketplaces, are developing fast and changing the way firms cooperate.

In this chapter the importance of a detailed analysis of the purchase situation is discussed. The author points out the significant changes in procurement (paragraph 2.1). Then different classification models of purchase situations are structured by identifying the underlying dimensions (paragraph 2.2). The different indicators are grouped in four dimensions. Based on the literature review (paragraph 2.3) the commonly used portfolios are discussed (paragraph 2.4). Then by combining the major dimensions an overall integrated classification model is developed (paragraph 2.5).

2.1   Developments in procurement

The field of procurement has evolved significantly in the last two centuries. The growing pressure of global competition and less internal value creation has led both, academics and practitioners, to the recognition, that procurement is an important contributor to a firm's competitive advantage (Reck & Long 1988, Jekewitz 1992). An appropriate sourcing strategy can contribute significantly in order to increase profitability, market share and technological innovation. This increased importance of procurement relates to three classic criteria of industrial performance as "cost, quality and technology" (Donada 1999, p. 1). Clear developments include supply base rationalization, longer-term contracts and relationships, increased outsourcing of professional and staff functions and acquisition of components rather than individual parts (Lyons et al. 1990, p. 29). Companies increasingly outsource activities to suppliers in order to specialize and to focus on their core competences and thereby become more effective and efficient (Gupta & Zhender 1994). Due to this increased outsourcing of production to external suppliers (Brandes 1994, Dubois 1994) and the decreased degree of vertical integration (Grant & Gadde 1984, Lamming 1989, 1993, Ford et al. 1992) the suppliers are pushed to cooperate (Lilliecreutz 1998, p. 74). Specialization has been an industry trend for some time however it accelerated in recent years. "Increasing technical complexity and diversity that makes it more and more difficult for a single company to be at the edge of several different technological areas at the same time are pointed out as rationale" (Gadde & Snehota 1999, p. 1). Because purchase costs account on average for more than 40% of total expenses they are clearly a major area for potential cost savings (Arnold 1998, Droege 1998). Besides cost benefits purchasing and supply management has a major impact on quality. Companies have tended to concentrate on their core competences with the aim to increase effectiveness and efficiency (Hamel & Prahalad 1995). The need to nurture core competences has lead to an increased emphasis on outsourcing (Venkatesan 1992). This development reduced a company's internal added value in the product value chain to its core competences and at the same time the supplier's influence on quality increased to a dominant role in some cases (Cusumano & Takeishi 1991). A further lever for growing importance of procurement has been the shortening life cycles of new technologies. Companies have focused on highly customized supplies instead of purchasing commodities. They have handed-over product responsibility and risk to their suppliers to cope with increased product development pressure (McMillan 1990, Brown & Eisenhardt 1995, Freudenberg & Klenk 1996, Cooper et al. 1997). Early and extensive supplier involvement has shortened the product development process and has been an important source of innovation (Gadde & Mattsson 1987, von Hippel 1988, Kamath & Liker 1990, Cusumano & Takeishi 1991, Kamath & Liker 1995, Liker et al. 1996, Hartley et al. 1997, Bozdogan et al. 1998, Wasti, & Liker 1999, Dröge et al. 2000). Especially the need to ensure manufacturing flexibility, which enables a firm to introduce new products more quickly and to parry competitive threats by modifying existing products has also necessitated a more intense interaction with suppliers (Carter & Narasimhan 1990, Williamson 1991). By means of information systems integration, concepts such as vendor managed inventory and continuous replenishment (Scott-Morton 1991, Lamming 1996, Johnson et al. 1999), have lead to tremendous cost savings. Suppliers have been able to provide information about experience with competitors (Axelssons 1983, Heydebreck 1995). By implementing concepts, such as simultaneous engineering with the supplier, the innovations process has been speeded up (Simon 1989, Bullinger & Wasserloos 1990, Womack et al. 1990, Gerpott & Wittkemper 1991, Heydebreck 1995, Abmeier & Herold 1998). "Time is the secret weapon of business" (Simon 1989, p. 72). Apart from shorter cycle times in the development phase, intensive cooperation with suppliers can increase the product quality and the probability of technical product success (Vollmann & Cordon 1998, p. 686). The uncertainties that are inherent in market relationships coupled with the bounded rationality of decision makers have made it likely, that suppliers and buyers will seek to standardize their transactions by developing more established repeat relations with each other (Provan 1993) based on a long-term perspective (Kalwani & Narayandas 1995). Additional to improved product quality, a joint product development with the supplier has lead to more commitment of both parties (Johanson & Mattsson 1987, Burt 1989, Stuart & Mueller 1994, Ritter 1998).

The focus of attention has shifted towards the significance of cooperative buyer-seller relationships to "enable purchasing to support a firm's strategic positioning" (Harland et al. 1999, p. 659). Based on these trends one of the most important objectives of the purchasing function is the development of a supplier network (Ellram 1991, p. 8), since a firm's ability to produce a quality product at reasonable cost and in timely manner is mainly influenced by its suppliers' capabilities (Hahn et al. 1990). A company's strategy to operate with various suppliers utilizes a portfolio of relationships to meet the requirements of different types of transactions (Robert & Mackay 1998, p. 177). Cooperation with suppliers becomes a critical process, "which can significantly contribute to reaching the company's objectives in terms of cost, quality and time to market and to hedging risk, in particular strategic risk, in sharp increase as a result of the growing interdependence between the companies and their suppliers" (Bouchard 1998, p. 71). Sheth and Sharma (1997, p. 95) point out four underlying reasons for supplier relationships: "increased cost efficiency, increased effectiveness, enabling technologies and increased competitiveness". Firms conclude that they will more readily attain long-term cost reduction by forming closer working relationships with "key" suppliers (Harland et al. 1999). However, partnering does not necessarily guarantee success as it causes costs, high resource intensity and risk of dependency. The relationships need to be adapted to the specific purchase situation. Araujo et al. (1999) provide evidence through a case analysis, that the efficiency of the relationships is greatly dependent on matching the management of the interface with its requirements. Productivity-targeted relations require a different management than relations established for creating innovations (Moller & Halinen 1999).

Depending on external contingencies for the development of appropriate relationship types, different governance structures and relational designs might be used. Bensaou (1999) showed, that firms "balance a portfolio of different types of relationships rather than rely on one type" which leads to the key question: *Which kind of supplier cooperation needs to be established in which purchasing situation to contribute to the success of a company? Or in other words, under which circumstances should a firm try to establish a relationship with its suppliers?*

The appropriate analysis of the purchasing situation is even more important since the establishment of electronic marketplaces and web-supported trading (Kaplan & Sawhney 2000a, 2000b), builds a new dimension for purchasing with reduced interpersonal contact but transactional focus. In a nutshell E-trade offers an even more different approach to do business and as such the decision of how to interact with the supplier base or parts thereof becomes more critical.

In the literature various dimensions for structuring the purchasing situation have been developed. However an integrated model is missing (Kraljic 1983, Witt 1986, Hubmann & Barth 1990, Müller 1990, Krapfel et al. 1991, Mittner 1991, Metcalf & Frear 1993, Landeros et al. 1995, Lamming et al. 1996, Olsen & Ellram 1997, Cannon et al. 1998, Dyer et al. 1998, Baumgarten & Wolff 1999, Bensaou 1999, Bogaschewsky & Rollberg 1999, Fröhling 1999, Wildmann 1999, Cousins & Spekman 2000, Elliott & Glynn 2000, Möller & Törrönen 2000). For classifying industrial goods Copeland developed already in 1924 the "commodity approach". Based on this product typology various approaches for structuring industrial goods have been developed in the late 1960s and 1970s in the Industrial Marketing literature (Miracle 1965, Riebel 1965, Marrian 1968, Fisher 1969, Kirsch & Kutschker 1978, Kutschker & Kirsch 1979, Engelhardt & Günter 1980, Kirsch et al. 1980, Kleinaltenkamp 1997, Backhaus 1999).

The author tries to integrate several aspects by building a systematic and consistent framework, which enables managers to identify the appropriate purchasing strategy depending on the situational circumstances.

2.2   Purchase situation classification dimensions

In the past, portfolio models have been successfully used for assessing more efficiently a company's position in respect to its current position, the projected future and the future desired positions in various dimensions (Markowitz 1952, Ansoff & Leontiades 1976, Wind & Douglas 1981). The pioneering portfolio theory for management of equity was developed by Markowitz in 1952. In the field of industrial marketing and purchasing several portfolios have been developed for evaluating customer and supplier relationships since the early 1980s. The different approaches can be structured by four segmentation dimensions: product, market, supplier and relationship characteristics.

With the term *purchase situation* the author considers all relevant forces and influences related to the acquisition of required materials, services and equipment, which have a potential impact on the way buyers and sellers work together. The following four dimensions underline the magnitude of various aspects impacting the sourcing environment.

2.2.1   Product characteristics

The most frequently cited product characteristic is the *purchasing volume* (Robinson et al. 1967, Marrian 1968, Howard & Sheth 1969, Webster & Wind 1972, Kirsch et al. 1980, Hubmann & Barth 1990, Müller 1990, Mittner 1991, Baumgarten & Bodelschingh 1996, Elliott & Glynn 1998, Baumgarten & Wolff 1999, Bogaschewsky & Rollberg 1999, Orths 1999, Wildemann 1999), which can be measured in three dimensions: monetary spent, number of parts or physical size. The economic volume is analyzed by applying an ABC-analysis, which clusters the spent in three categories (Leenders & Blenkhorn 1988, Corsten 1996).

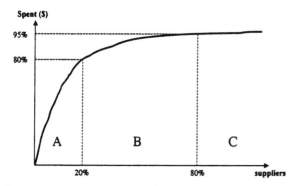

Figure 2.1 ABC-Analysis in the chemical industry

This classification differentiates suppliers with significant spent from the mass of suppliers with only small purchase volume (Bogaschewsky & Rollberg, 1999) and clearly demonstrates the economic importance of the supplier (Baumgarten & Wolff, 1999). Especially in the industrial production industry the ABC-analysis is very helpful, since the majority of the purchase spent is usually caused by only few material categories in this industry (Corsten 1996). Another volume characteristic is number of parts, which is particularly important in discrete production But besides economic volume and number of parts the physical size can also have an important business impact, especially for products, which need large storage space. In order to reduce inventory-carrying cost for large products, just-in-time order policies are widely applied. Therefore, some authors not only categorize the monetary sourcing spent, but also number of parts and physical volume (Bogaschewsky & Rollberg, 1999).

Nevertheless, relying on purchase volumes alone can sometimes be misleading. The cheapest component is, in the long run, not necessarily least expensive. Once the cost of poor quality is factored, the cheapest component may well be the most expensive one (Burt 1989). Decisions on sourcing strategies cannot only be based on purchase value or volume; the perceived risk has to be evaluated (i.e. financial risk, performance risk, social risk etc.) (Gemünden 1985, p. 84, Tanner & Stephen 1993, p. 43). Therefore some researchers emphasize *product and purchase importance* (Marrian 1968, Karljic 1983, Metcalf & Frear 1993, Stuart 1993, Van den Bulte 1994, Homburg 1995, Matthyssens et al. 1995, Olsen & Ellram 1997, Cannon & Perreault 1999, Homburg 1999). Olsen and Ellram (1997) detail the importance by economic factors in terms of "dollar value and the impact on the company's profits" (Olsen & Ellram 1997, p. 103), by competence factors, which "describe the extent to which the item purchased is part of the company's core competences" (Olsen & Ellram 1997, p. 103) and by strategic importance. The closer the purchased product is to the core competences of the firm, the greater is the strategic importance of the purchased good. Product importance as "the extent to which a consumer links a product to salient enduring or situation specific goals" (Bloch & Richins 1983, p. 71) is a broader definition for product characteristics. Bloch and Richins (1983, p. 71) suggested measuring the product importance by assessing the centrality of the product to the customer's goals with the dimensions "neither important nor unimportant" to "absolutely essential". This evaluation criterion is based on the Industrial Marketing literature, where authors argue the "degree of essentiality" (Marrian 1968).[2] For Metcalf and Frear (1993) the product importance is not an inherent product characteristic. The way it is perceived by the buyer will rather depend on the "product's ability to satisfy the goals of the buying firm" (Metcalf & Frear 1993, p. 66). Product importance is also influenced by the risk of the supply for the production process, if the delivery is delayed (Mittner 1991, p. 22). However, not only risks due to delays have to be included in the product importance evaluation, but also functional and qualitative aspects relating to product performance, financial factors or social effects (Gemünden 1985, p. 90). The potential risk or uncertainty can be differentiated in exogenous or endogenous components (Backhaus et al. 1994, p. 78). Exogenous uncertainty cannot be influenced by buyer or supplier, since it is more market driven, whereas endogenous uncertainty can be influenced by buyer or supplier. Product importance also refers to the position of the supply in the value chain of the producing company, which then determines a potential impact of short innovation and product cycle of the supply. The last characteristic, determining the purchase importance, is the number of purchase transactions caused by a supply. Products with an extremely high number of transactions have a high importance, as they cause a dominant amount of transactions costs. Correspondingly, the Organizational Buying Behavior Theory distinguishes between "heavy versus light" used products (Webster & Wind 1972, p. 118). The number of purchase transactions determines the intensity of personnel involvement, which has a direct impact on the purchase importance.

Another product segmentation dimension that is used to evaluate the product complexity and standardization is the *degree of product customization* (Pugh 1963, Fisher 1969, Hakansson & Östberg 1975, Metcalf & Frear 1993, Cannon et al. 1998, Dyer et al. 1998), which can be reflected in product specification, delivery agreements and specific payment schemes. Although Levitt (1980) postulated, that "there is no such thing as a commodity; all goods and services can be differentiated and usually are; though the usual presumption is that this is true more of consumer goods than of industrial goods and services, the opposite is the actual case", a differentiation by degree of product customization is key for an appropriate management of the purchase situation (Evans & Berman 2001). Hakansson and Östberg (1975) differentiate in three product categories: completely standardized products, moderate complex products and highly complicated products. Depending on the complexity of the

---

[2] For a literature overview on the related Organizational Buying Behavior literature see Backhaus (1999, pp. 284).

purchased goods they separate three organization types along with the marketing functions of Pugh et al. (1963): N-organization (i.e. referring to the exchange of a completely standardized product), A-organization (i.e. referring to the exchange of a product of moderate complexity) and C-organization (i.e. for exchanges of highly complicated products). Ford (1980), Hallén et al. (1991)[3], Hakansson and Gadde (1992), Metcalf and Frear (1993), Brennan and Turnbull (1995) as well as Wilson (1995) mention adaptations, which occur, when "one party in a relationship alters its processes or the item exchanged to accommodate the other party" (Wilson 1995, p. 339). Adaptations develop over time by implying cost intense learning process (Johanson & Mattsson 1987, p. 38). Some of the adaptations take place in form of specific investments or projects, such as the acquisition of particular machinery or a change of systems. Adaptations can be grouped in different types, such as technical, knowledge-based, administrative, economic and legal adaptations (Johanson & Mattsson 1987, p. 38, Hakansson & Gadde 1992, p. 408) and may include customizing products, financial terms, information sharing routines, pricing, inventory stocking policies, delivery schedules and production processes (Cannon & Narayandas 2000, p. 412). Johanson and Mattsson (1987, p. 38) go further by specifying adaptations between buyers and suppliers in terms of knowledge by acting together in some technical development matters. The product specification dimension is frequently used in the automotive industry, where only a limited number of suppliers deliver highly customized products. In Dyer's (1994, p. 177) study of the Japanese automotive industry, Japanese suppliers reported, that roughly 22% of their total capital investments were so dedicated to their primary customer, that these customized physical assets could not be redeployed if the customer walked away. They fall in the "keiretsu-category" (Herbig & Shao 1993, p. 11, Dyer et al. 1998, p. 60;), with roughly 30 suppliers of more than 300 suppliers. Keiretsu suppliers in the automotive industry deliver parts, such as engine parts, body panels or seats (Dyer et al. 1998). The relationships to those keiretsu-suppliers can be characterized by a "particularly high degree of stability and structure" (Lincoln et al. 1998, p. 242). The degree of customization underlines the supplier willingness to invest in the relationship. On the other hand it shows the trust and commitment (Morgan & Hunt 1994) of the buying company to rely on a single source, which decreases its replaceability of a certain supplier (Heide & John 1988, p. 24). Stump and Heide (1996, p.

---

[3] Hallén et al. (1991) give a detailed overview of the different approaches for defining adaptations.

432) proved, that specific investments by buyers are positively associated with specific investments by the suppliers.

The *demand pattern* defines the continuity and age of the relationship (Baumgarten & Bodelschwingh 1996, Baumgarten & Wolff 1999, Bogaschewsky & Rollberg 1999). Suppliers use this measurement as a key indicator for planning the production. As a result of derived demand, Fiocca (1982, p. 54) emphasizes the importance, that "industrial marketers must always be up to date about the current and prospective trends". The demand pattern has been already discussed in the early Organizational Buying Behavior literature. In 1967 Robinson et al. developed the "BUYGRID-Model", where they separated buying behavior in three groups: "new tasks, modified rebuy, straight rebuy".[4] The demand pattern of a straight rebuy has to be analyzed differently compared to the demand pattern of a new task, where no experience exists.

After reviewing these four sub-criteria of product characteristics the author concludes, that they are all too important to be excluded. However they need to be weighted according to their relevance in specific circumstances. A balanced scorecard approach can help to simplify this evaluation process (Friedag & Schmidt 2001, p. 122).

2.2.2   Market characteristics

For classifying a supplier relationship not only the product specific characteristics are important. Many different market aspects influence the purchasing situation, although they may not be fully influenced by both parties of the procurement process. One frequently used segmentation dimension is the *supply risk* determined by production shortages, product availability and availability of alternatives, which is the "degree to which a buying firm has alternative sources of supply to meet a need" (Cannon & Perreault 1999, p. 444), on time delivery, quality acceptance or seasonality (Witt 1986, Hubmann & Barth 1990, Müller 1990, Homburg 1995, Baumgarten & Bodelschwingh 1996, Baumgarten et al. 1999, Orths 1999, Wildemann 1999). Wildemann (1999, p. 441) differentiates between "internal and external supply risk". Company external risks are influenced by supply problems with substitutes, seasonality, transport logistics complexity and delivery time, whereas internal risk factors

---

[4]   For further details of this model refer to Anderson et al. (1987, pp. 71).

comprise the possibility of indoor production, availability of production know-how and product and production complexity (Lamming et al. 1996, Wildemann 1999).

The second market characteristic besides supply risk is the *buying power* (Lamming et al. 1996, p. 176). For defining the buying power, which describes the governance in the purchasing situation, several market indicators have to be summarized, such as industry growth and exit barriers, number of competitors, the number of suppliers and an understanding of the rivalry in the market (Porter 1996, p. 23). Following traditional economic theory, when many suppliers compete to sell comparable goods, the market becomes a ready source of information on prices and quality (Cannon & Perreault 1999), which strengthens the position of the buyer. The opposite occurs if only limited suppliers are in the market and the buying company has to cope with the uncertainty and dependence. The buying power is further described by Geck and Petry (1983, p. 17) with three characteristics: dominant size of the buying company compared to the supplier, market knowledge advantage of the buyer and the service function of the supplier ("customer is king"). The geographic spread is a further sub-criterion of the buying power, which defines the buying company's opportunities concerning global sourcing strategies (Kiedaisch 1997, Monczka et al. 1998). Similar to the buying power definition, Cannon et al. (1998) talk about situational factors such as dynamism of price and quality. Especially if a buyer is implementing a multiple sourcing strategy, this is an indicator that the buyer's power is dominant to the seller's power. Thus, the buyer's bargaining position is particularly advantageous in a short-term and operational perspective (Watts et al. 1992, p. 4).

The third individual category of market characteristics represents the *legal regulation factors*. An identification of all legal aspects, that affect both the way commercial affairs should be conducted and also the way organizations should be managed, is relevant (Saunders 1997, p. 60). The present legislation of the countries involved in the purchasing process clearly has to be taken into account in the development of strategies for organizations in general and purchasing and supply management in particular. Specific regulations such as company law and laws governing the operation of public sector organizations, commercial and consumer law, health and safety legislation, employment and industrial relations and last but not least the law of carriage and transport have to be taken into account when characterizing the supplier market (Saunders 1997, Monczka et al. 1998).

Summarizing the market attributes characterizing the purchasing situation, these factors are highly correlated to the product characteristics. As such they need to be integrated in an evaluation model together with the product aspects.

2.2.3   Supplier characteristics

Supplier characteristics are only used by a few researchers for supplier relationship classification (Bensaou 1999, Wildemann 1999, Elliott & Glynn 2000), whereas many supplier aspects have been evaluated in the literature dealing with the supplier evaluation and selection process (Ellram 1990, Thompson 1991, Hartmann 1992, Pearson & Ellram 1995, Koppelmann 1997, Saunders 1997, Monczka et al. 1998, Hildebrandt & Koppelmann 2000, van Weele 2000).

The first group of characteristics is the supplier's *resource base* by means of revenues, assets, employees, R&D, production capacity and information (Koppelmann 1997, p. 71). The definition of resources goes along with Hofer and Schendel (1978, p. 145), Helfert (1998, pp. 51) and Ritter (1998, pp. 82), who cluster the resource base in four groups: financial resources, physical resources, personnel resources and information resources. In business market the buying company depends in part on these resources of the supplier (Ford et al. 1999, p. 76). Skarmeas and Katsikeas (2001, p. 229) discuss the extent to which a trade partner provides important and critical resources by measuring the "interdependence magnitude". Standard performance indicators as given in the annual report enable a differentiated judgment for the procurement management concerning financial stability of the supplier. For a better basis of price negotiation, supplier's margins need to be recalculated or at least estimated (Olsen & Ellram 1997). The resource potential describes the supplier's commercial and financial competence, but the technical perspective is important as well (Olsen & Ellram 1997). Weber (2001) is clustering resources depending on their sustainability for the relationship. He defines less-sustainable resources as financial, special and human resources, e.g. diverse locations or managerial skills. More sustainable resources are relational and organizational resources, e.g. cooperation and loyalty or operational linkages. Information sharing is considered to be the most sustainable resource.

The next dimension characterizes the supplier's *competences* including product, process, support functions and management capabilities, which is correlated to the previously mentioned dimension resource base. On the one hand the production process needs to be described concerning specific technology, but also reliability in respect to quality, delivery and punctuality of delivery is included in this segmentation dimension (Koppelmann 1997). An overall strategic fit between buyer and supplier has to be approved. Additionally, characteristics such as flexibility, service and communication are integrated in the competence perspective (Hartmann 1992, p. 32). Another main competence characteristic is the innovation competence of the supplier (Lamming et al. 1996, p. 175), which is a "longer-term factor". Due to expanded emphasis on outsourcing (Venkatesan 1992) the supplier's impact on a buyer's value chain has increased tremendously. Suppliers, who are delivering complete system solutions, have major influence on the buyer's product and process innovativeness. Therefore the supplier's innovation potential can be critical to the buyer's innovation success (Heydebreck 1995, p. 115).

A further supplier characteristic is the company *network*, in which the supplier is embedded. The network of further relationships of the supplier can be described by the effect, these other relationships may have on the buyer: "neutrality effect, duplication effect, reference effect, prohibition effect, combination effect, deficiency effect, competition effect, access effect, avoidance effect and hierarchy effect" (detailed discussion in Ritter 1998, pp. 20). These criteria evaluate the benefits of the supplier's network for the buying company and influence the buying company's network position. Based on its network position, the buying company gets access to external resources, which it is depending on (Johanson & Mattsson, 1987, p. 36).

For evaluating the future potential, Wildemann (1999, p. 442) defines the dimension of *supplier development potential* by classifying the supplier as "standard" or "key supplier". This development potential of the supplier company has to be determined along the supplier's business processes in production, logistics and R&D. Olsen and Ellram (1997, p. 106) measure a similar aspect, which they call "relative supplier attractiveness" with respect to future changes. They use factors such as "the ability to cope with changes in technology, the types and depth of supplier's current and future technological capabilities, the supplier's current and future capacity utilization, supplier's speed in development, ability to cope with changes in the environments" (Olsen & Ellram 1997, p. 111). In this dimension the learning potential is also integrated, which the supplier offers to the buying company. These factors make a company choose a specific supplier. Some of the factors increasing supplier's attractiveness are also used in a supplier selection situation (Ellram 1991, Cousins 1992, Habermehl 1996, Fröhlich-Glantschnig 1997, Maron & Brückner 1998, Nachtweh 1998).

The last supplier dimension is the *supplier value*, which summarizes the various reasons why a buyer should work together with a certain supplier. Along with Walter et al. (2000), who analyze the value functions from a supplier perspective, the value functions are differentiated in direct (profit, volume and safeguard function) and indirect ones (innovation development, market, scout and access function). Direct value functions such as purchase cost savings, large purchase volume and safeguard suppliers (i.e. suppliers who deliver even if it may be a relatively unfavorable deal), contribute directly to the buyer's profitability independent from further supplier relationships. Indirect value functions such as joint innovation development with the supplier, development of further sources due to the reference of a supplier or information gathering due to the supplier's scout function capture connected effects in the future or in further supplier relationships (Walter et al. 2000). The fulfillment of these various value functions determines the buyer value of a certain supplier relationship.

2.2.4   Relationship characteristics

In the past decade relationship characteristics supporting the success of relationships have been in focus of relationship marketing research (Dwyer et al. 1987, Morgan & Hunt 1994, Norris & McNeilly 1995, Doney & Cannon 1997, Smeltzer 1997, Doney et al. 1998, Joshi & Stump 1999, Dyer & Chu 2000, Ryssel et al. 2000, Walter et al. 2000).

Basis of any form of cooperation is *trust*.[5] Smeltzer (1997, p. 42) describes a trustworthy supplier with the following attributes: "does not act in a purely self-serving manner, accurately discloses relevant information when requested, does not change supply specifications, standards or costs to take advantage of the other parties and generally acts according to normally accepted ethical standards". Another definition of trust is "confidence or predictability in one's expectations about another's behavior, and confidence in another's goodwill" (Dyer & Chu 2000, p. 260). Morgan and Hunt (1994, p. 23) conceptualize trust in terms of one party having confidence in an exchange partner's reliability and integrity. In a similar vein Moorman et al. (1992) define trust as the willingness to rely on an exchange partner in whom one has confidence. Trust occurs for Smeltzer (1997) because of corporate

---

[5]   For a detailed literature overview see Hosmer (1995, pp. 379).

identity, image and reputation. On the one hand a set of perceptions or personal constructs about the own company are important (corporate identity), on the other hand the outside view of the company (corporate image) are levers for trust. Additionally "supplier reputation" (Doney & Cannon 1997, p. 37) describes the actual attributes outsiders ascribe to the company. This describes the extent to which "firms and people in the industry believe a supplier is honest and concerned about its customers" (Doney & Cannon 1997, p. 37). Smeltzer (1997, p. 44) is linking trust with corporate identity, image and reputation as follows: "Identity equals the extent to which we believe we can be trusted. Image equals the extent to which we believe others think we can be trusted. Reputation equals the extent to which others actually trust us". Butler (1991, p. 648) identifies ten conditions of trust, namely availability, competence, consistency, discreetness, fairness, integrity, loyalty, openness, promise fulfillment and receptivity. Trust in supplier relationships is an important source of competitive advantage, since it "lowers transaction costs, facilitates investments in relation-specific assets and leads to superior information sharing routines" (Dyer & Chu 2000, p. 259). Especially for specific sourcing approaches such as "open book negotiations", where the supplier is required to "open its books" and expose secret and sensitive information to the customer (Lamming et al. 2000), a trustful relationship is required for taking the explicit risk of information transparency. A trustworthy party is "known to reliably make good faith efforts to behave in accordance with prior commitments, makes adjustments in ways perceived as fair by the exchange partner and does not take excessive advantage of an exchange partner even when the opportunity is available" (Dyer & Chu 2000, p. 260). Trust in supplier relationship includes a certain degree of optimism, that vulnerable know-how will not be exploited or transferred to third parties without prior consent (Gemünden 1999, p. 242). Helfert (1998, p. 114) is defining this optimism more specifically with perceived honesty, perceived benevolence and perceived competence. The degree of trust can be measured by social embeddedness, institutionalized processes or routines for fairly and reliably dealing and alignment of economic incentives between the business partners. "Social relations, rather than institutional arrangement or generalized morality are mainly responsible for the production of trust in economic life" (Granovetter 1985, p. 491).

The second important lever for successful relationships is *commitment*. Commitment is defined along with Walter et al. (2000, p. 4) as "a kind of lasting intention to build and maintain a long-term relationship". They differentiate between three types of commitment: affective commitment, i.e. the positive attitude towards the future existence of the relationship, instrumental commitment, i.e. whenever some form of investment (time or other resources) is made and temporal commitment indicating the timely component of the relationship. These three types point out, that "the exchange partner believing that an ongoing relationship with another is so important as to warrant maximum efforts at maintaining it" (Morgan, Hunt 1994, p. 23). Bensaou (1999) refers to the instrumental dimension by analyzing the buyer's and supplier's willingness for specific investments, similar to Dwyer et al. (1987, p. 15), who evaluate the seller's and buyer's motivational investment. However, once specific investments have been committed, the buying situation becomes fundamentally transformed (Stump 1995, p. 146). Due to higher switching costs the specific supplier is not one alternative out of several any more.

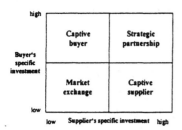

Figure 2.2 Types of relationship (Bensaou 1999)

High commitment reduces the possibility to break a supplier relationship and increases the tendency to adapt to organizational and environmental changes (Gemünden 1999, p. 243). Due to high commitment the willingness is intense to accept common norms, procedures and interfaces. According to Siguaw et al. (1998, p. 103) commitment is dependent on trust. They proved that the greater the intensity of trust in the supplier the greater the commitment to the relationship.

This high level of commitment creates stability or *continuity*, which is another segmentation dimension of relationships (Dyer & Chu 2000). In their study Dyer and Chu refer to the automotive industry, where continuity is extremely important due to the regular model change and the need for a supplier to re-win the business. Continuity cannot only be expressed by re-winning the business after a model change, but also by the overall length of the relationship (Doney & Cannon 1997). Heide and John (1990, p. 25) define continuity as "the perception of the bilateral expectation of future interaction". While conventional relationships are discrete or short-term events, closer relationships tend to be continuous or open-ended (MacNeil

1980). Researchers have proved a strong correlation between the length of a relationship and trust (Ganesan 1994, p. 4, Wildemann 1997, p. 421), since trust develops and builds over time. Another lever for continuity is the reinforcement of relationships through adaptations; those adaptations make the relationship more endurable (Johanson & Mattsson 1987, p. 39). Suppliers are especially committed to make "expensive adaptations when it is assured that the relationship will last long enough, so that the relationship specific investment [...] will pay off " (Rexha 2000, p. 4). Landeros et al. (1995, p. 9) use the word adjustments instead of adaptation and classify three types, operational unilateral adjustments (e.g. process control procedure for the supplier), operational bilateral adjustments (e.g. joint quality problem solving by buyer and seller) and managerial bilateral adjustments (e.g. joint reexamination by decision makers on the buyer and seller side, if performance problems can not be resolved by operational adjustments).

Gadde and Snehota (2000, p. 5) define the fourth dimension of relationships *involvement* by three characteristics: "coordination of activities, adaptations of resources and interaction among individuals". The activities carried out by the supplier and buyer can be more or less tightly coordinated, more or less specifically adapted to the requirements of the counterpart and the interactions can be more or less intense. Brennan and Turnbull (1999) found out that the level of involvement is dependent on the relationship duration. Gadde and Snehota (2000) underline that close interaction among supplier and buyer makes their choices more interdependent and affects both, commitment and trust, in the relationship, which in turn influences coordination and adaptations.

The fifth factor characterizing a relationship is *satisfaction*. Satisfaction can be defined as "the degree to which the business transaction meets the business performance expectations of the partners" (Wilson 1995, p. 337). According to Lingenfelder et al. (2000, p. 170) the overall satisfaction is a complex multi-dimensional construct, which is built out of four dimensions: quality aspects, time constraints, cost aspects and relationship issues. Wilson (1995) specifies satisfaction with the addition performance satisfaction, which includes both product-specific performance and non-product attributes. The level of performance satisfaction in the relationship is determined by the resources committed to the partnership and by the degree of commitment of the parties involved. Unless the buyer's needs can be satisfied, it is doubtful, that the relationship can achieve the desired level of success (McQuinston 2001). For Gruen (2000, p. 369) satisfaction is "the member's assessment of the relative value of the basic exchanges in the relationship". Satisfaction includes various characteristics of a relationship, such as "rewarding, profitable, instrumental, frustrating, problematic, inhibiting" (Ruekert & Churchill 1984, p. 227), thus dissatisfaction with an exchange partner may hinder morale, impede cooperation, precipitate litigation and fuel initiatives for protective legislation (Dwyer & Oh 1987, p. 349). The primary linkage between satisfaction and suppliers and buyers behaviors is generally considered to be loyalty, which is a sub-dimension of commitment (Helfert 1998, p. 15). Satisfaction is likely to have some impact on retention and co-production. A relationship will not endure, if the supplier is unable to meet the buyer's expectations, then the buyer will seek alternative partners (Wilson & Jantrania 1996). For Tuten and Urban (2001, p. 152) satisfaction is even a success indicator of the relationship.

A sixth relationship characteristic is the existence of *relationship promotors* (Walter 1998). Since all previously mentioned dimensions are subjective and dependent on personal judgment a relationship promotor has the important role to manage the interaction between supplier and buyer, so that trust, commitment, satisfaction, involvement and continuity can be built (Hauschildt & Gemünden 1999). The relationship promotor influences the stability effect of these characteristics, which guarantees a successful supplier relationship (Stoelze 2000, p. 11). He acts as an intermediator between supplier and buyer, who supports information exchange, identification and meeting of key players, coordination of activities and realization of negotiation results (Walter 1998, p. 126).

Reviewing the relationship characteristics emphasizes the correlation and interdependence of all participating groups. These dependencies are also stressed by the analysis approach of Elliot and Glynn (2000), who have chosen the dimension of loyalty, which is a combination of trust, commitment, involvement and satisfaction. Little satisfaction has a negative impact on the degree of trust, which then has an impact on commitment (Walter et al. 2000) and also describes the degree of involvement.

All in all, these six factors need to be integrated within one dimension to be able to judge the weakness or strength of the relationship and its easiness or problematic nature.

2.3   Purchase situation classification models

In the following table, the contributions of various authors are displayed. None of the 34 researchers has covered all four dimensions and only six researchers have at least covered three. 15 out of 25 classification models have included two dimensions. The product characteristics have been used in nearly all segmentation portfolios.

Researcher	Product characteristics	Market characteristics	Supplier characteristics	Relationship characteristics
Baumgarten & Bodelschwingh 1996	-Purchase value -Demand pattern	-Delivery risk		
Baumgarten & Wolff 1999	-Purchase value -Demand pattern	-Delivery risk		
Bensaou 1999	-Buyer's specific investment	-Supplier's specific investment		
Bensaou & Venkatraman 1995	-Task uncertainty	-Environmental uncertainty		-Partnership uncertainty
Beßlich & Lumbe 1994	-Purchase volume	-Supply risk	-Supplier power	
Bogaschewsky & Rollberg 1999	-Purchase volume -Purchase value -Demand forecast accuracy			
Campbell & Cunningham 1982	-Product technology -Production process	-Competitor analysis (# buyers, # suppliers, growth rate, market share)		-Life cycle of relationship
Cannon et al. 1998	-Product features	-Situational factors		-Relationship factors
Cannon & Perreault 1999	-Product importance	-Availability of alternatives -Supply market dynamism		
Copenland 1924	-"Commodity approach"			
Dubinsky & Ingram 1984	-Profit contribution (present and potential)			
Dyer et al. 1998	-Degree of product customization			
Elliott & Glynn 2000	-Buyer loyalty		-Relationship value to supplier	
Engelhardt & Günter 1980	-Purchase importance			
Fiocca 1982	-Sales concentration -Derived demand	-Structure of the power in the market		-Buying process complexity
Hakansson & Östberg 1975	-Product complexity			
Homburg 1995	-Economic importance of purchase	-Complexity of supply situation		
Homburg 1999	- Economic importance of supply	-Complexity of supplier situation		
Hubmann & Barth 1990	-Buying company dimension (e.g. purchase value)	-Supplier market (e.g. Risk)		

Researcher	Product characteristics	Market characteristics	Supplier characteristics	Relationship characteristics
Kleinaltenkamp 1997				-Relationship intensity -Customer involvement
Kraljic 1983	-Strategic importance of purchasing	-Complexity of supply market		
Krapfel et al. 1991				-Relationship value -Interest commonality
Lamming et al. 1996	-Type of commodity, part or service	-Functional and organizational structure		
Marrian 1968	-Degree of essentiality			
Matthyssens & Van den Bulte 1994	-Complexity of purchasing needs and requirements	-Complexity of supply market		
Metcalf & Frear 1993	-Degree of standardization/complexity -Importance of purchase -Novelty/frequency of transaction -Importance of product			
Mittner 1991	-Purchase value	-Supplier market		
Müller 1990	-Purchase value -Technical complexity	-Delivery risk		
Olsen & Ellram 1997		-Relative supplier attractiveness		-Strength of current supplier relationship
Orths 1999	-Purchase value	-Delivery risk		
Robinson et al. 1967	-Demand pattern			
Webster & Wind 1972	-Purchase importance			
Wildemann 1999	-Purchase value	-Delivery risk	-Supplier power -Supplier development potential	
Witt 1986	-Cost of purchase -R&D potential of buyer	-Competitive advantages on supplier market -Technology development -Supply risk		

Table 2.1   Overview literature review on supplier relationship classification

2.4   Combination of major dimensions

After the literature review of various different dimensions for characterizing a purchasing situation the most frequently used portfolio models are discussed.

Most researchers combine product characteristics with market factors (Heege 1987, Beßlich & Lumbe 1994b, Matthyssens & Van den Bulte 1994, Homburg 1995, 1999). The standard variable for the product perspective is purchase dollar volume, disregarding, if number parts or storage capacity are more expressive. For characterization of the market situation the supply risk is frequently selected.

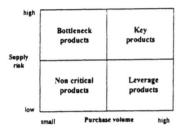

Figure 2.3 Supplier classification (Heege 1987)

Referring to Turnbull and Zoljiewski (1995), who discuss the classification matrix of Shapiro (1987, p. 104) evaluating customers from a supplier's perspective and Krapfel et al. (1991) classifying customers from a supplier's perspective, four relationship types can be built: partner, friend, rival and acquaintance. However, these classification models only focus on the supplier's perspective and therefore only incorporate aspects relevant for the supplier, e.g. cost to serve a customer, net price realized by the customer.

Other researchers such as Olsen and Ellram (1997) and Wildemann (1999) have used a sequenced approach for defining the purchasing situation characteristics. Wildemann (1999) even combined three dimensions: product, market and supplier perspective.

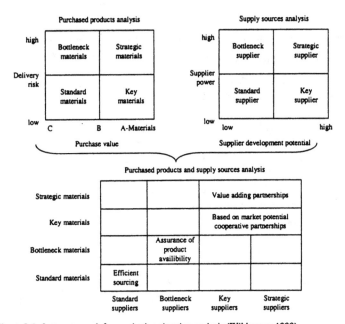

Figure 2.4 2-step approach for purchasing situation analysis (Wildemann 1999)

Various portfolios only focus on the relationship characteristics and combine several relationship factors for a very detailed understanding of the purchasing situation in respect to the relationship (Bensaou 1999, Elliott & Glynn 2000).

2.5   Relationship fit

The author recognizes the need to combine all four characteristic types discussed above within one classification model by simultaneously minimizing the interdependence between the different dimensions. Such an approach offers a meaningful tool for both academics and practitioners. It has to be stressed that due to the specific situational circumstances a contingency approach, which enables to respond to the importance and weight of the various factors. The buyer business impact dimension summarizes product characteristics (purchase volume [monetary, units and physical space] and the degree of customization) and all supplier characteristics (supplier resource base, competence, network and value) by relating their importance to the buying company's business impact. The supplier market competitiveness dimension is an accumulation of supply risk, buying power and legal regulations. The third dimension - the relationship attractiveness - refers to the relationship characteristics, i.e. trust, commitment, continuity, involvement, satisfaction and existence of relationship promotors.

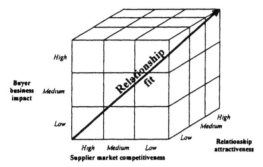

Figure 2.5 Relationship fit

An important item characterizing the dimension of the buyer business impact is the purchase volume (Hubmann & Barth 1990, Müller 1990, Mittner 1991, Baumgarten & Bodelschingh 1996, Baumgarten & Wolff 1999, Bogaschewsky & Rollberg 1999, Orths 1999, Wildemann 1999). If measured by monetary spent, number of parts or physical size has to be decided on individually depending on the product. The second item chosen by the author for characterizing the buyer business impact is the degree of product customization. Highly customized products have a higher business impact for the buyer, since the buyer is dependent on the one specific supplier concerning product performance (Morgan & Hunt 1994) and shifting cost are very high. The third major lever determining the buyer business impact is the supplier resource base (Koppelmann 1997, p. 71). The resource potential describes the supplier's commercial and financial competence (Olsen & Ellram 1997). Related to the commercial and financial competence are the supplier's competences, including product, process, support functions, management capabilities and innovation competence. These build the fourth aspect for the buyer business impact dimension. Besides the different areas of competences the supplier's network is an important driver for the business impact. Depending on potential business partners in the supplier's network further benefits can be defined. The last item chosen is the value function of a supplier relationship, which summarizes all relevant benefits and advantages achieved by close interaction with a certain supplier. As the intensity of these six factors increases, the importance of the buyer business impact also grows. High buyer business impact leads to the hypothesis, that a high relationship quality, or in other words a more relational approach, is necessary to guarantee any kind of success.

Detailing the supplier market competitiveness dimension, the author has used the three aspects that define market characteristics in the literature: supply risk, buying power and legal regulation. Most important is the supply risk, which is the "degree to which a buying firm has alternative sources of supply to meet a need" (Cannon & Perreault 1999, p. 44). Additionally more general market factors such as industry growth rate, exit barriers and number of buyers and suppliers have also to be included in the evaluation of the supplier market competitiveness. The third supplier market competitiveness item is the legal regulation, which determines all legal aspects and restrictions. The extent of those three items characterizes the strength of the supplier market competitiveness, which has an indirect impact on the need of relationships. Low or no supplier market competitiveness (i.e. limited competent supplier base) supports the necessity of relationships to successfully handle the purchase situation.

The third dimension is the relationship attractiveness. The author has chosen all six items - trust, commitment, continuity, involvement, satisfaction and relationship promotor – which have been commonly discussed in literature to define the extent of relationship attractiveness. Although those items are not completely independent and have some overlaps they are necessary to cover all different aspects influencing relationship attractiveness. High intensity of those items leads to high relationship attractiveness, which supports the establishment of successful relationships. However, it is the appropriate fit of these three dimensions that guarantees a long-term relationship success. Low business impact, high supplier market competitiveness, but high relationship attractiveness predict poor or no relationship success, since the benefits of the supplier relationship are only limited due to the business environment. In purchase situations with high business impact, limited supplier market competitiveness, but only low relationship attractiveness only poor relationship success can be expected based on a reduced level of trust, commitment, satisfaction, continuity, involvement or missing relationship promoters. On the other hand in a procurement environment with high business impact, limited supplier market competitiveness and high relationship attractiveness, the probability of relationship success is very high.

The author has aggregated the four dimensions described in literature into three, which are independent from each other and have a linear correlation to the necessity of relationships, whereas the four dimensions discussed in the literature are not independent and show some overlap. For example supplier characteristics are not independent from product and purchase importance for the buyer. On the other hand product and purchase importance are high, if the purchase volume is high. Demand pattern is especially important, if purchase volume is high. Supplier competences determine further supplier development potential. These examples justify, why the author has focused only on three dimensions, which seem to have the major impact on differentiating a purchase situation.

With a special emphasis on the increased complexity of the procurement function due to the internet, these three dimensions seem especially important. Diverse solutions of electronic business (e.g. electronic marketplaces) enforce the need to be able to define a target procurement strategy, since the internet opened new opportunities to the purchasing situation.

2.6   Implications for the management of the purchase situation

For sustainable procurement management it is very important to have a deep understanding of the purchase situation, i.e. sourcing environment. Based on the dimensions detailed above the purchase situation can be classified. Evaluating the existing purchase situation provides the basis for further management decisions. Thus, this classification is the cornerstone for establishing an appropriate purchase management. Depending on the situation, suppliers can be targeted and links to the suppliers can be built. The author deliberately uses the word link here, because it will not always be a relationship, which needs to be built. Finally, the sourcing strategy can be implemented keeping in mind that the implementation depends on other actors as well as on the firm's own abilities.

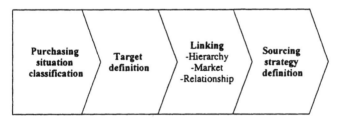

Figure 2.6 4-step approach for a consistent procurement management

This systematic approach that facilitates taking strategic sourcing decisions has to be analyzed, especially with respect to the new trends of electronic commerce, which have created different ways in doing business. The impact of these new types of doing business via electronic marketplaces is discussed in the following chapter.

3 Classification of B2B electronic marketplaces: a relational approach

The internet is not a mere alternative channel for marketing or selling products online, instead electronic marketplaces enable buyers and sellers to innovate whole business processes from sourcing, production to customer service. These changes will significantly impact business-to-business interactions and relationships as it offers new ways of collaborating across organizational boundaries (paragraph 3.1). After discussing the new developments in E-business a clear definition of B2B E-commerce is developed (paragraph 3.2). Then the author shows the variety of B2B electronic marketplace characteristics by grouping them into four dimensions (paragraph 3.3). In paragraph 3.4 a literature overview is given. Then the most commonly used portfolio models for characterizing B2B electronic marketplaces are discussed (paragraph 3.5). Based on the given variety of electronic marketplaces and the different assumed effects on relationships, a systematic approach to classify electronic marketplaces from a relationship perspective is developed (paragraph 3.6).

3.1   Developments in E-commerce

Over the past two decades, business in virtually every industry of the world economy has benefited from or at least has been influenced by the technologies of electronic commerce. We are witnessing a revolution in commerce and society primarily due to an explosion in information technology and the resulting rapid emergence of electronic commerce. However, severe interest is relatively recent, especially in research. Most transactions and profits in electronic commerce have been realized in business-to-business (B2B) commerce and not in business-to-consumer (B2C) commerce, which is no surprise, since business-to-business transactions outnumber consumer sales ten to one (Westland & Clark 2000, p. 2). Some estimates put the B2B electronic commerce market to be close to 78% of the overall electronic commerce market (Shaw 2000, p. 12). A Forrester Research forecast of 1997 was, that business-to-business electronic commerce would grow to $327 billion in the year 2002, measured as value of goods and services traded via the Internet (Timmers 2000, p. 4). Even though realism has entered the once euphoric E-arena, it continues to be an important part of managerial action in these days.

Companies can profit from various benefits of B2B electronic marketplaces. Organizations may adopt their trading processes to electronic marketplaces to lower transaction costs (Schlueter-Langdon 2001) and improve information flows, thus facilitating improved planning and more coordinated actions to reduce uncertainty (Roberts & Mackay 1997). The major benefits of electronic marketplaces can be clustered in three groups: process improvements, cost reductions and new business generation.

Figure 3.1 E-Sourcing benefits (Baker 2000, p. 105)

Process improvements are understood as simpler and faster ordering procedures, reduced paper work, easy online comparison and less human errors streamline the workflows (Kajüter & Ruland 2000). These operational benefits lead to significant time savings and an increase in the performance of inter-organizational information channels (Bakos 1991b, p. 33). Free time comes from shorter research and development time, more responsive reaction time, shorter cycle time and more efficient order handling (Sauter 1999, p. 103), which have caused a clear "time compression" (Hammer & Mangurian 1987, p. 65). B2B marketplaces can also free up procurement personnel (Baker 2000), so that they can do more strategic work such as negotiation preparations.

Aspects as transparency of spend, comparability of products, prices, suppliers, buyers and availability and efficient market and pricing mechanisms lead to a significant cost reduction (Schneider & Schnetkamp 2000). An electronic marketplace can reduce customer's costs of obtaining information about prices and product offerings of alternative suppliers as well as supplier's costs of communicating information about their prices and product characteristics to additional customers (Bakos 1991a). This information transparency leads to a "shift to the customer" (Hagel III & Rayport 1997, p. 55). Due to bundling business the scale effect has reduced cost in transaction processing (Berryman et al. 1998). But cost savings cannot only be realized in procurement, but also in production, inventory management, marketing, distribution, administration and customer service. Another advantage related to pricing is, that prices can be customized, not only by country level, but also by individual users. Therefore, pricing becomes less standardized and more volatile. But users will quickly become aware of such price discrimination and may not tolerate it (Quelch & Klein 1996). Summarizing the cost benefits caused by B2B E-marketplaces along with Malone et al.'s (1987) definition of production cost, which includes physical or other primary processes necessary to create and distribute the goods or services being produced, and coordination cost, which includes the transaction costs of all the information processing necessary to coordinate the work of people and machines that perform the primary processes (Benjamin & Wigand 1995, p. 64), both cost components can be reduced by using electronic marketplaces.

Automated trading and anonymity can eliminate many market inefficiencies, so that liquidity can be built at much lower cost (Sculley & Woods 1999). But marketplaces have not only improved efficiency and effectiveness, they have generated totally new business opportunities due to various kinds of transaction fees for running market places, online information generation, access to new customers and suppliers, increased market share and revenue, higher customer satisfaction, price increase for surplus material and development of completely new markets (Baker 2000, p. 105). The low cost of getting connected, irrespective of geographical distance, enables fragmented buyers and seller to find each other through B2B marketplaces without incurring real world search, travel expenses or high commissions for using intermediaries (Stundza 1999, p. S14). The elimination of geographical barriers and time zone differences has significantly improved the reach (Schmid 1991, Sculley & Woods 1999), which means "access and connection or how many customers a business can connect with and how many products it can offer to those customers" (Evans & Wurster 1999, p. 86). Due to the increased availability of buyers and sellers companies gain more flexibility (Krähenmann 1994). For suppliers B2B marketplaces aggregate buyers and suppliers discover new customers, for buyers these marketplaces aggregate suppliers and they can discover new sources (Reim 1997, p. 21). Using electronic marketplaces facilitates information exchange and enhances communication between companies and may reduce costs, risk and uncertainty while also increasing interdependency and joint investments (Roberts & Mackay 1998). Traditional decision trees are outdated, since the B2B marketplaces enable access to potentially all information needed (Evans & Wurster 1998). Especially beneficial are marketplaces for small buyers and suppliers. Buyers can aggregate small orders and small suppliers have broadened their reach (Phillips & Meeker 2000).

Besides all these benefits mentioned above, the E-hype causes also disadvantages (Bacheldor 2000), because inter-personal interactions are reduced as the focus is on optimizing the transaction and its related costs. Due to the process automation various job positions are redundant. Commitment and goodwill due to inter-personal relationships will be reduced. Therefore a company has to differentiate carefully. Different B2B electronic marketplaces concepts and approaches have to be thoughtfully analyzed before implementing to gain sustainable and tangible success. Weiber and Krämer (2001) emphasize the important role of the procurement personnel, since the success depends on their know-how, motivation and their willingness to implement new processes. Besides the internal acceptance of the procurement organization the supplier acceptance is also important (Weiber & Krämer 2001). By reviewing the literature, the author categorizes different criteria for classifying B2B electronic marketplaces and builds an integrated analysis tool. With this consistent framework, managers are able to identify the appropriate procurement strategy in the electronic market depending on the situation.

3.2   B2B E-commerce – a definition

Since industrial and academic interest in business-to-business electronic commerce is very new and still evolving, any definition of what is or is not included in E-commerce is bound to be controversial. The author goes along with the definition of Westland and Clark (2000, p. 1): "Electronic Commerce - or e-commerce - is the automation of commercial transactions using computer and communications technologies". Rebstock (1998, p. 265) uses a similar broad definition, which says that electronic commerce summarizes all opportunities, which support commercial transactions with electronic communication technologies. To narrow the definition commercial refers only to activities that create transactions between firms (business-to-business or B2B), excluding transactions between firms and individuals (business-to-consumers). These transactions involve the exchange of money, goods, obligations, information or ideas (Zwass 1996, Guay & Ettwein 1998, Bieberbach & Hermann 1999, Standifird 2001).

Shaw (2000, p. 12) differentiates in two types of B2B E-commerce markets. One is related to the management of material flows in production oriented supply chain networks and the other is related to the procurement of maintenance, repair and operating (MRO). His definition is focusing on physical material flows disregarding exchange of digital products, such as services or ideas. Contrary for Kollmann (2000, p. 126), electronic marketplaces are defined as "virtual markets within a data network, where virtual business transactions take place, which are supported by information technology by the marketplace operator at any time of the transaction process". By virtual Kollmann means digital in contrast to physical marketplaces (Müller-Merbach et al. 2001). Bakos (1991a, p. 296) is focusing in his definition of electronic marketplaces only on digital products, excluding physical product exchanges by relating an electronic marketplace to an "inter-organizational information system that allows the participating buyers and sellers to exchange information about prices and product offerings". Similar to Malone et al. (1987), Nokkentved (2000) is using a definition which says, that "the unique feature of a B2B exchange is that it brings multiple buyers and sellers together in a virtual sense in one central market space and enables them to buy and sell from each other at a dynamic price, which is determined in accordance with the rules of the exchange". Schmid (1993, p. 3) builds on this definition, since in his view "the electronic marketplace contributes to the realization of the ideal economic market as an abstract place of exchange with complete information where transaction costs do not apply".

The author includes both aspects in her electronic marketplace definition. From a relational perspective both, the physical product exchange and the more digital service offering, are important (Hallén & Johanson 1985, p. 495). Furthermore in theory the split between physical and digital product offering is criticized by researchers focusing on relationship marketing. B2B electronic commerce has a potential impact on any area of business, from the supplier's side, the company's infrastructure, company's management processes, the interface with the customer to linkages to the distributors.

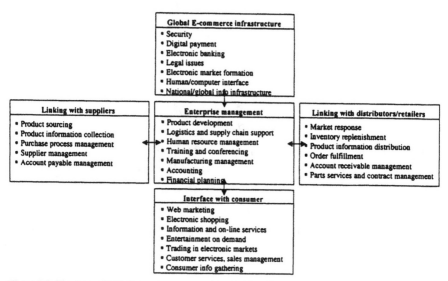

Global E-commerce infrastructure
* Security
* Digital payment
* Electronic banking
* Legal issues
* Electronic market formation
* Human/computer interface
* National/global info infrastructure

Linking with suppliers
* Product sourcing
* Product information collection
* Purchase process management
* Supplier management
* Account payable management

Enterprise management
* Product development
* Logistics and supply chain support
* Human resource management
* Training and conferencing
* Manufacturing management
* Accounting
* Financial planning

Linking with distributors/retailers
* Market response
* Inventory replenishment
* Product information distribution
* Order fulfillment
* Account receivable management
* Parts services and contract management

Interface with consumer
* Web marketing
* Electronic shopping
* Information and on-line services
* Entertainment on demand
* Trading in electronic markets
* Customer services, sales management
* Consumer info gathering

Figure 3.2   The scope of B2B electronic commerce (Shaw 2000, p. 7)

In this variety of diverse transactions the author focuses on transactions between buyers and suppliers and analyzes new opportunities based on electronic commerce for handling the purchasing situation. The number of various transactions between suppliers and buyers supported by E-commerce and handled on electronic marketplaces is in the center of analysis. Various notions are used in the literature: electronic marketplace, electronic market, electronic trades, electronic exchange, electronic hubs, electronic platforms, whereas different dimensions for a more specific structure of electronic marketplaces for suppliers and buyers have been developed.

3.3   Electronic marketplace classification dimensions

Commercial transactions between suppliers and buyers have taken place forever, but currently a revolution is taking place transforming the marketplace. This transformation is occurring, because exchanges between firms are increasingly being facilitated through electronic commerce (Strader & Shaw 2000, p. 77). In the literature these new electronic marketplaces can be differentiated along five segmentation dimensions: business model, order processing mechanism, revenue model, market characteristics and product specifics. These diverse dimensions are partially related to each other, but they are important for an integrated marketplace characterization.

3.3.1   Business models

The dimension business models is a common segmentation criteria for electronic marketplaces which has been used by various authors (Thorelli 1986, Kaplan 1999, Lief 1999, Merz 1999, Sawhney et al. 1999a, Schwartz et al. 1999, Wichmann & Weitzel 1999, Windham 1999, Woods 1999, Gulley et al. 2000, Kafka 2000b, Kaplan & Sawhney 2000a, 2000b, Lee et al. 2000, Müller & Preissner 2000, Nokkentved 2000, Phillips & Meeker 2000, Ploss & Johnson 2000, Rosson 2000, Skinner 2000, Scheer 2000, Schneider & Schnetkamp 2000, Stearns & Sgarioto 2000, Timmers 2000, Wirtz 2000, Shaw et al. 2000, Butscher & Krohn 2001, Picot et al. 2001, Sander & Behlke 2001). The business models vary by the number of buyers and sellers trading on the electronic marketplace. The author differentiates three types: marketplaces focusing on sellers, marketplaces focusing on buyers and neutral marketplaces, which do not favor either sellers or buyers but attract both (Kaplan & Sawhney 2000a, 2000b, Rosson 2000).

The author talks about *procurement hubs*, if the buying firm restructures its procurement process by establishing an electronic marketplace for its suppliers to receive an optimal offer for any predetermined sourcing good (MacLeod 2000, p. 27, Schneider & Schnetkamp 2000, p. 55,). The ratio between the business partners can be described by 1:n (buyer to supplier). Buyer-controlled marketplaces are set up with the aim of shifting power to the buyer's side (Berryman et al. 1998, Roberts & Alaniz 1999, Pfeiffer & Tomkins 2000). Typical for procurement hubs is the openness to any potential supplier with the goal of receiving the best product and service at the lowest price. Procurement hubs support the sourcing process by reducing product, process and inventory costs. Depending on the market, either process or product cost reduction or both can be realized. Kollmann (2000, p. 133) calls procurement hubs "buyer hierarchies" to underline the ability of the buyer to define and determine the type of the marketplace by means of transaction mechanism and revenue model. To strengthen the buying power by volume consolidation some buyers build cooperative procurement hubs (e.g. the hub Covisint) or so called "sourcing networks" (Phillips & Meeker 2000, p. 39), to further increase the cost reduction potential.

The counterpart of "buyer hierarchies" is *supplier hierarchies*" (Kollmann 2000, p. 133) or so called *portals* (Schneider & Schnetkamp 2000, p. 147), which are supplier-controlled (Berryman et al. 1998, Patel 1999, Skinner 2000). They can be characterized as n:1-relations (buyer versus suppliers) or n:m-relations, where n is much larger than m, which are coordinated by the suppliers. A typical example is the McOffice portal, which offers everything concerning indirect materials, such as materials not required directly for production but still essential for continued production (e.g. office supplies). Portals provide the full product range including key products, but also non-key assortment and related services. In many cases supplier hierarchies are conglomerates of marketing, distribution and service providers (Schneider & Schnetkamp 2000, p. 56). Focus of portals is not the product offering but customer orientation (Windham 1999, p. 93), because the buyer has the opportunity to buy a customized product package. Kajüter and Ruland (2000, p. 239) call a supplier-hierarchy bilateral E-trade to underline, that sellers try to enhance the customer relationship by offering superior value through customized features (e.g. portal Cisco).

The third business model is the *pure marketplace*, where many buyers and many suppliers come together. A marketplace is called neutral, if it is not buyer or seller controlled. It is either set up by a third party (e.g. a software provider) to match many buyers to many sellers (Berryman et al. 1998) or several companies form together a marketplace as for example 14 chemical and petroleum companies have created Envera as a global electronic marketplace for B2B services and transactions in the chemical industry (Chang 2000, p. 5). The main optimization potential can be realized through transaction cost reduction due to network effects of bringing together many market participants (Schneider & Schnetkamp 2000, p. 56). Additionally the marketplace enables a real time virtual come-together of the participants, which would have been more difficult in reality (Müller & Preissner 2000). Especially for non-transparent industries the marketplace offers efficient opportunities for matching demand and supply (Kollmann 1999, p. 30). Also in industries with temporary overcapacity the marketplace model offers significant optimization opportunities for establishing an efficient and effective matching process between demand and supply (David et al. 1998, p. 42).

Due to market automation traditional channel intermediaries will be eliminated (Ghosh 1998, p. 90) or replaced, as electronic commerce enables manufacturers to sell products directly to their customers (Choudhury et al. 1998, p. 478, Evans & Wurster 2000, p. 94). But electronic commerce will expand the role of intermediaries (Palmer & Johnston 1991, p. 5). New services and more efficient intermediaries can emerge (Timmers 1999, p. 39, Westland &

Clark 2000, p. 6). Especially on neutral marketplaces the intermediary gains an important role of collection, collation, interpretation and dissemination of vast amounts of information (Quelch & Klein 1996). It is needed to provide secure means of exchanging information quickly and effectively between the transaction partners (Bichler et al. 1998, p. 27). The intermediary can either act as a coordinator without actively participating in the transaction process or as E-distributor, who is equivalent to a trading company, which takes the title and decides on pricing (Kajüter & Ruland 2000). He can assist buyers and sellers in locating one another, in negotiating terms of trade and in executing secure transactions. ChemConnect is an example for an active intermediary; companies like Metalsite or PaperExchange are marketplaces with an intermediary virtually managing the transaction. The intermediary has the market coordination power, which can decide, how the virtual transaction will be processed (Kollmann 2000, p. 133). Some authors see this coordination function as disadvantage, since it causes a certain dependency to the "gateway keeper" (Kollmann 1999, p. 30). But not only on neutral marketplaces the intermediary gained a new importance, many buyer-controlled marketplaces also involve intermediaries. Some strong buyers have developed marketplaces for themselves. Then buyer's intermediaries act as agents or aggregators (Berryman et al. 1998).

3.3.2   Order processing mechanisms

Independent which business model has been chosen, the value generation process has to be defined. Different transaction mechanisms can be used (Thorelli 1986, Elofson & Robinson 1998, Lief 1999, Sawhney & Kaplan 1999, Schwartz et al. 1999, Sculley & Woods 1999, Wichmann & Weitzel 1999, Windham 1999, Gulley et al. 2000, Kaplan & Sawhney 2000a, 2000b, Kusterer 2000, Lee et al. 2000, Nokkentved 2000, Phillips & Meeker 2000, Ploss & Johnson 2000, Rosson 2000, Skinner 2000).

The first mechanism is the *aggregation or catalog model*, which brings large numbers of buyers and sellers together. Virtual distributors aggregate, standardize and index product catalogs or content and make these available in a centralized location to suppliers and buyers (Skinner 2000, p. 44). They offer products together with identical, similar or simply supplementary products in a joint electronic catalog. By aggregating various product catalogs, the product offering is a streamlined combination of many different suppliers (Sculley &

Woods 1999, Kusterer 2000). The aggregation mechanism is a static process with pre-negotiated prices, but can be different for different buyers (Kaplan & Sawhney 2000a, 2000b). By providing one-stop shopping opportunities on an easy to use web-site transaction costs can be reduced. Mostly the products are non-commodities or MRO (maintenance, repair and operating) products, low value goods with relatively high transaction cost. Those aggregated product catalogs made up of the regular offers of different suppliers, permit both, a greater selection and a comparison of price and quality (Wichmann & Weitzel 1999). Buyer and sellers have the opportunity to identify each other. Since catalog-based services group the demand of a large number of buyers, they strengthen their market power, which can lead to better conditions for the buyers (Zimmermann 2000, p. 4). The critical challenge of the catalog mechanism is the creation of a master catalog, which is gaining supplier critical mass (Alaniz & Roberts 1999).

The *auction mechanism* is a spatial matching process. Typical products are used capital equipment, perishable capacity or hard-to-specify products (Alaniz & Roberts 1999, Kafka 2000a). Auctions are a revolutionary new pricing model for many markets, in which multiple buyers and sellers bid competitively on a contract (Sculley & Woods 1999). E-auctions allow companies to take literally hundreds of bids from all over the world, which would not be possible in the convenient way of purchasing (Porter 2000b), especially in this very short timeframe (van Heck 2000). This method is ideal for liquidating surplus at best possible prices (e.g. e-Steel). Auctioning involves infrequently traded or unique items that can significantly vary in value depending on the buyer (Phillips & Meeker 2000). Auctions are commonly used in industries that are trading redundant, time sensitive or specialized goods and services. They work across multiple products and industries and typically in closed or pre-qualified marketplaces. Online auctions are not only a labor-saving device, they also widen the market and force suppliers to share the squeeze on margins (Thomas 2000, p. 36). By dynamic pricing the auction market enhances efficiency while maximizing the return for the buyer and seller. The seller-driven auction is less favorable to buyers, because there is no negotiation between the buyer and the seller. The buyer-driven or reverse auctions are favorable to buyers, especially if there are multiple sellers able to offer items that come close to meeting the buyer's requirements.

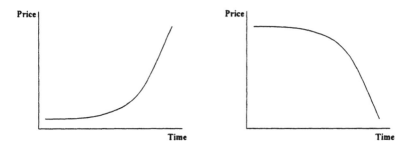

Figure 3.3 Seller-driven and buyer-driven auctions (Sculley & Woods 1999, pp. 81)

Both seller- and buyer-driven auctions are very common, due to the scale, reach, interactive and real-time attributes afforded by the internet. The auctioned article or service must be clearly described, so that the price alone is a sufficient criteria for the selection and acceptance of offers. The duration of auctions is limited. The technical implementation is relatively easy to set up and operate (Wichmann & Weitzel 1999). We differentiate between six types of auctions: English, Dutch, best-price, Vickrey, reverse and Yankee auction (Beckmann et al. 1997, Wichmann & Weitzel 1999, Picot et al. 2001, Raisch 2001). In the English or normal (forward) auction different bids are transparently submitted by the market participants and the highest is successful. In the Dutch auction price drops at fixed intervals by a certain sum and the bid of the first person to agree to a sum is accepted. In the best-price auction, a sealed-bid auction type, the participants bid in a written and sealed manner, winner is the bidder with the highest offer. The Vickrey auction is similar to the best-price auction besides that the winner, who has offered the highest price, only has to pay the second highest price (Chen & Wilson 2000). Buyers may be able to view all bids. In a reverse auction the seller defines the price, he is willing to sell his products for. This amount is hidden from the buyers. In case that the reverse price is not met, the seller is not obligated to sell the item. In a Yankee auction the seller offers multiple identical items with or without minimum bid. Bidders can bid any amount at or above minimum bid for a specific quantity (Raisch 2001, p. 135).[6] The auction organization offers the trading rules, that structure the bidding process and trade settlement best, additionally the intermediary organizes publicity, clerical work and bidding space (Lee & Clark 1997). Key challenge of auctions is building liquidity of buyers

---

[6] Besides these six auction types further auction models are in use, which have been developed by adapting and combining these six models.

and sellers and the ability of players using auction mechanisms to extend offers to include post sales customer support (Skinner 2000). Buyers benefit from broader supply base, lower search and transaction costs and more dynamic pricing, whereas sellers benefit from broader customer access, lower transaction costs and a better understanding of market pricing.

The third mechanism is the *exchange model*, which creates value by temporal matching of supply and demand. This model performs well for near-commodity items and can create substantial value in volatile markets, allowing companies to manage excess supply and peak load demand (Schwartz et al. 1999, Rosson 2000,). Exchanges smooth out peaks and valley in demand and supply by rapidly exchanging the commodities or near-commodities (Kaplan & Sawhney 2000a, 2000b). Besides getting the lowest possible prices from a buyer's view the suppliers have access to more buyers with only a modest increase in marketing cost (Wise & Morrison 2000). The process is a competitive bidding between multiple buyers and sellers with automated matching of orders. It creates an efficient price-setting mechanism online (Sculley & Woods 1999). The matching of buyers and sellers is controlled by the intermediary similar to the process at a stock exchange. A seller announces, that he wishes to sell a certain product and has a minimum price in mind. The potential buyers do not contact the seller directly, but submit their offers to the intermediary. He examines the offers and passes the best one on to the seller. Then the seller can decide whether to accept or not. Depending on the price and mix of participants a purchase contract may or may not materialize. In some marketplaces the purchase transaction takes place in each case with the intermediary, so that neither party knows the eventual buyer or seller. The anonymity prevents from getting any insights into strategic plans of the buyer or seller company. Cost savings are primary in focus for buyers, who can obtain products more cheaply, whereas for sellers these services represent a new sales market for previously difficult or impossible to sell products (Wichmann & Weitzel 1999). Exchanges exist in central, neutral locations, that offer defined processes for the trading of goods and services between buyers and sellers. The mechanism is more flexible than the auction model and allows both, buyers and sellers, to make bids and offers for some underlying commodity. Offers can be made at any time and can often be withdrawn or revised. Exchanges are common in markets with highly volatile prices. Buyers benefit from better matches and better prices as well as the ability to hedge risk in volatile markets. On the other hand sellers benefit from grater access to buyers as well as the ability to liquidate excess supply and manage volatility. The main challenge lies in the value proposition that is attractive to the majority of the dominant businesses, easy to implement and with low installation cost (Sawhney & Kaplan 1999, Skinner 2000). The barter model is a subgroup of the exchange mechanism, where the value creation is done by matching two parties that have reciprocal assets. (Sawhney & Kaplan 1999, Rosson 2000).

The last transaction mechanism is the *bulletin board* or *pinboard*, which is a sophisticated bulletin board, where buyers and sellers can post expressions of interest to buy or sell. After meeting through the postings, the parties negotiate a deal between themselves. The internet enables buyers and sellers from all around the world to participate online, which is ideal for fragmented markets with non-standardized products, since each contract is quite different and requires one to one negotiation (Sculley & Woods 1999, p. 35). The bulletin board creates a virtual community, which is interested in buying or selling a particular product and which can make a connection through the bulletin board (Ploss & Johnson 2000). Besides basic match-making functionality, the exchange must provide other services in order to attract new users and to support existing users of the systems. Many users will want to retain anonymity. Pinboards are the simplest kind of B2B marketplaces. Only limited transactional functions are provided. They offer the opportunity of announcing specific buying or selling requests and are initiating transactions. Prices are freely agreed between buyers and sellers. Transactions take place offline, whereas the marketplaces simply facilitate the coming together of buyers and sellers. The intermediaries systematize the notices on the pinboard and offers notification functions. In principle bulletin boards are only slightly different from small advertisement sections in specialist publications and they are technically very easy to set up and operate. They offer participants ample leeway in placing advertisements and setting prices. Typically the products offered on bulletin boards are very complex and need further detailed description, so that price alone is not the decision maker. A good example for a pinboard is yet2, which is bringing together supply and demand of intellectual capital (Du Pont 2001, p. B2). On this pinboard technology transfer is enabled via internet. Everybody can search for a specific technology by paying a certain access fee. Yet2 delivers the requests to the supplier. In case of a contract a transaction fee of 10% has to be paid. Due to the global offering of developments from all various industries totally new opportunities for implementation of innovations are created.

3.3.3   Revenue models

Revenue models for generating money in the online space vary from company to company. Some companies may believe more firmly in the subscription model; others may prefer the pay-per-use approach; while others rely on product sales margins as in more traditional retailing. Many marketplaces are not committed to just one revenue model and employ multiple strategies at the same time.

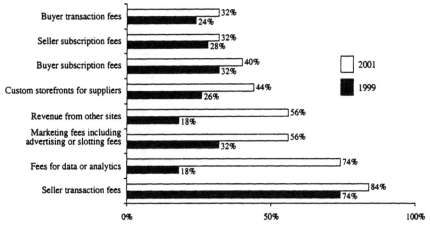

Figure 3.4 Electronic marketplaces diversify revenue sources (Lief 1999, p. 5)

The *transaction model*, in most cases used with the aggregation mechanism, calculates a percentage of the transaction volume, which has usually to be paid by the seller. A typical range varies from 0.5% to 8% of the transaction volume. Most of the transactions seem to be settling in the 1-2% commission range for catalog orders (Rosson 2000). Some electronic marketplaces have opted for standard annual *subscription fees*, based on assumptions about anticipated usage. Similar to the flat subscription fee is the *membership or storefront fee*, which is a charge to a merchant to list its catalog and promotional material in a segmented storefront in the marketplace. If the intermediary is just offering the software package for operating the marketplace a *license fee* is charged to the users (Windham 1999, p. 85). Flat fees encourage the marketplace usage and they avoid the occurance of tax associated with straight transaction fees (Phillips & Meeker 2000, p. 40, Kerrigan et al. 2001). Other marketplaces take the title to goods and *markup* the goods to what the market will bear. Typically the mark-up ranges from 5-10%, but varies widely. Mark-up introduces additional risk for the exchange, since the margin for the exchange is dependent on the product pricing above costs instead of fixed transaction fees.

3.3.4   Market characteristics

Depending on the market characteristics marketplaces have a different orientation, either vertical or horizontal, and focus on a specific dimension of context.

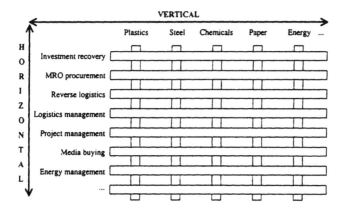

Figure 3.5   Vertical versus horizontal/functional marketplaces (Sawhney & Kaplan 1999, p. 6)

The majority of all marketplaces have a *vertical* focus. These vertical marketplaces are aimed at a very specific industry and are completely orientated toward the distinct needs of this particular group (Rosson 2000). The core element is the identification and solution of industry-specific problems that are connected to fragmented markets. These are markets, in which buyers and sellers have difficulty in coming together or can do this only with very high transaction costs. Markets with many geographically dispersed buyers and sellers are often not operating optimally in terms of transaction costs (Klein & Quelch 1997, p. 347). Lack of information or the use of temporarily under-utilized capacity can also be involved. Inefficiencies in traditional distribution channels can avoid, that buyers find all possible sellers or vice versa. Based on that, prices paid are too high or believed to be too high for either party (Klein & Quelch 1997). Verticals try to find a solution to these very specific problems. They focus on inefficiencies, that exist across a supply chain within a specific industry sector (Skinner 2000). Furthermore these vertical marketplaces try to improve market transparency and price transparency by providing additional industry information. "When you know one market [...] you know exactly one market" (Phillips & Meeker 2000, p. 9). Vertical marketplaces are increasingly supplementing basic transactions with content and communities, that provide advice on how and where products can be best sourced. The success of vertical marketplaces is determined by the generation of transaction revenue, buyer traffic and the recruitment of key suppliers (Rosson 2000). Verticals tend to be dominated by a buyer or seller group, mostly an industry consortium.

In contrast to vertical B2B marketplaces, *horizontal* or *functional* marketplaces are not tailored to the needs of a specific industry, but to functions or processes, which are important in many industries. They run across several or many industries and focus on precise knowledge of the appropriate processes for achieving optimal results. These markets can be characterized by common buyer needs and are addressed through supply of standardized goods and services (Rosson 2000). Whereas vertical marketplaces concentrate on one supply chain within a specific industry, horizontal marketplaces aim to improve inefficiencies within multiple supply chains. They center on a process or service or involve the trade of indirect goods and are usually independent (Skinner 2000). A typical process, which various functional marketplaces wish to simplify and automate, is procurement and especially procurement of MRO (maintenance, repair and operating) (Phillips & Meeker 2000, p. 10). Besides procurement functions such functions as marketing, logistics or human resources are in scope of horizontal marketplaces. They focus on process standardization and generalization. Their competence is process knowledge and workflow automation expertise. These horizontal and functional marketplaces provide the ability to complement process automation with industry-specific content and the ability to customize the business process to respond to industry-specific differences (Sawhney & Kaplan 2000a, 2000b). Successful horizontal marketplaces call for automating workflows and reducing process costs (Rosson 2000).

3.3.5 Product specifics

The last criterion for classifying electronic marketplaces is the dimension product specifics. Product specifics have a major impact on the focus and benefits of an electronic marketplace, its business model, order processing mechanism and the revenue model, since not all goods are equally suited for B2B E-markets.

Commodity type products with well-known technical specifications, manufacturer brands, that can easily be price-compared and do not require substantial after-sale service from vendors are especially suitable candidates for auctions, where the transaction has to be closed in limited time based on price negotiations only without any negotiations on product specifics (Klein & Quelch 1997). Suppliers of commodity products are typically driven by price, quality and delivery criteria and can be characterized by low asset specifity (Roberts & Mackay 1997). These product characteristics have the perfect fit for being traded on an electronic marketplace. Highly standardized merchandises that can be easily compared across suppliers are more suitable for certain B2B markets, than highly customized products with individual specifics and infrequent purchase pattern (Lee et al. 2000).

Another important factor is the *life cycle* of a product. Product markets with short life cycles create large quantities of obsolete and discontinued items, which are perfectly suitable to be market by the exchange mechanism. Customers may experience difficulties in finding spare parts or compatible accessories for earlier generation products. This is especially true in international markets, where product launches lag behind the U.S. market and foreign buyers are paying higher prices than captive customers of local vendors (Klein & Quelch 1997).

Another dimension for differentiation is the *product value*. In a survey of the Center for Strategic Procurement Management in 1997 Cox and Harris (1997, pp. 35) found out the top 10 problems with low value products. The major problem mentioned by the respondents was high transaction costs in relation to cost of product, staffing difficulties due to vast number of transactions and administrative burdens. Low-value goods with relatively high transaction cost are perfectly suitable to be traded on various B2B markets (Kafka 2000b), whereas products with high value are often technically complicated and very specific, although their transaction cost ratio is comparatively low.

Finally, *spot markets* for common operating resources like manufacturing capacity or labor are successfully traded on electronic B2B markets (Kaplan & Sawhney 2000b, p. 57). Especially products with highly volatile prices are purchased on spot markets. They have a perfect fit for auctions with transparent bidding processes. However, products with long frame agreements do not fit to be traded on an auction, but might be posted on pinboards.

3.4   B2B electronic marketplace classification models

The author tries to classify the different approaches, although often the dimensions business models and transaction mechanisms are not consistently separated. Different authors use same indicators for describing different characteristics.

Researcher	Business models	Order processing mechanisms	Revenue models	Market charac- teristics	Product specifics
Alaniz & Roberts 1999	-Direct transactions -Trading portals	-Exchange -Auctions -Buy-side solutions -Sell-side solutions -Supply chain optimization			
Baker 2000		-Auctions -E-Catalogs -Virtual exchanges			
Beckmann et al. 1997		-English auction -Dutch auction -Best-price auction -Vickrey auction			
Berryman et al. 1998	-Seller- controlled marketplaces -Buyer- controlled marketplaces -Neutral marketplaces				
Chen & Wilson 2000		-English auction -Dutch auction -Vickrey auction	-Listing fees -Transaction fee -Advertising revenue		
Daniel & Klimis 1999	-Biased market -Unbiased market -Personalized regional and global market				
Elofson & Robinson 1998		-Filtering model -Negotiation model -Auction model			
Gulley et al. 2000		-Virtual auction -Virtual exchange -Virtual catalog			-Com- modities -Special- ties
Harting 2000		-Auction -Exchange -Publishers -Distributors -Brokers	-Perpetual license -Subscription -Advertising -Transaction		

Researcher	Business models	Order processing mechanisms	Revenue models	Market charac- teristics	Product specifics
Kajüter & Ruland 2000	-Bilateral E-trade -Marketplaces -E-Distributors				
Kaplan & Sawhney 2000a, 2000b	-MRO hubs -Yield hubs -Exchanges -Catalog hubs	-Aggregation -Matching			-Operat. input -Manuf. Input
Klein & Quelch 1997		-Auction -Buyer markets -Pure exchange		-Market fragmentation	-Com- modities -Life- cycle
Kollmann 2000	-Buyer hierarchies -Supplier hierarchies -Marketplaces				
Kurz & Ortwein 1999	-Seller value network -Buyer value network -Electronic marketplace -Co-ops				
Kusterer 2000	-Context provider -Content provider -Commerce provider	-Agora -Aggregators -Alliances -Distribution networks -E-Hubs			
Lief 1999		-Auction -Aggregator -Bid system -Exchange	-Seller transaction fees -Fees for data or analytics -Marketing fees for advertising -Revenue from other sites -Storefronts -Buyer transaction fees -Seller/buyer subscription fees		
Müller- Merbach et al. 2001	-Aggregation -Adjustment	-Catalog -Auction -Exchange -Request for proposal	-Bonus -Participation fee -Subscription fee -Hosting fee -Advertising -Sale of info	-Vertical -Horizontal	
Nokkentved 2000	-Independent -Vendor focused -Consortium -Private -Collaborative	-Auction house -Exchange			

Researcher	Business models	Order processing mechanisms	Revenue models	Market charac- teristics	Product specifics
Patel 1999	-Seller-controlled -Buyer-controlled				
Phillips & Meeker 2000	-Buyer managed -Supplier managed -Distributors/ market makers -Content aggregator	-Catalog order -Dynamic pricing -Auctioning -RFP (request for proposal)	-Transaction fee -Subscription fee -Auction service -Mark-up -Membership/ storefront fee -License fee		
Ploss & Johnson 2000		-Trading floor -Catalog -Broker -Community			
Porter 2000a	-Sell.side -Buy-side -Neutral	-Demand aggregation -Supply aggregation -Matching			
Quelch & Klein 1996		-Electronic auctions -Exchanges			
Rosson 2000	-Buyer managed -Supplier managed -Distributor, market maker -Content aggregators	-Catalog models -Auction models -Exchange models -Barter models	-Transaction fees -Subscription fees -Auction services -Mark-up -Storefront fee -Fee for use of proprietary software	-Vertical markets -Horizontal markets	
Sander & Behlke 2001	-Product/service strategy -Platform strategy -Investment strategy -Participation strategy	-Catalog service -Exchange -Request for proposal -Auction			-C-parts -Raw materials -Industrial goods
Sawhney & Kaplan 1999		-Catalog -Auction -Exchange -Barter		-Vertical -Horizontal	
Schneider & Schnetkamp 2000	-Procurement hubs -Marketplaces -Portals		-Subscription fees -Transaction fees -Advertising fees -Sales market info -Fees for added-services -License fees	-Vertical -Horizontal	

Researcher	Business models	Order processing mechanisms	Revenue models	Market characteristics	Product specifics
Sculley & Woods 1999	-Aggregators -Trading hubs -Post and browse markets -Auction markets -Fully-automated exchanges	-Fixed pricing -One-on-one negotiation -Auction markets -Electronic auto-exectution systems			
Skinner 2000	-Sell-side applications -Buy-side applications -Market making applications -Supply chain applications	-Auctions -Exchanges -Aggregation -Community	-Transaction based pricing -Subscription based pricing -License based pricing -Advertising based pricing	-Vertical -Horizontal	-Direct goods and services -Indirect goods and services
Wichmann & Weitzel 1999		-Pinboards -Catalog-based -Exchanges -Auction service	-Participants subscription -Transaction fee -Receipts from advertising -Licensing of software -Ancillary service -Sale of transaction information -Fees for access to editorial content	-Vertical marketplaces -Horizontal market-places	
Windham 1999	-Portals -Virtual retailers -Auctioneers -Aggregators		-Transaction model -Reseller model -Advertising model -Subscription model -Pay per use model -License fee model -Hybrid model		
Wirtz 2000	-Content -Commerce -Context -Connection				

Table 3.1   Overview literature review on B2B E-marketplace classification

3.5   Combination of major dimensions

After reviewing various important dimensions for characterizing electronic marketplaces, typical portfolio models are discussed. For selecting the appropriate transaction mechanism, some authors have chosen the type of business model by referring to the number of buyers and sellers in the market. In electronic age the trend is from one-to-one relations towards many-to-many relations between buyers and sellers, which is controversial to the development of long-term relationships with a reduced number of suppliers from a buyer's perspective or focusing on key customers from a supplier's perspective.

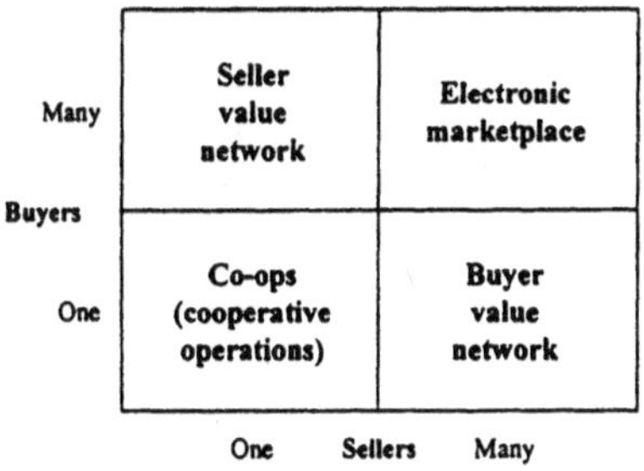

Many	**Seller value network**	**Electronic marketplace**
Buyers		
One	**Co-ops (cooperative operations)**	**Buyer value network**
	One Sellers Many	

Figure 3.6 E-Marketplace classification (Kurz & Ortwein 1999, p. 131)

For Berryman et al. (1998) the question about market share and buying power are in focus for determining, which marketplace model is most effective. If a product stands out from competitors and is strongly branded, its producer should consider selling from its own web site, whereas a seller of a product with a weaker market position should try to enter several marketplaces in order to broaden its reach. From a buyer's standpoint, the key variables are the size of procurement expenditure and the fragmentation of the supplier base. Large buyers in a market with many suppliers should set up their own procurement site to increase their buying power even more. Aggregators make sense for small buyers in a market with few suppliers, whereas in a market with many suppliers auctions lead to lower prices due to intense competition between the suppliers.

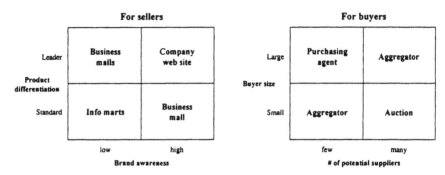

Figure 3.7 Marketplace models (Berryman et al. 1998, p. 134)

3.6   Relational B2B electronic marketplace model

All of these various portfolio models pick some single dimensions for determining the appropriate marketplace mechanism, but none of them have chosen attributes out of all five characterization dimensions (business model, transaction mechanism, revenue model, market characteristics and product specifics) discussed above. But more importantly, all models do not discuss the impact of different platforms on the inter-organizational relationships. This is insufficient, because electronic marketplaces do have an impact on the inter-organizational exchange and as such, it is necessary to understand, which characteristics do have an impact on relationships. Therefore, the author recommends the following systematic approach.

Figure 3.8: E-Marketplace classification model

With this approach the important dimensions mentioned in literature and characteristics referring to the impact on inter-organizational relationships are integrated within two segmentation criteria: product specifics and marketplace openness.

Four items can describe the first dimension, product specifics, by summarizing different aspects of standardization. Starting with the product type, commodities are differentiated only by price, quality and delivery criteria (Roberts & Mackay 1997) and do not require substantial after-sales service. They have only a low or nearly no necessity of relationship to be successfully traded on electronic marketplaces. They are perfectly suitable to be traded on B2B electronic marketplace without special relational focus. Different with customized products, they require a relational electronic marketplace setting, since they need conversation for product specification (Campbell 2000, p. 390). They are not only price-driven, here the fit of the supplier's offering to the customer's problem is essential. The second item for characterizing the level of product standardization is the purchasing method. Especially standardized products are bought on spot markets. Purchases sourced on spot markets can be successfully transferred to B2B electronic marketplaces without special attention to relational aspects. In the past, they have been bought in the right moment without any specific relationship to a certain supplier and in the same way they can be purchased via electronic marketplaces. But products, which have been bought from suppliers based on long-term frame agreements, have to be treated differently. They need an electronic marketplace setting with a higher degree of relationship. Long-term agreements have been closed only with suppliers, where a high degree of trust and satisfaction was basis of an intense relationship. The third item characterizing the degree of product standardization is the product value. Especially low value products with extremely high transaction cost can be traded via electronic marketplaces, which have only low to medium extent of relationship orientation. Often low value products are standardized and easy replaceable products. Then relationship is not needed for a successful sourcing process via B2B electronic marketplaces. But on the other hand, medium value products, as for example specialty chemicals require a higher degree of relationship on the electronic marketplace, since they are differentiated by quality and product specification. High value products, where the high price comes from intense customization, need such a high level of relationship, that they won't be suitable for electronic marketplaces. The fourth item in the product specifics dimension is the life cycle. A short life cycle leads to high extent of obsolete products. For those products electronic marketplaces open a new sourcing opportunity. But products with short life cycle are often technical complex or customized products (Günther & Tempelmeier 2000, p. 47), which require a certain extent of relationship to be successfully traded.

The second segmentation criterion evaluates the electronic marketplace openness. This dimension can be summarized by four characteristics: business model, number of participants, order processing mechanism and anonymity. Hierarchical business models, such as portals (supplier hierarchy) or procurement hubs (buyer hierarchy), require more relational support to gain market participants than neutral marketplaces, where no party is dominant. In the hierarchical constellation one buyer or supplier has the dominant position to control all others and to take the final decision. But on the other hand the one supreme actor also needs enough relationship competence to attract and convince enough business partners to make the marketplace a success. The second attribute characterizing the marketplace openness is the number of participants. In open situations with many participants, relational support is not possible. The number of participants is high enough to ensure the needed number of transaction for a profitable marketplace. Whereas on marketplaces with only limited participants, the environment requires more intense relationships to convince to execute the transaction. If we analyze the order processing mechanism in respect to the openness of the B2B electronic marketplace, the need for relationship support varies depending on the mechanism. Pinboards are just starting point for a supplier-buyer product exchange and require one-to-one interaction to finalize the transaction process. Here relational support might be key for success in order to finalize the supply transaction. This is different with auctions, where under time pressure the transaction has to be finalized. There is no time and no need for any relational support. The exchange mechanism is in-between. Although the transaction will be finalized via internet, a more inter-relational transaction is needed to find a solution, which is acceptable to both parties. The last characteristic of marketplace openness is the level of anonymity. N:m-relational electronic marketplaces operated by intermediaries, where no participant knows the other participants, have the highest level of openness. The market players have no risk to loose any company insight. Due to the high anonymity, no relationship support is necessary, transactions are without any obligations. On marketplaces with 1:n-ratio (portals or hubs), where the number of buyers or suppliers do not know the other participants, but all know the marketplace operator, a higher extent of relationship support is necessary to convince to participate. The lowest marketplace openness is on marketplaces without anonymity, where each participant knows all other participants. There the relationship support is key for the business success of the B2B electronic marketplace. Resistance against other competitors and market leaders has to be overcome. Summarizing the described four items, with decreasing level of marketplace openness the opportunities and need for relationship support increases.

These two dimensions seem especially important to cover all relevant issues and effects related to the new purchasing environment on B2B electronic marketplaces.

3.7   Managerial impact

Based on the mentioned segmentation criteria, a B2B electronic marketplace can be specified depending on the relevant circumstances. But for developing a sustainable successful marketplace, a detailed analysis of the purchase situation is necessary. Dimensions such as the buyer business impact, supplier market competitiveness and relationship attractiveness have to be detailed to get a full picture of the purchase situation. These characteristics determine the degree of relationship intensity needed to successfully manage the purchase situation. Dependent on the level of relationship necessity the B2B electronic marketplace has to be adapted. Then the target procurement strategy can be defined based on the existent purchasing environment and the relevant marketplace features. Blind action just for having any activities in the electronic market can be dangerous and will not be a guarantee for sustainable and tangible success. This relation between a given purchase situation and the characteristics of an E-marketplace will be detailed in this study. The author tries to define a fit between the two from a relationship perspective with respect to the interplay between purchase situation and E-marketplace concept influencing the success of supplier relationships.

For implementing the new E-tools discussed above most firms have defined a project for assuring a smooth and successful introduction of the B2B E-marketplace. This project organization and its success factors are discussed in the next chapter.

4   B2B E-marketplace introduction project

Some forecasts predicted, that in 2004 B2B E-commerce will hit $2.7 trillion (Kafka 2000b). While internet trade between individual partners (B2C or business to customer) will continue to flourish, B2B E-marketplaces are expected to fuel most of the growth, reaching 53% of all online business trade in five years. Especially from a buyer's perspective the B2B E-commerce activities have already been valued of high importance in 2000 as shown in below figure:

How important is online B2B E-commerce for your company today? In 2002?

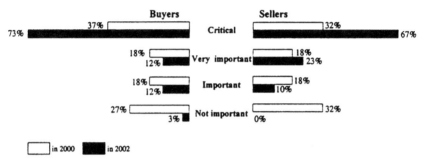

Figure 4.1   Importance of B2B E-Commerce based on 80 companies (Kafka 2000, p. 3)

To establish any B2B E-marketplace concept within the procurement organization, most companies have started specifically defined projects with a strict time line and cost budget. They have assigned a dedicated project team with the appropriate know-how of procurement, business experience, electronic commerce skills plus commitment and communication skills (Korper & Ellis 2000, p. 253). In this chapter the project organization is further detailed. Chapter 4.1 summarizes the set-up of such an introduction project. Furthermore, in chapter 4.2 the project success and its various levers are detailed, whereas in chapter 4.3 the different aspects of project management are discussed.

4.1   Set-up of the B2B E-marketplace introduction project

First the author wants to define the term project, how it is understood in this study. Along with Martino (1964, p. 17) "a project is any task which has a definable beginning and a definable end and requires the expenditure of one or more resources in each of the separate but interrelated and interdependent activities which must be completed to achieve the objectives for which the task was instituted". The purpose of the project in focus of this study is the introduction and implementation of new E-procurement tools supported by the internet, which have been discussed in chapter 3.

Depending on the overall firm strategy, the B2B E-marketplace project has to be set up. The way, in which the introduction project is structured, has a profound effect on the results. Most firms have had some experience with large and complex IT or business restructuring initiatives, so that they are familiar with the basic framework of enterprise-wide projects. However, there are some important aspects, such as supplier involvement, building a business case and developing scoring criteria for software platform selection, which are unique to a B2B E-marketplace project (Neef 2001, p. 161).

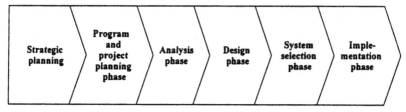

Figure 4.2   Key phases of an enterprise-wide E-procurement project (Neef 2001, p. 162)

Before beginning any major firm-wide project, the key organizational leaders convene to discuss and agree on the way the project is setup and executed (Corsten 2000, p. 12). The executive group has to be educated on the many aspects of E-procurement, to debate and agree on the case for action, to consider the need for business process restructuring, supplier involvement, risk and change management and to reach consensus on the basic scope of the project, including cost, resources and timescales. When the strategic setup is defined the operational perspective has to be clarified (Baguley 1999, p. 23). Experts from all relevant departments such as procurement, finance, management and information systems (MIS) and manufacturing have to review the strategic directions, guiding principles and the project goals (Neef 2001). The targets have to be set, critical areas to be identified (Litke 1995, p. 31). In the analysis and design phase, the project shifts from the planning to the doing modus. Based on the developed project plan, the procurement process can be redesigned. In the system selection phase the software requirements have to be identified and aspects such as cost, functionality, integration and interoperability have to be thoughtfully analyzed. Finally the project has to be implemented, which is the most critical and resource intense phase (Baguley 1999, p. 24).

4.2   Project success of the B2B E-marketplace introduction project

Although the idea of project management does exist for a long time, the technology, tools and methods for successfully carrying out projects have constantly been further developed.[7] The internet, networking and computers have all provided a basis for undertaking and managing projects with greater success (Yap 2001). But despite all of these advances, many projects still fail or run into severer trouble (Glass 1999, p. 17). Therefore evaluating and measuring project success continuous to be highly important.

In project management literature, a variety of empirical studies concerning project success factors do exist.[8] The complexity of the project success measurement is demonstrated by the outcome of past empirical studies. In one study 32 out of 200 potential success factors were identified (Murphy et al. 1974). In another study even more than 100 success factors were identified (Daum 1992). But, as McCoy (1986), Wateridge (1998) and Wells (1998) observed, neither a standardized definition of project success does exist nor an accepted methodology to measure it.

For defining the project success, as it is understood in this study, the author uses a definition of project success, which goes along with Lechler (1997). The project success of the B2B E-marketplace introduction project consists of three success areas: costs, time and performance (Lock 1997).

---

[7]   For further details on the origins and development of project management refer to Litke (1995, p. 21).
[8]   For a systematic approach on different studies concerning project success refer to Lechler (1997, p. 59).

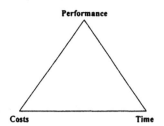

Figure 4.3 Triangle of project objectives (Lock 1997, p. 23)

Baguley (1999, p. 22) further differentiates the performance dimension into two sub-aspects: quality and execution.[9] Depending on the priority of the objectives, one specific success area can have a higher impact on the overall success than others.

In this study the success dimensions time and costs are covered by measuring efficiency. Along with Gemünden (1993), the author uses efficiency as a measurement of cost and time constraints. When projects are planned with the objective to stick to a certain time frame, the initial planning plays a vital role in the successful achievement of project deadlines (Dey & Ogunlana 2001, p. 24). For defining the project duration, several steps have to be executed. First the project scope has to be defined. Second, the work breakdown structure has to be derived, which is the basis for resource allocation. Finally, critical project tasks have to be identified to be able to estimate the related risk areas for planning a buffer time. Based on these steps the time target can be set. Only based on a thoughtful time definition, the risk of time overrun can be minimized (Williams 1995).[10] For controlling purposes, not only the total actual project duration is measured against the predefined plan (Gemünden 1990a, p. 8, Lechler 1997, p. 90, Högl 1998, p. 76), but also during the execution of the project the actual duration of single project tasks is measured against the plan, so that time overrun can be identified as early as possible to be able to take the appropriate action (Litke 1995, p. 106).

Similar to the time controlling, the cost controlling also depends on a detailed capacity plan on a single task basis. For each task the capacity requirement needs to be estimated. Then actual costs are measured against the plan.

It is an iterative process with the goal of optimizing the time constraints with given resources (Litke 1995, p. 115).

---

[9] For the quality aspect refer to Zenz (1981, p. 153).
[10] To get an overview on project risk management refer to Williams (1995).

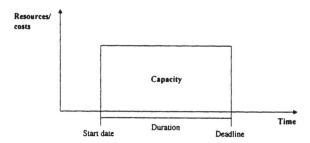

Figure 4.4 Interaction between time and cost constraints (Litke 1995, p. 115)

If time is the limiting factor, further resources can only partly compensate missing time, increasing project costs might occur as a consequence. Additional resources, which are added later on to the project, need to be well introduced to the project. Further time is lost and the coordination outlay increases exponentially with each added resource (Lechler 1997, p. 90). Therefore in most cases an overrun of time also leads to an overrun in cost as Brooks (1975, p. 25) states "adding manpower to a late software project makes it later". This assumption of strong correlation between cost and time constraints was positively supported in diverse empirical studies (e.g. Might & Fischer 1985, p. 73, Larson & Gobeli 1989, p. 122, Lechler 1997, p. 172).

As mentioned earlier, the success dimension performance can be further differentiated into quality and execution. For evaluating the quality as one sub-dimension, the measure effectiveness is used. The effectiveness measures the objective realization (Gemünden 1981, pp. 166, Scholz 1992, pp. 533). Although it is difficult to clearly define the objectives of innovative and mostly highly complex projects (Jenkins et al. 1984, p. 79, Hauschildt & Pulczinsky 1992, p. 74, Weltz & Ortmann 1992, p. 35), the objectives in the specific case of B2B E-marketplace introduction projects are a combination of process cost, material cost and inventory reduction. Additional objectives, such as price and supplier comparability, improvement of existent supplier relationships and supplier concentration are included to measure effectiveness. Clarity about the objectives of the project is key to the project success (Hendrix 2001, p. 122). Not only joint agreement on the project objectives by the top management, but also by the project team is required (Neef 2001, p. 161, Simpson 2001, p. 23). The project team needs to consist of highly goal-oriented individuals, strong-willed with high leadership skills (Seely & Duong 2001, p. 31). The project effectiveness evaluates the fulfillment of these diverse objectives compared to the targets defined at the project start.

The execution aspect of the performance dimension is evaluated by measuring the B2B E-marketplace acceptance. Along with Martin (1993, p. 18) acceptance summarizes on the one hand the attitude towards the new technology and on the other hand the readiness and willingness to use the new technology. Based on this definition Schönecker (1985) as well as Müller-Böling and Müller (1986) diversified the acceptance measure into four different groups depending on the intensity of the attitude towards the new technology and the willingness to use the new technology. For the B2B E-marketplace acceptance the author uses the following three measures: B2B E-marketplace acceptance evaluated from the project team and B2B E-marketplace acceptance evaluated from the procurement organization. In both measures the attitude towards the new system as well as the willingness to use it is evaluated. As a third dimension the supplier's willingness to use the new technology is incorporated. This dimension is also critical to the project success, since it measures, how successful the project team has convinced the supplier about the benefits of the new E-procurement environment.

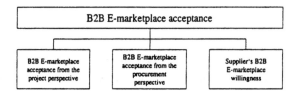

Figure 4.5   B2B E-marketplace acceptance

Joseph (1990) developed a model for analyzing the acceptance of CAD systems. He classified four areas of impact on the acceptance measure: people care, personal aspects, organizational issues and technology. These factors properly applied lead to the above-defined B2B E-marketplace acceptance.

To summarize above: the project success of the B2B E-marketplace introduction project can be seen as the first step towards the new procurement environment. Due to project termination on time and within the given budget the project team can provide the deliverables in a very efficient manner. But efficiency is just one aspect of project success; same importance should be attached to the content of the deliverables. They need to fulfill the required objectives. The third contribution to the project success is the acceptance of the B2B E-marketplace.

Figure 4.6 Definition of project success

4.3   Different facets of the appropriate project management of B2B E-marketplace introduction projects

After a clear understanding of project success and how it is measured in this study, chapter 4.3 focuses on the project management, which enables a successful project. The project resources, including budget, people and other resources, need to be managed. In the B2B E-marketplace introduction project team members come from different organizations as the procurement department, IT department, production or R&D (van Weele 2000, p. 229). The cross-functional project team has to be able to provide the appropriate qualifications. Together the team members can cover all technical and social questions related to the new procurement environment. Each organization within the firm has its own interests, agenda and management contributing to the joint workload. Although new support tools do exist, there are fewer constants, more challenges, reduced resources and increased risk (Lientz & Rea 2001).

The first area of importance concerning successful project management of B2B E-marketplace introduction projects is the top management support. Top management refers here to upper management being able to take overall decisions. The top management is responsible for the overall guidance and to set project rules (Lechler 1997, p. 96). Furthermore, the top management is responsible for more specific project related issues. Priority setting between different project tasks, definition of the project leader and the project team, fine-tuning of project objectives, definition of budget and time constraints are also responsibilities of the top management. In case of high-level problems and conflicts, the top management has to solve those. The appropriate conflict management for achieving resolutions is key for the project to keep on time and within the defined budget. Major project decisions, such as additional resources or additional time, have to be taken by top management. Additionally, the top management has to inform all relevant departments within the firm about the ongoing project, the importance and the status. They are responsible for the satisfaction of all parties involved in the project by managing the strategic aspects of the project.

In this study the second important area of successful project management is the team competence, which consists of different aspects: project leader qualification, project team qualifications and project communication.

The project leader is responsible for managerial items but also for administrative items (Rinza 1985, p. 133, Schmelzer 1986, p. 69, Litke 1995, p. 174, Maddaus 2000, p. 88). First he has to manage and direct project resources to achieve the project objectives. Secondly, he has to supervise the project work. Furthermore he has to develop the project plan and ensure that the work is completed on time, within budget and with satisfying quality. The project leader has to anticipate and plan ahead, since anything unforeseen can reflect poorly on the project leader, even if it is not his fault (Maddaus 2000, p. 89). Another responsibility is the interface with upper management regarding project review, approval and addressing project issues. Highly important is the motivation aspect; the project leader has to motivate the team in the presence of normal pressures of work as well as political realities and pressures. Conflict management is often required to solve intra-team conflicts, but also conflicts with other organizations or suppliers (Corsten 2000, p. 56). A project manager must be able to act as a problem and conflict solver. He needs to be able to identify and understand problems, put them into perspective and then develop and implement solutions (Lock 1996, p. 44). The project leader needs to select the right approach depending on the type of conflict. Forcing an individual to accept the others opinion might create an apparent removal of any conflict, but brings feelings of resentment and causes deterioration in the relationship between the persons in conflict. Solving the conflict by withdrawing from the conflict issues is also not appropriate as such an approach does not eliminate the conflict. The emphasis on smoothing is to focus on similarities rather than on differences over issues. This approach may not address the real issues; the differences remain under the surface. Bargaining and searching for a solution is a compromise, which is often achieved at the expense of optimum results. The confrontation approach involves a rational problem-solving approach, where disputing parties solve their differences by first focusing on the issues, then looking at alternative approaches and finally selecting the best alternative.[11] Effective conflict management is essential to assure the team motivation. Finally, the team leader is responsible for the appropriate qualifications of his team, he has to train members of the project team in project management methods and tools, in which they are involved. To be able to achieve the expectations, the project leader needs to be backed by the required power (Zogg 1974, p. 260, Lechler 1997, p. 98, Baguley 1999, p. 138). Therefore, he needs the formal authority to make decisions and decide issues. This may have to be used occasionally, but it can easily be abused. Then he needs to rely on reward and penalty power, so that he is able to reward or punish team members. Furthermore, the project leader requires the power as a technical authority. Otherwise the team members would not accept him as an expert and would not respect his judgment and maturity (Sotiriou & Wittmer 2001, p. 12). Through the experience and behavior of the project leader, the project leader installs a sense of respect among the project team. This is probably the best type of power. Power should be invoked as little as possible in a formal way. Instead the project leader should develop and apply skills of collaboration, which appeals to the self-interest of the team members (Lientz & Rea 2001, p. 108). A project leader should have the following qualities to be able to develop respect among team members and management as a source of power: A project manager needs to communicate well verbally and in writing within and outside of the project. Communication problems have been identified as a major source of project failure (Lientz & Rea 2001, p. 111). The project leader has to be able to see the big picture and then relate it to the current project situation. Furthermore, the project leader has to be able to effectively manage people. He has to be able to take his experience, integrate it and then apply it to the current project. Based on the appropriate level of ambition and energy the project leader must work hard and be able to take measured risk (Sotiriou & Wittmer 2001, p.12). It is highly important that the project leader is able to step back from the project and take the overall view, otherwise symptoms of problems may be overlooked. A project leader should be able to show initiative and be willing to take risk (Neef 2001, p. 195). Due to their dual role of project manager and project administrator, they have to be organized. This includes managing time and being able to allocate time and energy to issues that are important (Corsten 2000, p.53). A good project manager has to be able to admit that there is a problem and accept responsibility as well as to be able to accept suggestions, hints, and criticism and turn it into positive action. It is highly important for strategic decisions, that the project leader

---

[11] For a more detailed review of different approaches of conflict management refer to Singh & Vlatas (1991), Al-Tabtabai et al. (2001).

is familiar with the organization, how it works and who the key players are. The project leader has to be prepared concerning all new E-procurement tools and possibilities. Otherwise he will lack credibility within the team. All these skills are interdependent. Experience and knowledge facilitate problem solving, as managing people and communicating go hand in hand.[12]

The project team is responsible for producing the project output, although the determination of the project purpose is beyond their responsibility (Baccarini 1999, p. 28). Based on the team work, complex and innovative tasks can be efficiently realized (Schmelzer 1992, p. 298, Lechler 1997, p. 101). Basis for solid project work is the appropriate know-how, experience and the relevant technical skills of the project team (Skulmoski 2001, p. 13). High motivation of the project team is key for the successful achievement of the project objectives. Only supported by high motivation, the project team can overcome many challenges related to individual differences and unexpected circumstances (Dunn 2001, p. 4). The project team must be well trained on specific issues concerning new technologies (Rothman 2000, p. 39), since the team members must be able to identify all critical issues beforehand during the execution of the project. When the project is finished, they need to be able to hand-over the new procedures and concepts to the operational workforce, who is working in the E-procurement environment. A poor hand-over is a major reason for a project failure.

Clarity concerning the individual tasks between the various team members enables a smoother project execution. In case of questions the appropriate responsibility can be easily identified.

The third aspect of team competence is the project communication. Effective communication has to be planned in two ways: internally within the project team and externally to all relevant organizations and even to the suppliers. Different types of information are available and can be used in the appropriate circumstances, oral communication especially useful for team internal use and written information for external communication (Maddaus 2000, p. 304). The information and communication plan has to be adapted to the project organization with different people at different locations. Different mediums have different advantages; for example the advantage of verbal communications in the sense that you can convey tone and yet not be pinned down to a specific text (Lientz & Rea 2001, p. 281).

The last area of importance of project management is the planning and steering aspect. All projects are built around standard business objectives for success: achieving high

---

[12] For a detailed discussion on the attributes of a successful project manager refer to Lientz & Rea (2001, p. 111).

productivity, improving quality, delivering at the appropriate time, utilizing resources effectively and efficiently and managing costs (Stewart 2001, p. 41). The goal of every project is to do more, better, faster and with less. In order to be able to achieve this goal, project leaders need to be able to measure, what they are doing and how well they are achieving their goals against an initial benchmark or baseline. Therefore various activities have to be considered (Lientz & Rea 2001, p. 167). The status of the work on the project has to be determined on a regular basis, e.g. once a week. A standard format should be used covering the status on active tasks, additions and changes to the schedule, identification and discussion of any issues and the projected schedule for the next reporting period. Based on this information, the status of the project has to be analyzed. In case of any delay, appropriate actions can be taken to compensate the delay. Either the project objectives can be adapted or additional resources can be staffed on the project or time lines can be extended (Rinza 1985, p. 23). A continuous comparison between targets and actual status is key for an early recognition of any delay. The quality has to be assessed, so that poor quality can be directly adapted. The quality assessment has to be done on a detailed level to be able to identify weaknesses in quality, content, completeness and other attributes. Motivating and encouraging the team is an ongoing process to keep the team up to speed with the required quality level. Upcoming issues and opportunities have to be addressed. On a regular basis the management needs to be informed about the project status and occurring problems. Many project failures are caused by poor planning and controlling (Rothman 2000, p. 40). As Stewart (2001) recommends in order to better manage the ongoing project and to provide an organization-wide response to increasing pressures for excellence in project management, a balanced scorecard approach can be used to perform health checks throughout the project life cycle. Another possibility is the usage of computer packages for deterministic project management such as CPM (critical path method) (Dey & Ogunlana 2001), although their appropriate usage requires time-intense adaptations in the software to define the corresponding project set-up. Furthermore, during the ongoing project various indicators have to be continuously adapted (Kueng 1997, p. 50). However, before investing in any project management software, various criteria as the existent features of the software packages, the market presence of the producer, experience of reference customers and training offering should be evaluated (Martin 1997, p. 49).

Summarizing the aspects of project management, which are important in this study, for a successful project management of B2B E-marketplace introduction projects the above discussed three components need to be optimized: top management support, team competence and project planning and steering.

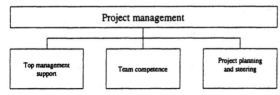

Figure 4.7 Definition of project management

5   Theoretical framework and hypotheses of the study

B2B E-marketplaces offer tools and processes, such as business rules, technology, transaction support, that help companies conduct business with other entities more effectively. What separates this new marketplace from the old can be summed up in two words: efficiency and change (Cunningham 2001, p. 9). However, these new processes and tools must also comply with existing standards of doing business and the technology must support rather than impair those standards. The key to success is the appropriate fit between the given circumstances and the new methods of doing business. Not every B2B E-marketplace concept fits to every purchase situation. The purchase situation determines, which kind of relationship support is required. This has to be taken into account, when defining B2B E-marketplace concepts. Furthermore, the cornerstone of the appropriate fit is a successful project management of the introduction of the B2B E-marketplace concept.

In the following chapter the theoretical framework is derived. The main research questions analyze the relation between the purchase situation and the characteristics of the B2B E-marketplace. Can a fit between the purchase situation and the B2B E-marketplace be defined from a relationship perspective? Since the relationship perspective is in center of analysis, the influence of the interplay between purchase situation and B2B E-marketplace characteristics on the success of a supplier relationship is analyzed. For reducing complexity, the theoretical framework is divided into three models. In the *first model* the impact of the appropriate fit between purchase situation and B2B E-marketplace characteristics on the direct and indirect value functions of a supplier relationship is discussed (chapter 5.1). With the *second model* the effects of successful project organization concerning the introduction of B2B E-marketplace concept is further detailed (chapter 5.2). In chapter 5.3 the *third model* is introduced covering the impact of a successful project organization on the fit between the purchase situation and the B2B E-marketplace. Chapter 5.4 provides a summary of the derived hypotheses and gives an overview of the theoretical framework of the study.

5.1   Model 1: Fit between purchase situation and B2B E-marketplace

Before discussing the impact of the appropriate fit between purchase situation and B2B E-marketplace on the relationship success the author wants to define the term "relationship success" as it is understood in this work.

Relationships have always mattered in business markets "when the interaction between a customer and a supplier has economic consequences that go beyond the simple transfer of products for money in a single transaction. [...] Relationships matter when the value to the parties involved in an exchange stems from interaction in its entirety, rather than simply from the tangible resource transfer between the companies involved" (Ford et al. 1999, p. 66). Relationships in traditional marketplaces developed organically as the key individuals in each firm built close personal or business friendships. Due to their mutual trust firms made specialized non-retrievable investments that created structural bonds, which hold the relationship together (Williamson 1975, 1979, Wilson & Jantrania 1996). Nowadays, the purpose of the development of relationships is to achieve strategic goals. A synergistic combination of individual and mutual goals encourages suppliers and buyers to invest time, effort and resources to create a long-term collaborative effort and thereby achieve individual and partnership strategic advantages (Wilson & Jantrania 1996, p. 56). Along with Walter et al. (2001) different value functions can be utilized in a partnership between a supplier and buyer. In order to be able to create value through these supplier relationships, it is highly important for the buyer to understand the functions of relationships properly. In the context of this study, value is understood as "the perceived trade-off between multiple benefits and sacrifices" gained through a supplier relationship by key decision makers in the buyer's organization (Walter et al. 2001, p. 369). The success of a relationship can be determined by summarizing the output of these various value functions. Only with an optimized utilization of the diverse value functions the buyer creates high relationship success. Some researchers define only monetary value functions (Anderson et al. 1993), whereas others also include non-monetary benefits, such as competence, market position and social rewards (Zeithaml 1988, Wilson 1995, Wilson & Jantrania 1996, Johnson et al. 1999).[13] In this study, relationship success is measured by two components: direct and indirect value functions (Walter et al. 2001). While the direct value functions characterize the monetary outcome in cost savings, the

---

[13] For a literature overview on value definitions refer to Woodruff (1997, p.141).

indirect value functions summarize the non-monetary benefits.[14] The latter comprise innovation functions, which express the potential of innovation development due to the supplier relationship, and the access and market functions, which cover the supplier's competence of being able to help in getting better access to "official authorities as chambers, banks or trade associations" (Walter et al. 2001, p. 373). The author has translated the seller's perspective into a buyer's perspective with special reference to E-markets. The conceptualization of relationship success can be seen as following figure:

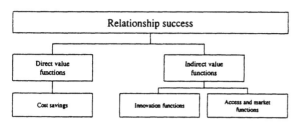

Figure 5.1 Relationship success

After getting clarity on the definition of relationship success the author wants to focus on the different reasons, which lead to the assumption, that the appropriate fit between purchase situation and B2B E-marketplace has a direct positive impact on the relationship success. The following figure gives an overview of the first derived model:

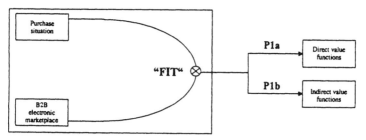

Figure 5.2 Model 1: Fit between purchase situation and B2B E-marketplace

The two propositions 1a and 1b are based on the following considerations:

---

[14] The other dimensions of direct value functions as defined by Walter et al. (2001), i.e. volume function and safeguard function, have not been incorporated in this study. The reason is that the volume function can be expressed by cost savings and the safeguard function is not relevant in the content of the B2B E-marketplace introduction project.

(1)   The existing purchase situation has to be appropriately understood and interpreted.

(2)   The B2B E-marketplace concept should not be a limitation to the potential success factors of the corresponding purchase situation.

(3)   Limitations in direct or indirect value generation should be accepted.

(4)   The real potential of indirect and direct value generation of the existing purchase situation has to be appropriately identified.

Ad1:   The purchase situation is the basis for supplier relationship development. The indirect and direct value generation of such relationship will be determined by the ability of the firms involved to exploit the given purchase situation in a relational sense and to adapt the B2B E-marketplace concept to these requirements.

The purchase situation as detailed in chapter 2 describes a specific position with respect to its current position, the projected future and the future desired positions in various dimensions, such as product, market, supplier and relationship characteristics. Based on this position, the buyer has to develop the appropriate strategy to utilize the direct and indirect value functions for optimizing the relationship success. The purchase situation predefines the areas of high and low potential. For example, in markets with only a limited number of suppliers the dependency of the buyer on the supplier is extremely high, which leads to only limited potential of the cost savings function, whereas the innovation function could deliver comparatively high value. On the other hand an extremely high purchase volume supports the volume and cost savings function. Based on these circumstances the B2B E-marketplace concept has to be adapted, otherwise the requirements cannot be fulfilled.

Ad2:   Only if the purchase situation is matched by the B2B E-marketplace concept relationships can exist and prosper, because the B2B E-marketplace concept fosters interaction between partners.

The intensity of the required relationship support can be determined by the purchase situation. The higher the buyer business impact (refer to chapter 2) the more relationship support is needed. Similar to Dubinsky and Ingram (1984, p. 34), who rate customers depending on their profit contribution, which is decisive for the customer relationship, the supplier relationship should be carefully cultivated, if the utilized supplies have a high business impact on the buyer's business. In highly competitive markets the buyer receives increased quality and reliability in products, more choice in existing product ranges as well as through new products, more customization, faster satisfaction of need, freedom to change late in the order cycle and increased level of customer service (Gules & Burgess 1996, p. 32). The buyer is not limited to one specific supplier. In case of poor service or quality, he is able to switch to another supplier. In this purchase environment close relationships are not on the top agenda, they can be better characterized by "low cooperation and high competition" (Wilkinson & Young 1996, p. 71). The B2B E-marketplace concept must be flexible enough to foster the development of supplier relationships, if required by the purchase situation. As the critical dependency on products or services increases, the need for trust and established relationships increases proportionally (Raisch 2001, p. 6). For example, if a company is planning to purchase some standard maintenance, repair and operations products, then it may be willing to try some suppliers, it has never heard of and worked with before to try to save on price. On the other hand, if a company intends to arrange steady procurement of mission-critical parts that feed the production, it would most likely rely on trusted relationships with established suppliers. While independently owned and operated B2B E-marketplaces are the venues for transacting commodity trades, that require less established relationships, industry-backed consortia have the support of major companies to move beyond commodity buying and selling (Raisch 2001).

Ad3:   If the B2B E-marketplace concept focuses on anonymous transactions in a highly open environment, the indirect value generation due to the supplier relationship is limited, whereas the opportunity of direct value generation does exist.

New information technologies have enabled and stimulated new organizational forms. As competition intensifies, innovation can no longer be attained solely within the integrated industrial enterprise. Companies must work together to create online networks of customers, suppliers and value-added processes. The internet is the new platform for collaboration and competition. Firms must learn to create favorable conditions for all players (Ticoll & Lowy 1998). The internet has changed partnership evolution and development. In the past, organizations spent months and sometimes years building their partnership networks. In the internet age, speed is extremely important and has a major impact on a partnership approach

(Cunningham 2001, p. 56). The B2B E-marketplace concept of auctions uses speed as its key strategic element besides volume and price (Cunningham 2001, p. 18). The auction model is considered as a more open method of trading with full automation. In a limited time frame bids can be entered. In case of success the auction site is providing all information for the transactions. The bidder will receive an email with the price, availability and the shipping details (Thomas 2000). Disputes are handled by automated customer-support tools. The complete process is fully automated, and the development of relationships is neither in focus nor desired. In a limited time frame price and volume should be optimized. The auction format enhances efficiency while maximizing the return for the buyer or the seller. In addition, an auction concentrates liquidity into one specific point in time, when the auction closes (Sculley & Woods 1999, p. 79). Before the internet age, companies were forced to pay fixed or negotiated prices for standardized goods, because one-on-one negotiation was inefficient for centralized mass producers. However, the development of relationships for gaining strategic advantages and optimizing any value function has never been stressed. Internet-based auctions provide the opportunity for a more efficient and more satisfying transaction process. Buyers bid no more than they are willing to pay, so that sellers who ask for too high prices must soon lower their price or choose not to sell (Lee 1998). Buyers have a wider selection to choose from, more convenience and the opportunity to pay less. Sellers benefit from a larger market and the opportunity to sell higher volumes (Sculley & Woods 1999).

Ad4:   In a highly competitive market of commodity products, the buyer should focus on a
        B2B E-marketplace solution for price optimization without relational focus.

In a highly competitive market of commodity products the correct purchase strategy focuses on price optimization. Buyers will typically choose seller with the lowest total cost. These cost will usually include the price paid to the seller plus any search, transportation and other similar costs (Bakos 1991a, p. 298). The buyer has different options to focus on. He can put all efforts in volume concentration within his diverse departments and sites or use one global source. Based on the new increased volumes he can execute a best price evaluation (Soellner & Mackrodt 1999, p. 90). The new E-procurement environment makes various opportunities possible. First, the buyer might select an auction concept with focus on cheapest price in shortest time, or second, he might use the exchange mechanism and thereby emphasize price with more closed regulations. A third opportunity would be using an E-catalog. Due to the new volumes the buyer has an improved market position but can also decrease process cost by decentralizing the purchase process. The final B2B E-marketplace concept has to be adapted to the strategic goal defined in the procurement department. Short-term price optimization demands for exchange or auction, whereas the E-catalog system enables a long-term strategy with respect to indirect value generation due to relationship development. But those relationships would become more impersonal and more formalized (Leek et al. 2000), which limits the indirect value generation. Therefore, the buyer should focus on the strategic goal without any relational focus by choosing the appropriate B2B E-marketplace concept in order to gain the most benefits for the company.

It is not true, however, that the internet is close to producing an entirely automated, electronic market, where buyers and sellers turn every good and service into a commodity, comparable only on price (Booker 2000). Summarizing all diverse aspects of the appropriate fit between a given purchase situation and the B2B E-marketplace concept for optimizing the direct and indirect value generation of the supplier relationship the following hypotheses can be formulated:

Proposition 1a: *The higher the fit between purchase situation and B2B E-marketplace characteristics is, the higher is the outcome of the direct value functions.*

Proposition 1b: *The higher the fit between purchase situation and B2B E-marketplace characteristics is, the higher is the outcome of the indirect value functions.*

5.2   Model 2: Successful project organization of the B2B E-marketplace introduction project

Apart from the fit model discussed above, the author examines the project organization of the B2B E-marketplace introduction project, since the project organization is the cornerstone of a successful implementation of the new procurement environment. The following figure gives an overview of the five derived hypotheses of the second model:

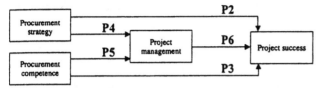

Figure 5.3 Model 2: Project organization

In chapter 5.2.1 the impact of the procurement competence and procurement strategy on the project organization is discussed. Then in chapter 5.2.2 the project management is focus of analysis.

5.2.1   Impact of the business environment on the project organization

Basis of a successful project organization of the B2B E-marketplace introduction project is the right business environment. As Dobler and Burt (1996) outlined, an integrated well structured and managed business environment within the procurement organization is key for controlling costs, improving quality, increasing productivity, shortening concept to customer delivery times, and strengthening the integration of materials management. This business environment should be built on two pillars: procurement strategy and procurement competence.

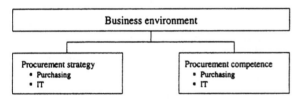

Figure 5.4 Two pillars of an integrated business environment in the procurement organization

In order to establish a competitive procurement strategy addressing strategic direction, productivity and value advantage, managers are urged to look beyond the traditional touchstones of the experience curve and the link between relative costs and market share (Christopher 1998, p. 33). As the competitive context of business continues to change due to the internet, causing new complexities, companies need to seek out and develop strategies to increase efficiency and productivity. Most of these changes are not mere trends, but the result of large, unruly forces, which have a lasting effect on the world economy (van Weele 2000, p. 5). Answers to questions such as global versus local sourcing, single versus multiple sourcing, partnership or competitive bidding, buying on contract or buying on spot basis, or price agreement versus performance agreement need to be found (Kaufmann 1995, Göltenboth 1997, Faber 1998).

In this study procurement strategy is understood as the overall procurement direction with special emphasis on a successful supplier relationship development. This strategy covers on the one hand the purchasing approach with all the strategic directions, such as insourcing versus outsourcing decisions, objectives setting concerning arm's length relationships versus collaborative relationships etc. (Dobler & Burt 1996, p. 37), and on the other hand the strategy concerning the appropriate information technology support (Monczka et al. 1998, p. 638). Due to the tremendous changes caused by the internet, it is today even more important that the procurement strategy includes the information technology perspective. Electronic data interchange is outdated, new internet-based solutions provide further optimization potential within the procurement environment.

However, to successfully implement a defined procurement strategy the appropriate competence also needs to be available. As in the case of the procurement strategy, does the procurement competence also comprise two factors: operative purchasing know-how and IT competence. Operative purchasing know-how means that the procurement professionals need to know the different tasks of the various steps of the procurement process (Seggewiß 1985, p. 27, Hammann & Lohrberg 1986, p. 7). Furthermore, they have to possess know-how concerning all activities of materials management, activities such as the definition of the spent, identification of relevant supply specifics and purchasing needs, market studies, supplier selection process (long and short list), request for proposal process, analysis of proposals, negotiation preparation and execution, controlling of the contract fulfillment, the physical supply transaction and storage policies, supplier relationship development etc. (Piontek 1997, p.1). The operative purchasing know-how alone is not sufficient. Additionally, the procurement professionals need to provide know-how concerning the relevant information technologies in the procurement environment. Due to the complex network of available data sources fast information gathering is key for a successful procurement management. With the implementation of new internet technologies the internal and external corporate information flow can be optimized (Köglmayr & Strub 1998, p. 72).

Only by a combination of all these diverse aspects, the procurement team is able to optimize the procurement process on an overall basis, especially with respect to the many internal interfaces of the procurement function (Dobler & Burt 1996, p. 31).

5.2.1.1   Impact of the procurement strategy on the project success

A clear and uniform understanding of the procurement strategy enables the realization of a higher project success. This assumption is based on the impact of the procurement strategy on

(1)   Project efficiency

(2)   Project effectiveness and

(3)   B2B E-marketplace acceptance.

Ad1:   A clear procurement strategy enables a better project performance concerning time and cost constraints.

In firms with clearly defined strategic goals for the procurement organization, the process of objective definition of all various projects is much smoother and more efficient, since all projects have to contribute to the overall strategy. The procurement strategy gives direction and guidance. For the definition of the project objectives the team can benefit from this know-how by applying it to the project target setting of the B2B E-marketplace introduction project. Companies with a clear focus on cost optimization are likely to establish project targets with the same direction, such as finding the cheapest supplier, decreasing material cost, reducing process cost. Contrary to that, companies stressing quality optimization will probably define other project goals, e.g. improving the existing supplier relationships or using the internet to improve the value-added service offerings. Solid project objectives provide the basis for a realistic development of the time line and the project budget. Thus, the author draws a similar assumption as Saad (1998, p. 120), who analyzed the positive impact of clearly defined project goals on the project success (Farr & Fischer 1992, Sakakibara 1993, Wolff et al. 1994).

Ad2:   The more clearly the procurement strategy is defined, the more easily the project objectives can be defined and reached.

For B2B E-marketplace introduction projects the objectives vary from process cost, material cost or inventory reduction, price or supplier comparability, access to new suppliers or supplier base reduction. Project effectiveness measures the fulfillment of these diverse objectives compared to the targets defined at the project beginning. In companies with clear procurement strategies, the project objectives support the overall strategy. Therefore the target realization is much easier, with all participants in the procurement organization focusing their efforts on the same targets. Similarly, Hakansson and Lorange summarized the results of their study on cooperative R&D projects as follows: "a critical finding is the importance of shared commitment to a clear purpose" (Hakansson & Lorange 1989, p. 21).

Ad3:   A well-defined procurement strategy has a positive impact on the B2B E-marketplace acceptance.

"The internet changes everything" (Venkatraman 2000, p. 15). However, these new internet-based solutions will only be successful, if they are accepted. If a clear strategy concerning E-procurement is defined, the next important step is the acceptance to guarantee a successful implementation. Diverse research is focusing on customer acceptance (Seybold 1998, Newell 2000, Reichheld & Schefter 2001, Wirtz & Lihotzky 2001). Although successful implementation of E-marketplaces may be found in several industries, some implementations have failed or their penetration pace is slower than projected, which is indicating, that significant barriers remain (Lee & Clark 1997). Lee and Clark (1997, p. 120) are differentiating two types of adoption barriers: (1) transaction risks created by the new alternative market form and (2) lack of the market power, necessary to enforce the change. On E-marketplaces buyers have to make purchasing decisions based on information without physical inspection, increasing the risk of incomplete and distorted information. On the other hand sellers may doubt that their goods would be appropriately valued by the buyers. Along with Lee and Clark (1997) the author assumes that the B2B E-marketplace acceptance requires a top-down approach. The introduction of radical changes needs to be supported by top management (Davenport & Short 1990, Hammer & Champy 1993), who has the authority to lead the reengineering concept through the organization. As long as the procurement strategy determines the implementation of E-procurement solutions, the implementation of new processes will be supported by the procurement personnel. In this case, less resistance has to be overcome especially from the operative workforce in the procurement department.

By summarizing the above-mentioned assumptions, a clear procurement strategy enforces diverse success factors of the project:

Proposition 2:   *The more clearly the procurement strategy is defined, the higher is the project success.*

5.2.1.2   Impact of the procurement competence on the project success

Besides the positive impact of the procurement strategy on the project success, the author assumes also a positive impact of the procurement competence on the project success. This assumption is based on the various areas impacting a successful project:

(1)   Time and budget constraints

(2)   Project deliverables

(3)   Limited resistance against new IT systems

(4)   Awareness how to handle implementation problems

Ad1:   The more procurement competence is available the higher is the project efficiency.

Yet, a clear procurement strategy alone is no guarantee for project success. The procurement professionals also have to provide the appropriate procurement competences. They need to prove capabilities in diverse areas, such as technical capabilities. For a solid supplier selection approach they need to be able to judge on the different product features and advantages (Hahn et al. 1990, p. 6). Additionally, they have to recognize process advantages and disadvantages. Besides technical capabilities they have to possess quality know-how, which includes knowledge on where the specification limits are, or which testing equipment is still economically. On top of technical and quality capabilities the procurement professionals need to be able to assess delivery capabilities, including evaluating, which materials lead times are feasible for the production, if the risk is too high or which process flexibility needs to be buffered by safety stocks of raw material. Last but not least the cost capabilities are important. The procurement professionals need to be able to develop a value analysis examining indirect costs, which are related to a raw material shift from one supplier to the other (Hahn et al.

1990, p. 6). A Total Cost of Ownership (TCO) analysis might be helpful to have a complete understanding of the product concerning quality, management, delivery, service, communication and price (Ellram 1993, p. 7). All these technical skills are not sufficient enough, the procurement professionals need to be excellent communicators. They have to interact between many different organizations and departments, firm-internally but also externally with suppliers. A smooth information flow is essential for a efficient procurement department (Monczka et al. 1998, p. 638) Based on such broad procurement know-how, covering all diverse aspects, the project team is better able to define solid cost targets and time schedules. Backed with this manifold procurement knowledge the project team members are able to evaluate potential risks and delays in advance, which can be included in the time and cost plans. If the project team is able to predefine realistic budgets and time schedules in advance, the project efficiency is promoted.

Ad2:   The better the procurement competence is, the better is the project effectiveness.

Similar to the efficiency, the effectiveness of a project is positively affected by the appropriate procurement competence. Procurement professionals need to develop differentiated strategies towards their supply markets. Purchasing managers need to be able to judge, if the present procurement strategy supports the business strategy and if it meets the long-term requirements (van Weele 2000, p. 145). They are asked to apply the appropriate strategy to the different suppliers depending on the supply risk and on the purchasing impact on financial results. Based on their procurement know-how the project team members are able to define realistic project targets, which they are able to implement in time and within the defined cost budget. Due to their experience and expertise they are able to define a realistic project plan, especially if they have to implement this plan themselves.

Ad3:   Due to procurement competence the companies have to handle less resistance against the implementation of a B2B E-marketplace.

The various E-procurement solutions allow companies to streamline the procurement process and employ human resources on more value-added activities. Following on Goldman Sachs' evaluation (1999), with B2B E-procurement solutions companies can decrease the unit cost of a single procurement process by 10 to 25 percent. According to Oradanini and Pol (2001, pp.

279) companies are able to improve three resource networks due to the usage of the new E-tools: (1) logistic resources including managing all the complementary transaction processes such as ordering, procurement, transportation or storage; (2) transaction resources related to reducing information asymmetry, which means the business opportunities linked to a potentially broad transaction market and the definition of a more transparent exchange context with an impact on trust resources and (3) knowledge resources referring to the marketplace participants, who can share experiences more easily and explore new business opportunities. It is critical for companies to focus not only on their own internal operations, but also on being an active participant in the global internet revolution, that is changing the dynamics of business. Companies must take an external viewpoint of their operations and look outside of their enterprise to the entire value chain, from customer demand to production to final product and service delivery (Raisch 2001, p. 299). However, in order to be able to recognize, implement and utilize all these advantages the procurement professionals need to have the appropriate know-how concerning the purchasing skills as well as the IT skills. They are required to understand the possible realization potential. Successful leaders that implement these new business concepts possess an adequate mix of industry and technology skills. Procurement professionals are for the most part characterized by having comprehensive backgrounds. Their management profiles show that their expertise expands to much more areas than just their industry expertise. The typical mix includes information technology, strategic financial management, consulting, sourcing, distribution and logistics (Harbin 2001). A broad procurement background simplifies the recognition of the competitive advantages of B2B E-marketplaces, which reduces eventual resistance against change.

Ad4:   Companies with appropriate procurement competence are aware of the problems and issues of implementing a B2B E-marketplace.

The internet and its associated network technologies are "stimuli", which means making something necessary, and "facilitators", i.e. making something possible (Kanter 2001, p. 231). On the other hand, it is like a spiral of increasing force: "The more the Web is used, the more uses are identified, and the more it must be used to do more things. Change produces the need for more and deeper change" (Kanter 2001, p. 231). Mastering these changes caused by E-commerce organizations need to do more than just adapt to changes already in progress. E-commerce requires them to be fast, agile, intuitive and innovative. Procurement professionals need to continuously learn and adapt, spread knowledge, and share ideas. Based on her global E-culture survey of 785 companies, Kanter (2001) reported that a positive approach to change is strongly associated with empowerment. Decisions are made by people, who know most about the issue regardless of rank. The other lever for change is collaboration; departments and functions working actively with other departments on a regular basis. Cunningham (2000) compares the introduction of B2B E-marketplace initiative with a merger or acquisition. "Successful acquisitions have aggressive cultural and system integration programs" (Cunningham 2000, p. 152). A successful implementation of new systems and processes requires a clear understanding of what would happen in the market if the organization did nothing or executed its plan poorly. By developing a plan to integrate all aspects of the new E-procurement strategy, a tight integration plan with new work processes, technology and business goals and an education and change transfer program at all levels in the procurement organization, the procurement professionals have the appropriate know-how to handle diverse potential problems.

By combining these aspects, it can be concluded that the procurement competence has a positive impact on the project efficiency, effectiveness and the B2B E-marketplace acceptance. More generally the following hypothesis can be defined:

Proposition 3:   *The more competent the procurement professionals are, the higher is the project success.*

5.2.1.3   Impact of the procurement strategy on the project management

In 1990 already, Carter and Narasimhan (1990, p. 2) stated "the importance of the linkage between the purchasing functions and the other functions within a firm is becoming more evident with each passing year". However this emphasis on procurement has even increased due to the introduction of new purchasing methods via electronic commerce. The author based her assumption on the following arguments:

(1)   A clear strategic focus simplifies the definition of project objectives.

(2)   Top management is interested in a project, which is aligned with the overall strategy.

Ad1:   A clearly defined procurement strategy simplifies the definition of project objectives.

In most companies the procurement function has gained a more strategic role, as a key component of firm competitiveness and involved at the highest level of corporate strategy formulation and decision-making (Carter & Narasimhan 1996b). Therefore the procurement strategy is no longer focusing on mere material cost reductions, although intense international competition increases the pressure to reduce cost. It is rather additional aspects, e.g. the need for manufacturing flexibility, shorter product development cycles, stringent quality standards and ever-changing technology that have to be included (Carter & Narsimhan 1990, p. 3). Concepts such as Just-in-Time and Total Quality Management have to be evaluated (Carter & Narasimhan 1994, p. 7). Quayle (1995) specifies different procurement strategies such as single-sourcing, which may lead to partnership sourcing, multi-sourcing, which may lead to parallel sourcing and backward vertical integration by buying the source itself.

In 1996 Carter and Narasimhan (1996a) developed a vision of what the procurement function will be in the next century, how roles, responsibilities, capabilities, organizations etc. will look like, which was validated by roundtable sessions with senior purchasing and materials management executives of U.S. and Europe. They identified various commonly used sourcing strategies, which depend on the competitive priority of the company. Firms, whose competitive direction is differentiation and customization, stress the material sourcing strategies of total quality management, time-based sourcing, internal organizational integration and environmentally sensitive purchasing. Firms, whose competitive priority is total quality management, rely on material sourcing strategies and transactions cost management. Other firms, whose competitive direction is traditional and manufacturing oriented, focus on the materials sourcing strategies of time-based sourcing and external organization integration.[15]

Narasimhan and Carter (1998) provide evidence, that there is a relationship between sourcing strategies and competitive priorities of a firm. Based on their findings, the author assumes an impact of the procurement strategy on the definition of objectives for the B2B E-marketplace introduction project. Depending on the strategic focus of a company, the goal of such a project can vary. Firms with a clear focus on low prices and fast delivery, which corresponds to more traditional sourcing approach, try to implement E-procurement solution to support

---

[15]   For further detailed results of the study see Narasimhan & Carter (1998).

this strategic orientation. On the contrary, firms with procurement emphasis on total quality management force the quality assurance aspect within the implementation of specific E-procurement solution. Irrespective of the focus of the procurement department the procurement strategy has a strong impact on the definition of objectives for such a B2B E-marketplace introduction project, since the project should support the overall procurement strategy. But as long as a company has a clearly defined procurement strategy, the direction is given and predetermines the objectives of the E-procurement project.

Ad2:   Due to a clearly defined procurement strategy the top management is more willing to support the project team.

In case of a clearly defined procurement strategy, the company's direction is fix and supported by the top management, who have been involved and are responsible for the definition of the procurement strategy. In order to measure the importance of the procurement function as a strategic component of the overall business success, Carter and Narasimhan (1996b) introduced benchmarks as the degree of top management emphasis on the procurement function, the existence and the importance of the planning process in the procurement function, procurement's emphasis on total quality management and customer satisfaction in defining its mission and the procurement's role in the corporate business planning process. Nowadays the procurement function is seen as a key component of firm competitiveness and involved at the highest level of corporate strategy formulation and decision-making. The historical role of procurement, where procurement's major contribution to an organization's success has been ensuring the timely availability of required materials and services and obtaining the materials and services at reasonable prices has definitely changed (Anklesaria & Burt 1988, p. 9). While the importance of a strong marketing function is universally recognized and most companies invest enormous effort in "out-thinking the customer" (Kapoor & Gupta 1997, p. 21), it is just since the 80's that companies focus on "reverse marketing" (Leenders & Blenkhorn 1988). However, there are still limitations to direct purchases or cost of goods sold, whereas the vast array of expenditures went almost untouched (Kapoor & Gupta 1997). During the past few years, the procurement function has gained major importance, models of purchasing excellence have been implemented with special focus on indirect products. Companies such as American Express, Sears or Chase have launched campaigns to tackle indirect purchases with impressive results, between 10 to 15 percent reduction in the expenses without any changes in quality or functionality (Kapoor & Gupta 1997). These impressive savings opportunities raised the top management attention, especially in situations with high competitive pressure. Stuart (1993) analyzed the levers for high top management commitment in procurement, such as competitive pressure, importance of purchased inputs and purchasing capabilities and opportunities. The author assumes, that as long as the B2B E-marketplace project supports the overall procurement strategy and even pushes the savings potential, top management is highly supportive and positive about this project.

Summarizing those two aspects, the new position of procurement, which is integrated within the overall strategic development of a company's business success with a clearly defined strategic orientation as part of the overall business strategy, simplifies the project management of such a B2B E-marketplace introduction project. All employees have the same vision and understanding on what the company wants to reach. The B2B E-marketplace project is one part of this overall strategy, which enables a better result. Consequently the author proposes the following:

Proposition 4:   *The more clearly the procurement strategy is defined, the better the project can be managed.*

5.2.1.4   Impact of the procurement competence on the project management

Having a strategic direction alone is not enough for a successful procurement function. Moreover, the appropriate competences are necessary. The assumption that the procurement competence has a positive impact on a successful project management is based on the following aspects:

(1)   Due to the appropriate lessons-learned from previous projects and experience the project objectives can be defined more easily.

(2)   Adequate competences enable the top management to recognize the need for supporting the project team.

(3)   Project milestones are more realistic.

(4)   Assessing the need for communication in general and the kind of communication, that is appropriate, is better recognized by more competent and experienced professionals.

Ad1:   High procurement competence simplifies the definition of project objectives.

Before procurement can become a "competitive weapon" (Reck & Long 1988, p. 8), procurement executives and procurement managers must understand the essential components of the chosen competitive strategy and set their developmental priorities accordingly. They need to gain expertise and experience focusing on decision areas such as suppliers, personnel and information, but also on interfaces with other functions within the company, such as production, R&D or marketing. Procurement competence must involve the "concept of appropriateness" (Cox 1997, p. 25) by contributing strategically and operationally to the business success. On the one hand procurement professionals have to forecast the demand by developing annual buying plans (Dobler & Burt 1996, p. 618). But on the other hand they need to be good negotiators. They are required to develop precise objectives for the negotiation. Additionally they have to be experts in negotiation techniques backed with solid know-how on pricing. Besides the specific negotiation know-how and know-how on the products they want to buy, they should possess a good working knowledge of all the primary business functions, such as accounting, human relations, economics, business law and quantitative analysis. Only by combining their skills, knowledge and judgment, procurement professionals develop superior tactical and strategic plans (Dobler & Burt 1996, p. 381). This broad and profound know-how simplifies the definition of objectives for a B2B E-marketplace introduction project, since the team is able to judge, if the defined targets and goals are realistic and promise success. Apart from the maturity to judge on the feasibility, the team is also able to implement the set targets.

Ad2:   Due to excellent procurement competence the top management is more willing to support the team.

Procurement competence not only helps defining the right project objectives, it also helps gaining top management support. Top management is happier to support projects, if the department has already proofed its capabilities. Then the risk for the top management is minimized, since they can rely on their procurement professionals, that the feasibility of the objectives is realistic and already approved.

Ad3:   With the appropriate procurement competence the project plan can be better realized.

Due to its central and linked position the procurement function has excellent connections to diverse business functions, since purchasing decisions cannot be made in isolation and should not be aimed at optimization of purchasing performance only (van Weele 2000, p. 99). Purchasing decisions should be made by taking into account the effects of these decisions on the other primary activities, such as production planning, materials management and transportation. Therefore, purchasing decisions need to be based on balancing total cost of ownership (Ellram 1993, p. 4, Handfield et al. 1999, p. 72). This approach is often used for the supplier selection process, where aspects such as cost and availability of raw materials, difficulty of the process matched against the supplier's capabilities, waste generated in the supplier's process, environmental compliance or technical competence are relevant. Procurement professionals are not only able to interact with other departments within the own company, they also have to handle interfaces to logistics providers and finally with the suppliers. Therefore, they have deep know-how in risk management, how to prevent any delays in production. Furthermore, they have the ability to recognize any problems with the diverse partners they have to work with. Additionally, due to the analytical skills of the procurement professionals they are used to system support such as MS Excel or similar calculation programs, which enable an automated target controlling system. More sophisticated professionals are even experienced in project management software packages, which even better enable an on-time project management.

The author assumes that the procurement know-how builds a profound basis for a solid and realistic project plan development with clearly defined milestones, which enable an early recognition of any delay or other problems.

Ad4:   The better the available procurement competence is, the better the project information and communication work.

Besides an accurate project time plan a successful project management requires an appropriate information and communication plan. Due to the above detailed integrated position of the procurement function, communication is key for the success. Information has always been central to the efficient management of logistics but now, enabled by technology, it is providing the driving force for a competitive procurement strategy (Christopher 1998, p. 199). The procurement professionals need to search for the appropriate information on available suppliers and their products, but then they also need to be good internal communicators to their internal customers, e.g. the production personnel. In the negotiation process excellent communication is a driver for success (van Weele 2000, p. 284). This includes knowing which information they should provide to the supplier and which information better to hide. This broad know-how concerning communication tactics and information delivery enables the author to assume, that this is the perfect basis, which makes the project better work.

Summarizing the above-mentioned four aspects, the conclusion can be drawn, that procurement competence is a prerequisite for a successful and smooth project management.

Proposition 5:   *The higher the available procurement competence is, the better the project can be managed.*

5.2.2   Impact of project management on the project success

As already demonstrated by the empirical study of Lechler (1997) and various studies in the project management literature, the author assumes a strong positive correlation between the project management of the B2B E-marketplace project and the project success. The arguments can be structured into four aspects:

(1)   In projects with top management support and commitment the pressure for on time and within budget project termination is much higher.

(2)   Based on a detailed project plan with continuous controlling, time and cost constraints are better under control.

(3)   A solid communication strategy simplifies the achievement of the defined targets.

(4)   The project team's competence has a major influence on how well the new E-tool is utilized.

Ad1:   With the appropriate top management support it is easier to terminate the project on time and with the given budget.

"We must find the radicals, the true revolutionaries, and support them" (Louis V. Gerstner, Jr. Chairman and CEO, IBM).[16] Change moves faster, and so do the reactions to change, but E-commerce protestors create bad news almost as quickly. Thus leadership for change is necessary for a successful and fast implementation of E-commerce. Kanter (2001, p. 256) defines ten classic reasons, why people resist change, which also apply to the resistance of the E-commerce environment:

"(1)   Loss of face. People have fear that dignity will be undermined; they are embarrassed since change feels like exposure for past mistakes.

(2)   Loss of control. People are angry since power is shifting.

(3)   Excess uncertainty. People are feeling uninformed about where the change will lead and what is coming next.

(4)   Surprise. People react automatically defensive, since they had no advance warning and no chance to get ready.

(5)   The "different" effect. People are rejecting changes because it does not fit to existing mental models, seems strange and unfamiliar, and challenges usually unquestioned habits and routines.

(6)   "Can I do it?" People have concerns about future competence, they worry about whether they will still be successful after the change.

(7)   Ripple effects. People are annoyed at disruptions to other activities and interference with the accomplishment of unrelated tasks.

(8)   More work. People have resistance to additional things to do, new things to learn and no time to do it all.

(9)   Past resentments. People remember past hostilities or problems that were never resolved.

(10) Real threats. People are angry that the change will inflict real pain and create clear losers."

With resistance to change even under benign circumstances, leaders must be even more skillful at handling the human side of change, when the environment is turbulent and the

---

[16]   Citation in Kanter (2001, p. 255).

impact of change revolutionary. The pace and complexity in the New Economy is much more demanding. Along with Lee and Clark (1997) the author assumes that the successful deployment of electronic purchasing solutions requires an appropriate management of barriers. Most risks, uncertainties and barriers stem from social and economic factors rather than IT-related obstacles (Davenport & Stoddard 1994, Stoddard & Jarvenpaa 1995). Only with an adequate support by top-management the E-procurement project team is able to handle all kinds of resistance and convince the people to strive for the predefined time and cost plan (Lee & Clark 1997).

Ad2:   A detailed project plan and controlling process enables a project termination within given time and cost constraints.

Top management support is one lever for a successful project, but well organized teamwork is another component.[17] Högl and Gemünden (2000) underline the importance of a structured project plan with clearly defined work packages. The project team has to differentiate between tasks, which are to solve in a collaborative joint effort and tasks which are to be accomplished individually. Therefore "team coordination is the essence of teamwork" (Brannick et al. 1995). Another determinate for a successful teamwork is the balance of the different work packages (Högl & Gemünden 2000). The contribution to the project content has to be balanced between the different team members. Referring to the individual capabilities of the team members, the work packages should be defined. Only a balanced and healthy relationship between the different team players supports a solid project solution. With an appropriate and detailed project plan and monitoring process these diverse restrictions on the teamwork can be properly managed. As a starting point clear team rules (Pinto et al. 1993) should be established, which clarify workload, time engagement, priority setting and workload sharing (Högl & Gemünden 2000). Similar to Kern and Knauth (2000, p. 107), who have proved the impact of a steering tool on the intensity of delays it can be argued, that a realistic project plan and steering process support the project success.[18]

---

[17] For further details on the impact of top-management support on the project success refer to Lechler (1997, p. 95).

[18] For further details on research concerning project steering tools and project success please refer to Lechler (1997, p. 105).

Ad3:   A structured project information and communication plan supports the achievement of objectives.

Besides team spirit, social support and workload sharing, Campion et al. (1993, pp. 829) defines communication and cooperation as a major component of successful team interaction. An honest communication strategy gives the team the feeling to be up-to-date. Detailed information upfront supports the team motivation. A uniform communication strategy within the project team enables the team members to build group cohesion. They are experts and have more information about this topic than anybody else in the firm. They are part of the decision team, which is responsible for major changes within the firm. In his study in the automotive industry Clark (1989, p. 1256) proved a positive impact of strong communication and clear project information on the project objective fulfillment. Based on regular information exchange between the team members complications and potential conflicts can be discussed at an early point of time to prevent potential project delays. Concerning the analysis of the impact of project information and communication on the project success extensive literature reviews do exist (Gerstenfeld 1969, Utterback et al. 1976, Clark 1989, Keplinger 1991, Lechler 1997). With a regular communication plan, e.g. "Jour fix" once a week, the team members have the opportunity to discuss any problem or question. On the other hand strategic changes or novelties can be directly communicated. With a tight communication plan for the team but also for the employees outside the project team the risk of conflicts can be minimized. Conflicts arise due to different recognition of project goals (Högl 1998, p. 47, Levine & Moreland 1990, p. 605.). Besides conflict resolution skills and social skills, the team members need to have excellent communication skills to cope with conflicts and to minimize their occurrence (Stevens & Campion 1994). To have a structured way of information, an information and communication plan may be helpful for clarifying the project objectives.

Ad4:   The project team's competence has a major impact on the B2B E-marketplace acceptance.

Besides an accurate project termination the project acceptance is key to the project success. Therefore, the competences in the team play a major role to create the appropriate conditions, which lead to a satisfying B2B E-marketplace acceptance. In a first step the project team must be able to improve the current processes (Lientz & Rea 2001, p. 125). As long as the new processes have been optimized (e.g. EDI transactions have been replaced, the coordination of the purchase transaction is simplified or the physical product or service transfer has been simplified) the resistance is at minimum level. The next determinate of the acceptance is the work environment in the procurement organization (Corsten 2000, p. 51). The acceptance is positively impacted by less redundant work process, less routine tasks and more transparency. The third effect on the acceptance of B2B E-marketplace projects is determined by the supplier's attitude. If the procurement personnel expect reluctance from the supplier side to use the new procurement environment, they have a highly negative attitude (Neef 2001, p. 166). But if the supplier has already experience with these new E-procurement solutions or is even willing to invest in these solutions the acceptance of B2B E-marketplaces is positively impacted. To avoid or minimize negative influences and developments of these three areas of impact the project team's competence is fundamentally. The process improvements must be clarified upfront. The impact on the work environment has to be detailed before prejudices occur. The supplier's competences have to be proved early enough to take any initiative. Finally, a smooth and detailed hand-over is required to enable an ongoing implementation of the project.

All in all, a properly managed project has a positive impact on the project success defined by efficiency, effectiveness and B2B E-marketplace acceptance.

Proposition 6:   *The better the project is managed, the higher is the project success.*

5.3   Model 3: Impact of a successful project organization on the fit between purchase situation and B2B E-marketplace

After discussing the first model (i.e. the fit between purchase situation and B2B E-marketplace) and the second model concerning the project organization, the third model combines these concepts and discusses the links and impacts between the project organization on the fit between purchase situation and B2B E-marketplace. Additionally, the impact of the project success on the direct and indirect value functions is analyzed.

The following figure gives an overview of model 3 and the corresponding hypotheses:

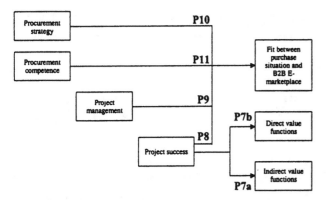

Figure 5.5 Model 3: Impact of the project organization on the fit

5.3.1   Impact of the project success on the relationship success

In this chapter the hypotheses concerning the impact of the project success on the direct and indirect value functions are derived. The argumentation is based on four keystones:

(1)   The project success confirms the first step in the right direction.
(2)   The project success supports the development of trust and commitment in the new E-tools.
(3)   A cost-benefit calculation of the project motivates the realization of further improvements.
(4)   The procurement professionals are interested in proving their own competences by topping the improvement results of the project team.

Ad1:   The project success is the first step towards the new procurement environment, therefore it has a positive contribution to the relationship success.

Initiatives for new IT-solutions often fail to appreciate the need for an integrated program of change management. In case of the B2B E-marketplace introduction project, change management is not only required for the relevant procurement professionals, but also for the corresponding sales people at the supplier side (Neef 2001, p. 187). A successful project shows that traditional processes and procedures can substantially be improved. Backed with the project success the procurement professionals can more easily convince the broad supplier base to adapt to the new processes and to transfer the current transactions on the E-procurement tools.

Ad2:   The project success helps to build trust and commitment in the new procurement environment and thereby generates a motivation, which further supports the relationship success.

Introduction projects offer a first opportunity to get familiarized with the new E-procurement environment. With close guidance of the project team the buyer is able to gain first experience with the new processes and job requirements. Within organizations trust contributes to more effective implementation of strategy, greater managerial coordination and more effective work teams (McAllister 1995, Doney et al. 1998, p. 601). Based on the definition of trust by Walter et al. (2000, p. 4) the buyer can develop trust concerning the "motivational or intentional trust dimensions". First success indications support the establishment of benevolence, since the buyer can see first savings and improvements. Trust also encompasses honesty, which the buyer can develop based on the tight involvement in the project. The buyer can be convinced, that the optimization of the purchasing environment is the major goal of the project by reducing material cost on the one hand, but also by optimizing the work process by eliminating routine-work. The skepticism about the new E-procurement solution being able to improve and replace the common procurement processes can be reduced after first pilot runs. As Doney et al. (1998, p. 603) posit, "in trusting situations the sources of risk generally are related to vulnerability and/or uncertainty about an outcome". Moreover, based on the first positive results the buyer can also build confidence in the competence of such B2B E-marketplaces. The trust in these first results of the project helps to build commitment. The buyer can be convinced that the B2B E-marketplace is able to deliver the predicted objectives. Consequently the author argues that project success helps to convince and motivate procurement personnel to go forward with the project by implementing the new procedures in the day-to-day business. The success of this implementation can be measured by the indirect and direct value generation of the supplier relationship with a more long-term perspective.

Ad3:   For justifying the investment of the project, certain improvements are required, which support the motivation to realize further improvements and savings.

Part of many project evaluations is a calculation comparing the project cost and the predicted benefits. Only if this equation is balanced the project is profitable. It is the responsibility of the project leader to control this balance. He needs to guide the project in the right direction. As Hauschildt and Chakrabarti (1988, p. 385) found out the "process promotor" is responsible for the management of the process. He needs to be able to have a larger picture based on economic and social aspects. Hauschildt and Keim (1999) conclude that the project leader is the perfect "process promotor", managing the project depending on the specific circumstances. In case of budget conflicts the project leader needs to motivate the team to develop more creative solutions, which can be faster implemented. In case of time constraints the project leader needs to filter the more important tasks and prioritize them. The process promotor has the function of a cost controller, who has to keep the equation between cost and benefits of the project in balance. Based on this balance his job is it to convince his team that the project is just a first step of the B2B E-marketplace implementation, which will continue after the project. With a successful project rollout long-term savings can be realized.

Ad4:   The improvements and savings of the project prove the optimization potential of the new procurement environment, which motivates the procurement personnel to realize even further improvements and savings than the project team.

Often projects have a "teaching" character, which gives the feeling to prove that someone could do better. In this study a "radical innovation" (Leifer et al. 2000), the B2B E-marketplace, has to be implemented, which will have decisive impact on the day-to-day purchasing work. Since the B2B E-marketplace is new, the teaching character is limited. But the project work enforces some kind of competition between the project team and the regular procurement professionals. The project team shows, that saving potentials can be realized with the project. The procurement professionals are under pressure to show, that they can do at least as good as the project team or even better. This competition forces the motivation for further realization of optimization potential. Additionally, the project causes learn-effects. The procurement professionals have learned during the project, so that they are able to implement and apply the new processes after the project.

Combining these arguments the author draws the conclusion:

Proposition 7a: *The higher the project success is, the higher is the generation of indirect value functions.*

Proposition 7b: *The higher the project success is, the higher is the generation of direct value functions.*

5.3.2 Impact of the project success on the fit between purchase situation and B2B E-marketplace

The author assumes a strong positive correlation between the project success and the appropriate fit between purchase situation and B2B E-marketplace. She bases her argumentation on two thoughts:

(1)   The project success can be interpreted as a confirmation of the right fit.

(2)   The satisfactory usage of the new B2B E-marketplace can be interpreted as a confirmation of the right fit.

Ad1:   The project success confirms the right assessment of the purchase situation, which defines the requirements of the B2B E-marketplace concept.

The B2B E-marketplace introduction project with its different project phases (Baguley 1999, p. 24) cannot be seen as an independent unit. Although the project has a definite end, this end is the starting point for the rollout of the implementation in the entire procurement organization. The project success is only an indicator, if the project team has successfully achieved the project objectives. The project success confirms, that the method, how to define the fit between purchase situation and B2B E-marketplace, is correct. But the long-term success of the project needs also to be assured. Therefore, the hand-over and knowledge transfer of the project team to the procurement professionals is crucial (Lock 1997, p. 370). The procurement managers need to fully understand the method on how to determine the purchase situation and how to develop the appropriate B2B E-marketplace concept. Based on a successful project hand-over and knowledge transfer (Körbs 2000, p. 170) the long-term success (i.e. relationship success) can be enhanced.

Ad2: The satisfying B2B E-marketplace acceptance confirms that the appropriate B2B E-marketplace concept has been selected.

The identification of the appropriate purchase situation is one indicator for the correct fit, but the second component is the suitable B2B E-marketplace concept. Along with Hilbig (1984) the acceptance of the new system is an indication of the satisfaction of the procurement professionals with the new E-tools. With increasing acceptance of the new environment the usage increases. This has a positive impact on the productivity of the procurement environment. Referring to Schönecker (1985), who defined three different levels of impact due to acceptance, the acceptance cannot only have a positive impact on the company level, but also on the individual level by improving the personal work atmosphere and on the society level. The positive correlation between acceptance and usage has already been tested by Martin (1993), who analyzed the impact of the acceptance of production planning systems (PPS).

Summarizing these arguments, it can be argued:

Proposition 8:   *The higher the project success is, the better is the fit between purchase situation and B2B E-marketplace.*

5.3.3   Impact of the project management on the fit between purchase situation and B2B E-marketplace

Besides the project success the project management is also positively influencing the appropriate fit between purchase situation and B2B E-marketplace. For validating this assumption the author has grouped her arguments in two classes:

(1) Top management supports the decision on the appropriate strategy concerning the B2B E-marketplace concept, so that the new environment goes hand in hand with the strategy of the company.

(2) Special know-how and experience is required to be able to anticipate critical issues before choosing the B2B E-marketplace concept.

Ad1:   Top management support enables the identification of a successful E-procurement strategy, which is in alignment with the overall firm strategy.

A successful E-procurement initiative requires dramatic changes in strategy, organization, process and systems (Choi et al. 1997, p. 51). It affects functions throughout the whole organization, changes the way employees work and how a company organizes its supply chain and purchasing processes (Shaw et al. 2000, p. 22). Therefore, executive sponsorship and participation is key. But the upper management can only provide full support, if they have a common understanding about the goals, scope and the purpose for action. A lack of clarity around the business context and the failure to understand the strategic importance of the B2B E-marketplace project can result in a lack of momentum and support from the key leaders. The top management needs to debate, define and reach consensus on what the project will entail, why the initiative is necessary, how it affects other current or planned projects, how long it will take, who will be involved, how much money it will cost and what the expected return on investment will be (Neef 2001, p. 143). The key executives have to define the project strategy, which is integrated in the company's overall strategy (Fingar et al. 2000, p. 267). Early decisions need to be made concerning, which products the key area of focus are, whether logical divisions between strategic and tactical commodities can be made, when and how supplier consolidation takes place and which processes should be restructured.

Ad2:   Based on the solid team competence, all critical issues can be identified beforehand, so that the appropriate B2B E-marketplace concept can be selected.

"Innovation begins with someone being smart enough to sense a new need" (Kanter 2001, p. 258). The project team must be adept at anticipating the need for change. It needs to sense problems and weaknesses before they represent real threats. The team members should identify gaps between what is and what could be realized due to the new E-procurement tools. Another desirable strength of the project team is the ability of change management (Schuh et al. 1998). The team members have to overcome resistance and fear regarding accepting and implementing the new system. The procurement professionals will be embarrassed, because the changes feel like exposure for past mistakes. They might be angry, since power is shifting elsewhere. A feeling of not being informed about where the change will lead might come up. The purchasing managers might reject the change, because it does not fit to existing mental models or seems strange and unfamiliar. People might be resistant to additional workload and new things to learn. The project team needs to remain impartial in order to be able to identify the different levels of threats and weaknesses of the new B2B E-marketplace concept. The appropriate actions have to be planned to convince the procurement professionals and to overcome any problems.

With the right project team, which is backed by the upper management, the right conditions are given to identify the appropriate B2B E-marketplace concept.

Proposition 9:   The better the quality of the project management is, the better is the fit between purchase situation and B2B E-marketplace.

5.3.4   Impact of the procurement strategy on the fit between purchase situation and B2B E₁marketplace

Not only the project success and the project management have a significant impact on the appropriate fit, the author also assumes a strong positive correlation between procurement strategy and the right fit between purchase situation and B2B E-marketplace. She has grouped her arguments in four categories:

(1)   The understanding of the purchase situation is determined by the procurement strategy.
(2)   The procurement strategy eventually restricts the selection process of the appropriate E-procurement solution.
(3)   Based on a clear procurement strategy the B2B E-marketplace concept seems not to be interesting for all product categories.
(4)   The characteristics of the B2B E-marketplace can be limited by the procurement strategy.

Ad1:   The procurement strategy influences the interpretation of the purchase situation.

Along with Dobler and Burt (1996, p. 41) the objectives of purchasing management can be viewed from three levels: a very general managerial level, a more specific functional or operational level and a detailed level at which precise strategic buying plans are formulated. From a top management perspective six elements are expected to be achieved by the procurement organization. They have to buy the right quality from the right supplier in the right quantity at the right time at the right price with the right service (Monczka et al. 1998, p. 18). From a more operational perspective the procurement organization has to support company's operations with an uninterrupted flow of materials and services. They have to buy competitively. Buying wisely involves a continuous search for better opportunities. Inventory investments and inventory losses should be kept at minimum. The procurement managers should develop effective and reliable sources. The procurement function needs to be handled proactively in a cost-effective manner. The overall procurement strategy defines the importance of the different tasks (Saunders 1997, p. 10, van Weele 2000, p. 8). Firms with major focus on cost cutting emphasize price more than service, which increases the risk of material flow interruption. On the other hand firms, which emphasize the service and quality reliability, have often to accept a compromise concerning price. Depending on the strategic orientation of the company the purchase situation may be seen differently. Low supplier market competitiveness is more critical to firms focusing on quality than on price. The relationship attractiveness is higher valued by firms focusing on service and reliability of suppliers.

Ad2: The procurement strategy gives directions for selecting the appropriate B2B E-marketplace concept.

Due to the challenges caused by new information technologies, the enterprises are under great pressure to act. At the same time the uncertainty has never been greater than today, since the changes are becoming increasingly more radical (Leifer et al. 2000). The ability to identify chances at an early stage is key, as well as understanding the rules of business in the information age and formulating procedures to ensure a successful transformation (Österle & Fleisch, Alt 2000, p. 19). Finding the right position in the new E-procurement environment goes hand in hand with the procurement strategy (Rodin & Hartmann 1999, p. 156). If the procurement strategy emphasizes the development of long-term relationships regardless the cost disadvantages the E-opportunities might be less meaningful. Then aspects as product quality and reliability of the supplier are more in focus. The procurement strategy can restrict the potential optimization opportunities of the new E-procurement environment.

Ad 3:   The procurement strategy determines, which products should be transferred to the new procurement environment.

Taking the existing procurement strategy in a company, the author has already shown that companies differentiate their product portfolio by different measurements, such as ABC-analysis (chapter 2). Bakos (1998, p. 40) shows that lower buyer search costs in electronic marketplaces promotes price competition among sellers, which will have most dramatic effects in the commodity markets, where intensive price competition can eliminate all seller profits. If no relationship is required by the existing strategy, a company may choose to source all commodity products through the B2B E-marketplace. For those product categories, where a closer relationship is required by the procurement strategy, the procurement professionals need to have a close look, whether they find a B2B E-marketplace concept that supports the sourcing of these materials.

Ad4:   The procurement strategy influences the openness of the chosen B2B E-marketplace.

Eisenhardt (2001) proclaims that in former times, when the business landscape was simple, companies could afford to have complex strategies. Nowadays, with business being that complex, they need to simplify. She suggests three approaches to strategy. First companies might establish their position by focusing on profitability. Another solution might be to leverage resources by establishing a vision, building resources and leveraging them across markets. This approach follows the performance goal of long-term dominance in moderately changing, well-structured markets. Her third strategy suggestion goes along with the strategic logic of flexibly pursuing opportunities in rapidly changing and ambiguous markets with the performance goal of growth. In stable markets, managers can rely on complicated strategies built on detailed predictions of the future (Eisenhardt 2001, p. 116), but in complicated, fast-moving markets due to new opportunities based on the internet unpredictability reigns. Depending on the procurement strategy the E-procurement solution should follow the same guidelines. "When business becomes complicated, strategy should be simple" (Eisenhardt 2001, p. 116). If organizations focus on cost cutting, the business model and order processing of the used E-marketplace have to support this goal. On the one hand the implementation cost of such an E-procurement solution has to be minimized and prices reductions need to be realized. For realizing only process cost reduction with minimum implementation cost an E-catalog might be the appropriate solution by leasing an internet-based software. Decentralized purchasing enables process cost savings and due to pre-negotiation material costs can also be reduced. A company focusing not only on process cost reduction, but also on price reduction, may focus on auctions, where within a limited time frame the products can be purchased for the cheapest market price. For companies, which want to access new suppliers exchanges, might be more appropriate, since time is not limiting, but they can gain market transparency on diverse suppliers. Firms, which want to be leading edge and want to actively develop the market, may build their own B2B E-marketplace.

The appropriate procurement strategy is essential for selecting the appropriate B2B E-marketplace concept. "Creating a sense of purpose, focus, and clear goals and objectives is critical for the success of any organization" (Raisch 2001, p. 306). Companies, which have already focused on strategic sourcing activities, are used to analyzing the underlying cost structure of the goods and services bought. Working to rationalize the supplier base is part of a standard process of their procurement activities. They are already managing their costs and trying to maximize use of suppliers (Avery 2000, p. 111). Those companies are ready for E-procurement, as long as the E-procurement strategy supports the normal business approach.

Proposition 10:   *The clearer the procurement strategy is understood, the better is the fit between purchase situation and B2B E-marketplace.*

5.3.5   Impact of the procurement competence on the fit between purchase situation and B2B E-marketplace

Finally, the assumption concerning the impact of the procurement competence on the appropriate fit between purchase situation and B2B E-marketplace are discussed. The following three thoughts provide basis for argumentation:

(1)   Only with the relevant knowledge the right products for the right B2B E-marketplace concept can be selected.

(2)   For convincing the right supplier to participate in the new E-procurement environment, a sound know-how is necessary.

(3) Only with the appropriate competence lasting supplier relationships can be built on the new E-procurement platform.

Ad1: Based on the appropriate procurement know-how, the buyer is able to identify the right products and the appropriate B2B E-marketplace concept.

For a solid purchase situation assessment the procurement personnel has to be specially trained. As soon as the supply needs have been established and precisely described, the buyer begins an investigation of the market to identify potential sources of supply. Depending on the product, if it is a routine item or a new item, the intensity of investigation varies (Dobler & Burt 1996, p. 66). In highly complex innovations the supplier selection process can already be started during the product development phase (Wolters 1999, p. 259). Procurement professionals have to assess diverse levels of abstraction (van Weele 2000, p. 269). Starting with the product level, they have to focus on establishing and improving the supplier's product quality, incoming inspections and quality inspections have to be approved. The next level is the process level, where the state of the supplier's machinery and the quality control system are subject to in-depth auditing. By proving the supplier's processes, if they are under control through consistent application of quality procedures, the buyer has clarity about the expressed quality standards and specifications. Further analysis is conducted in the quality assurance system level with focus on the way, in which procedures regarding quality inspection are developed, kept up-to-date, maintained and refined. Last but not least the company level has to be proved. Financial aspects have to be taken into account. The quality of the management has to be proved (Sebastian & Niederdrenk 1999). Based on this assessment the relationship attractiveness can be determined. The buyer needs to have a clear picture about the purchase situation to identify products, which can be successfully transferred to the new procurement environment. If the products are identified, the appropriate B2B E-marketplace concept has to be selected. Only based on procurement know-how the critical issues of the current process can be taken into account.

Ad2: With the right procurement competence the buyer has a realistic view of his strengths in negotiating with the supplier.

Bourantas (1989, p. 140) posits that "organizations are open systems which engage in exchanges and transactions with other organizations or elements of their environment and as a result, they inevitably become dependent upon their environment". Pfeffer and Salancik (1978, p. 141) define dependence as "the product of the importance of a given input or output to the organization and the extent to which it is controlled by relatively few organizations". In an effort to avoid or at least to minimize this dependence, the buyer should aim to understand the supplier market competitiveness. The buyer has to analyze in detail the substitutability of the source. He has to check the ability to replace the source of a particular resource with another one. The greater this ability, the lower is his dependence upon that source. Therefore, the buyer has to find out the existence of other sources of a given resource and he has to evaluate the cost incurred by such a substitution (Bourantas 1989). In case of only limited sources the buyer has to take into account costs occurring due to supply risk in case of delays caused by the supplier (e.g. production problems, delivery delays) (Homburg 1995, p. 817). For evaluation of these different drivers determining the dependence on the supplier, procurement professionals need to have the appropriate knowledge.

Ad3:   Competent procurement professionals are able to build successful supplier relationships, which survive the transfer to the new procurement environment.

The buyer must have the appropriate knowledge to build a trustworthy relationship with the supplier, so that he will support the new procurement environment and adapt his processes. Mutual dependence and trust are related to environmental uncertainty, transaction-specific investments, reputation and satisfaction in such a supplier relationship (Ganesan 1994, p. 1). The buyer needs to be able to evaluate, which investments to make, how to enable risk sharing and how to satisfy the supplier. Based on Ritter (1998) showing that network competence has a positive impact on the technological interweavement, the author assumes a positive correlation between procurement competence and supplier relationships. Due to the appropriate procurement know-how, the buyer is able to handle conflicts with the supplier concerning the new E-processes. The procurement competence enables the buyer to recognize further development potentials. He knows, how to utilize these to convince the supplier to keep the relationship. By appropriate information sharing and adequate communication frequency the buyer might gain the requested satisfaction of the supplier, which supports a long-term orientation even in the new procurement environment (Cannon et al. 1998). The underlying motivation for long-term co-operations is that of competitive advantage derived from the supply chain as a whole rather than individual companies (Zheng et al. 1998).

Combining all these aspects, the procurement competence is a main driver to define the right fit between purchase situation and B2B E-marketplace:

Proposition 11:	*The higher the competence in the procurement organization is, the better is the fit between purchase situation and B2B E-marketplace.*

## 5.4	Summary of the hypotheses and theoretical framework of the study

In this chapter eleven hypotheses are derived based on three models: the fit between the purchase situation and the B2B E-marketplace, the project organization of the introduction of the B2B E-marketplace and the impact of the project organization on the fit from a relationship perspective.

Model 1 analyses the fit between a given purchase situation (refer to chapter 2) and a B2B E-marketplace concept (refer to chapter 3) for optimizing the relationship success between supplier and buyer.

In *model 2* the project organization (refer to chapter 4) of the introduction of B2B E-marketplace solutions in the procurement organization is in focus. From the literature the impact of the business environment and the project management on the project success have been derived.

Model 3 draws the connection between the first two models by analyzing the impact of the project organization on the fit construct and the relationship success.

The following figure shows an overview of the eleven hypotheses of the theoretical framework. These theoretical thoughts are tested in an empirical setting, which will be described in the next chapter.

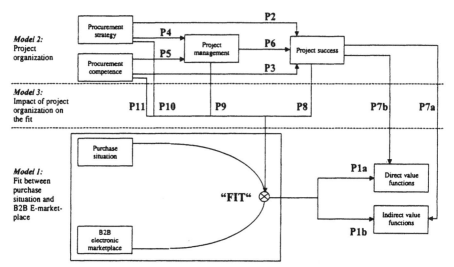

Figure 5.6 Theoretical framework

B   EMPIRICAL PART

6   Process of data gathering, sample description and process of data analysis

The following chapter describes the data gathering process. First the data gathering tool is introduced (paragraph 6.1). Then the approach of the pretest is described in paragraph 6.2. In a next step, the approach for the data generation is explained in detail (paragraph 6.3). The test sample is introduced in paragraph 6.4 by explaining selected characteristics. At the end a detailed description of the methodology and process of data analysis is given (paragraph 6.5).

6.1   Data gathering tool

The author has developed a standardized questionnaire[19], which was faxed or emailed to the potential participants. The questionnaire comprises two parts, which are attached in appendix A:

(1) The first part, the *project questionnaire*, referred to project characteristics of the introduction project of a B2B E-marketplace and more strategic aspects of the B2B E-marketplace. This questionnaire was addressed to the project leader.

(2) The second part of the questionnaire, the *supplier questionnaire*, addressed to a procurement manager referred to the supplier relationship and the operational experience with the B2B E-marketplace. This section was asked to be completed by different procurement managers.

Both types of respondents acted as key informants for optimizing the data gathering efficiency.[20]

---

[19] Standardized means that all participants have the same questionnaire with the same questions in the same order (see Stier (1999, p. 171)).

[20] Field survey research employing key informant reports is a common and well-accepted approach in marketing research (Anderson et al. (1994, p. 12)). For further details on this approach refer to Phillips (1981, p.396), and John & Reve (1982). For a discussion on advantages and disadvantages of the key-informant-approach refer to Stern (1988).

Ad1:   Project questionnaire

The project questionnaire contains five sections, which are explained in the following paragraphs.

- *General questions on the B2B E-marketplace introduction project*: In the beginning the respondent was asked to select the most recently finished B2B E-marketplace project and one specific product category. Referring to this project the respondent was asked to provide general project details as starting time, people resources, time frame and further projects. With this general section the respondent should get an easy introduction to the questionnaire, which should increase his motivation answering the questionnaire.[21]

- *Business environment:* In this section the respondent was asked to explain the company's procurement strategy and competence. A variety of different strategies was given (e.g. volume concentration, best price evaluation, global sourcing, relationship development), so that the respondent could rate them by importance. Then the respondent should provide information on the purchasing competence by referring to aspects as trainings, system support and performance tracking. Besides the purchasing aspects the information technology was the second topic in this section. Similar structured the respondent had first to give details on the IT strategy and then on the IT competence. Information on data transparency, process transparency, system support and classification systems has been questioned.

- *B2B E-marketplace introduction project:* This paragraph referred to the project management of the introduction project. First the respondent was asked about the project objectives. Aspects such as comparability of products, prices and suppliers have been discussed. Goals like access to new suppliers, improvements of existing supplier relationships or development of process and product innovations had to be differentiated. In the second section of this paragraph the respondent was asked to detail the project management with facets such as top management support, competence of project team and team leader, project planning and steering and project information and communication.

---

[21]   For structuring the questionnaire refer to Schnell et al. (1999, pp. 319).

The third section referred to the B2B E-marketplace specifics. Finally, the respondent was asked to name the B2B E-marketplace and the software provider.

■ *Success indicators of the B2B E-marketplace introduction project:* In section 4 the project success was in focus. The respondent should detail the project efficiency concerning time and cost. Then the project effectiveness concerning the objective fulfillment was questioned. Thirdly the B2B E-marketplace acceptance should be evaluated. Finally, the overall project success should be expressed by referring to project repetition or rollout.

■ *General questions about the firm:* In the last section the respondent was asked to provide general questions about the firm, such as revenues, number of employees, purchase spent, purchasing employees and percentage of purchase spent purchased via the B2B E-marketplace. Also the savings potential should be detailed, although this question was uncompleted in most cases due to confidentiality reasons. The respondent should provide this general company information for 1999, 2000 and 2001.

Ad2:   Supplier questionnaire

The supplier questionnaire was addressed to a procurement professional. This person should refer to his experience with the in the project questionnaire selected B2B E-marketplace and product category. It is divided into three parts referring to one selected supplier relationship, which is detailed in the following.

■ *Purchase situation:* According to the in chapter 2 detailed dimensions the respondent was asked to provide information on buyer business impact, supplier market competitiveness and relationship attractiveness.

■ *Changes due to B2B E-marketplace:* This section questioned aspects such as operational changes due to the usage of the new E-procurement environment. The B2B E-marketplace acceptance had to be evaluated. Finally, the supplier's IT competence had to be rated.

■ *Relationship success:* In the last section of the supplier questionnaire the relationship success after the establishment of the B2B E-marketplace has been discussed. Value functions as volume, cost savings, innovation function, scout, access and market function have been in center of analysis.

Then the respondent of the supplier questionnaire was asked to answer the same set of questions again referring to a second supplier, whose products are also bought on the selected B2B E-marketplace.

For most questions the respondent has been asked to provide his agreement or disagreement on a seven point rating scale. A seven point rating scale enabled the respondent to clearly differentiate and to express a neutral opinion due to the odd number of points.[22]

6.2   Pretest

After the development of the data-gathering tool, a detailed pretest has been executed (n=25). The questionnaire has been verified concerning appropriateness and answerability of the questions.[23] The duration of the exploratory pretest interviews varied between thirty minutes and one hour. For respondents industry experts, experts for the establishment of electronic marketplaces and sourcing experts have been selected. A small number of questions has been rephrased. A limited amount of items has been eliminated due to redundancy. Additionally, the experts had to validate the completeness of all relevant aspects, which led to introduction of further indicators.

Overall the feedback of the pretest was very positive. Only a limited number of changes had to be implemented into the questionnaire. The positive feedback of the pretest is also a result of various benefits, the author could build on:

■ The questionnaire development was based on an extensive literature research. The author had a clear understanding of the focus of research and could build on in the literature discussed operationalizations.

---

[22] Refer to Ritter (1998, p. 109) and Helfert (1998, pp. 95), who refer to empirical studies of Rohrmann (1978).
[23] For the necessity and execution of pretests refer to Schnell et al. (1999, pp. 324).

■ For the questionnaire development the author could benefit from the valuable know-how and experience of the Institute of Technology and Innovation Management at the Technical University Berlin and of the Department of International Economics and Management at the Copenhagen Business School, especially in areas as project management, value generation of relationships and IT.[24]

6.3 Data generation

The data generation took place from May 2001 until August 2001. In the following chapters the related activities are described.

6.3.1 Company selection process

Although the derived hypotheses have been formulated for no specific industry, the author has focused her study on the chemical industry in Germany.

Even in a troublesome economic slowdown, E-business is still a priority in strategies and operations of the chemical industry, however additional critical issues are confronting this industry, such as channel selection, outsourcing, value proposition determination and value chain alignment. The core topic is, how to best use E-business to foster customer and supplier relationships and to drive out market inefficiencies (Ravitz & Lee 2000, p. 26).

In the chemical industry several criteria are fulfilled, which enable the appropriate fit to various B2B E-marketplace concepts. The industry can be characterized by low concentration of buyers, a high number of geographically dispersed suppliers. A high number of existing intermediaries does exist. Typically there is a high number of transactions, low brand impact, but a complex distribution chain. The market is dominated by standardized products across all countries, which are purchased by repeat trades with low service levels. The industry is well known for excess capacity and unpredictable demand (Eastwood et al. 2000, p. 3).

Especially in an industry with low margins, cost-savings in the supply chain will continue to be a driving force, which supports the actuality of E-business activities in the chemical industry. Compared to the discrete part manufacturing industry, lean and efficient production

---

[24] Empirical work of Heydebreck (1996), Helfert (1998), Lechler (1998), Ritter (1998), Saad (1998), Walter (1998), Ryssel et al. (2000), Walter et al. (2000), Walter et al. (2001).

structures are much more difficult to realize due to the high complexity of the processing conditions and the limitation by improvements in the chemical process engineering (Blömer et al. 2000, p.401), thus any optimization opportunity is welcome. Although the B2B sector is in an early stage of its development the implementation of new E-business procedures and processes is further developed than in many other industries. Along with some forecasts the chemical industry is even the biggest B2B space in the future with a global sales volume of $400 billion, thereof 10 to 15% could be conducted online in 2003 (Ravitz & Lee 2000, p. 26). Industry changes are emerging as common standards are developed. The chemical industry Data Exchange (CIDX) forces the development of a broad set of nonproprietary, extensible markup language (XML) standards to facilitate B2B electronic data exchange across the chemical industry. In the first phase of standardizations companies as BASF, Dow and Dupont have been involved already in 2000 (Chemical Market Reporter 2001, p. 3).

Compared to the U.S., European chemical companies have been slower to adapt to E-commerce than North American firms (Gillies et al. 2000). Although first-mover advantages in E-Commerce have not resulted in sustainable competitive advantages, the only true losers are those, who are excessively slow to adopt the new technology or who rely on market inefficiencies (Ravitz & Lee 2000, p. 26). German chemical companies have to overcome barriers to the use of E-commerce such as technologies as Electronic Data Interchange (EDI), which have not always been successfully used (Doesburg et al. 1999, p. 113).

For this study the author has contacted several organizations of the chemical industry to get a full listing of all chemical companies. Basis of the database was the member listing of "Verband der Chemischen Industrie" (VCI) with all producing chemical firms. Firms focusing on trading of chemicals have been excluded. Besides the trading firms very small companies, which where listed in the VCI index without any telephone number or address have also been excluded.

This firm list was completed by adding chemical companies in Germany, which were participating on various conferences such as:

- 6. Deutsches Einkaufsleiter Forum 2000, 2-5 May, Mainz,
- E-Procurement in der Praxis, 18-19 September 2000, Thalwil,
- E-Plastics 2000, 21-22 September 2000, London,
- Zukunftsweisende Einkaufsorganisation, 10-12 October 2000, Frankfurt,

■ E-Procurement, 9-10 November 2000, Eschborn,

■ Elektronische Marktplätze für die Beschaffung, 12-14 December 2000, Frankfurt,

■ Der Einkaufsleiter, 15-16 January 2001, Eschborn,

■ Chemie 2001 – Quo vadis?, 28-29 May 2001, Bad Homburg.

Besides those various firm listings personal and professional contacts have been included. Combining all contacts in one database resulted in a total of 546 firms.

6.3.2   Acquisition of participating entities

The author has contacted all 546 firms of the developed database by telephone for identifying the appropriate contact person and for convincing him/her to participate in the study. Therefore the procurement director or leader has been requested, who the author tried to convince to participate.

First the author gave a short introduction about herself and then she detailed the research project. The topic and content of the questionnaire have been further explained. Furthermore the author explained the process, that the questionnaire can either be faxed or emailed to the respondent, so that the respondent has the flexibility to complete it any time. Then the timeline for completing the questionnaire has been discussed. In case of commitment, the author has faxed or emailed the questionnaire.

Most participants had to be contacted again as a reminder. This follow-up telephone call took place in a two weeks sequence.

Out of the 546 selected firms, only 248 firms confirmed that they have already B2B E-marketplace activities going on. That means that more than half of the contacted firms (52%) have no B2B E-marketplace implemented. Based on the remaining 248 firms, 26%, which equals 65 companies, participated in the study. The others rejected the participation due to time constraints or missing motivation. In most cases just one procurement professional per firm completed the supplier questionnaire, some completed the supplier section for two suppliers, others for more than two suppliers. In total, 121 questionnaires were completed.

6.3.3   Data documentation

The data of all returned questionnaires have been continuously archived by the author in a MS Excel table. For each item a separate column has been generated. Since archiving the data was done directly by the author the risk of errors was minimized, although any discovered mistakes have been directly corrected.[25]

In case of incomplete questionnaires the author contacted the respondents again by telephone and completed the open questions by interviewing the participants.

Finally the Excel file was transferred into a SPSS data file, SPSS for Windows, Version 10.0.

6.4   Sampling

During the data generation from May until August 2001, 121 questionnaires could be collected. Thereof one project questionnaire and two supplier questionnaires had to be excluded in the statistical analysis, as they were not sufficiently completed in both sections in the project questionnaire as well as in the supplier questionnaire.

In the following paragraphs the data sample of the participating firms is characterized by selected criteria.

As already mentioned before the author focused on the chemical industry. The data sample well represents the industry with a few very large companies, but a broad spectrum of small to medium sized firms. The average turnover of the sample amounted 7,684 mil. Euro in 2000, whereas the majority of the participating entities are small to medium sized firms with revenues below 500 mil. Euro.

---

[25] For correction of typing errors refer to Schnell et al. (1999, pp. 401).

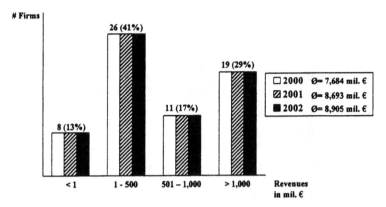

Figure 6.1 Overview revenues of participating entities in 2000

Regarding the employee structure, on average more than 23,000 headcounts have been employed in the companies of the sample. However more than 40% of the participants had less than 1,000 employees. Over the three years in focus of the study on average 3% of the overall headcount have been employed in the procurement organization.

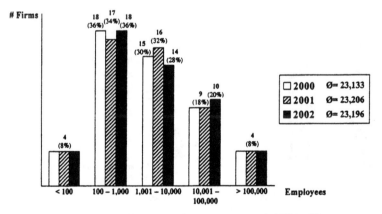

Figure 6.2 Overview number of employees of participating entities in 2000 (n=50)

Looking at the purchase volume the participating entities spent between 2,500 and 2,750 mil. Euro, whereas more than half of all participants spent less than 500 mil. Euro.

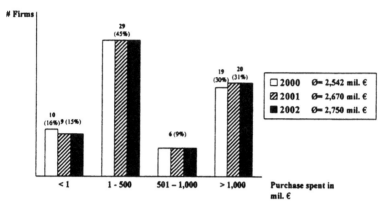

Figure 6.3 Overview purchase spent of participants in 2000

The data confirms that the E-business activities of most chemical companies are just at the beginning: in 2000 only 3.5% of the total spent have been purchased via B2B E-marketplaces, whereas the average forecast for 2001 amounted 5.5% and for 2002 even 8.1%. Since 2000 the spent purchased on B2B E-marketplaces has doubled each year.

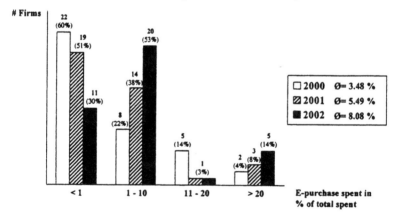

Figure 6.4 Overview purchase spent via B2B E-marketplaces in 2000 (n=37)

A similar situation can be observed with the number of suppliers, whose transactions are processed via B2B E-marketplaces. In 2000 the average was 6.6%, for the year 2001 the forecast sums up to 9.4% and the 2002 estimate is 15.5%.

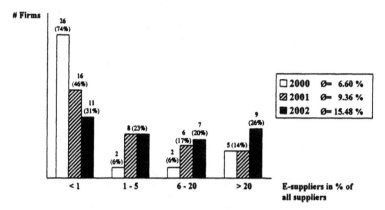

Figure 6.5 Overview suppliers with trading process on B2B E-marketplace in 2000 (n=35)

Although the E-purchase spent of 2000 was relatively small the number of procurement personnel using the new E-procurement tools already was relatively high. In 2000 a quarter of all procurement professionals have made use of the new technology, however the forecast for 2002 is that this number will double and more than half of all procurement professionals will be using E-procurement tools.

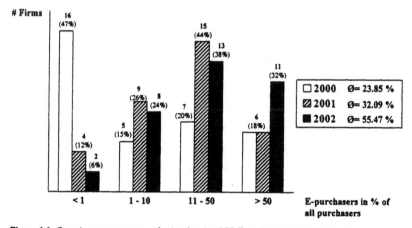

Figure 6.6 Overview procurement professionals using B2B E-marketplaces in 2000 (n=34)

Despite the fact that a quarter of the procurement professionals were already using E-tools in 2000, on average only 12.9% of all order transactions have been processed via a B2B E-marketplaces in 2000. The forecast for 2001 amounts to 17.0% and for 2002 to 20.9%. The following chart confirms that the E-business activities are just at the beginning, since most of the firms processed less than 1% of all their purchase transactions via a B2B E-marketplace.

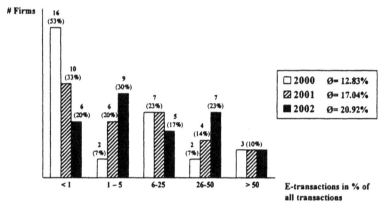

Figure 6.7   Overview number of transactions on B2B E-marketplaces in 2000 (n=30)

Most participants were not willing to release details on material cost savings and did not complete the questions relating to this issue. For n=26 in 2000 an average of 2.7% could be calculated and for 2001 the forecast is conservatively estimated at 3.8%. The highest realized material cost reduction in 2000 was 20%.

In the following paragraphs the author wants to focus on the product categories, which are transferred on B2B E-marketplaces.

In 2000 nearly a fifth of all product categories were processed on B2B E-marketplaces, although the majority of the participants purchased less than 1% of all product categories via the new E-procurement tools. In 2001 already a quarter was purchased via B2B E-marketplaces, whereas in 2002 more than 30% are expected to be bought via the new E-procurement environment.

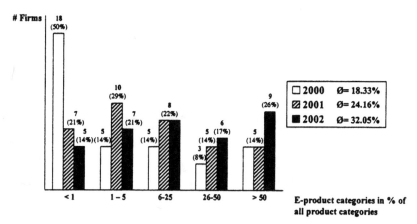

Figure 6.8 Overview number of product categories purchased via B2B E-marketplaces in 2000 (n=36)

Referring to the sample of 65 participating firms, all have chosen highly standardized products. 61% of the participants have picked standardized raw materials or commodities. 39% of all respondents have chosen indirect materials as offices supplies, MRO products (maintenance, repair and operating materials) or lab materials.

Comparing the two product groups, on average the spent of the indirect materials sums up to 361 mil. Euro. It has to be noted that the indirect material spent was below 1 mil. Euro for 45% of all participants.

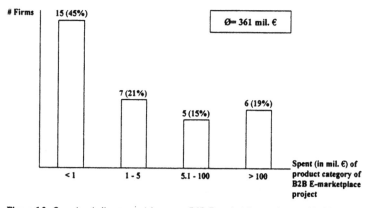

Figure 6.9 Overview indirect material spent on B2B E-marketplace project (n=33, 6 firms without details)

The average spent in the raw material category is nearly three times as high as the indirect materials cluster and sums up to 1,092 mil. Euro. Half of the participants have selected a raw material product with a volume ranging from 1 to 5 mil. Euro.

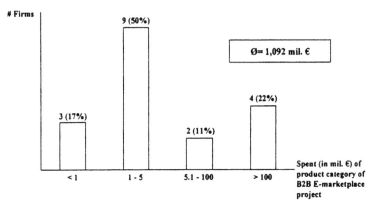

Figure 6.10 Overview raw material spent of B2B E-marketplace project (n=18, 7 firms without details)

Focusing on the project details most firms have started their E-procurement initiatives in year 2000. Only 4% of the respondents have already implemented their E-procurement tools in 1998.

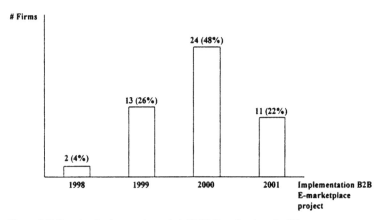

Figure 6.11 Overview implementation period of B2B E-marketplaces (n=50)

Regarding the project team on average the participants have staffed five internal and five external team members for the project execution.

6.5 Methodology and process of data analysis

In the theoretical part of this study the author developed concepts for operationalizing theoretical constructs, such as purchase situation or B2B E-marketplace, which can be characterized as "an abstract entity which presents the 'true', non-observable state or nature of a phenomenon" (Bagozzi & Fornell 1982, p. 24[26]). These constructs have been operationalized by various items in the questionnaire. For evaluating theoretical constructs, indicators have to be generated, which refer to the theoretical, directly not measurable construct. The quality of those indicators, how good they can describe the theoretical construct, can be tested by two tests: the reliability test and the validity test (Homburg & Giering 1996, p. 6).

The reliability test describes the probability of random errors influencing the test results of a study. A low impact of random errors is reflected in a high reliability (Atteslander 1995, p. 263).

The validity questions the correctness of the data gathering tool, if it is able to measure, what it should measure. Although validity has a broad definition (Jacoby 1978, p. 91) in this study only the convergent validity[27], the discriminate validity[28] and the validity of the content[29] are in focus.

For measuring the reliability and the validity, the reliability analysis (Cronbach's Alpha), the item-to-total correlation analysis and the factor analysis have been used, which have been computed by using the software package SPSS 10.0[30]. With the exploratory factor analysis[31], which confirms, if the selected indicators fit to one factor, the convergent and discriminate validity is tested.

---

[26] Citation in Ritter (1998, p. 119).
[27] "Convergent validity is the degree, to which two or more attempts to measure the same concepts are in agreement" (Bagozzi & Philipps (1982, p. 468)).
[28] The discriminate validity is defined along with Bagozzi & Philipps (1982, p. 469) as "...the degree, to which measures of distinct concepts differ".
[29] For measuring the validity of the content no objective criteria are available (Atteslander (1995, p. 343)). But based on the interviews with experts and the pretest the validity of the content can be assumed.
[30] For practical advice of the software package SPSS see Voss (2000).
[31] Factor analysis is used to reduce a variety of different items to a number of items, which are sufficient to characterize a certain factor (refer to Backhaus et al. (2000, p. 252)). The Kaiser criterion is used as exit function. The number of extrapolated factors equals the number of factors with Eigenwert larger 1 (Backhaus et al. (2000) and Janssen & Laatz (1999, p. 452)).

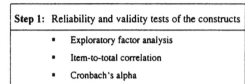

Step 1:	Reliability and validity tests of the constructs
	• Exploratory factor analysis
	• Item-to-total correlation
	• Cronbach's alpha

Step 2:	Analysis of the links between the constructs
	• Correlation analysis
	• Regression analysis
	• Hierarchical regression analysis
	• 2-factor variance analysis
	• Mean comparison

Figure 6.12 Approach of the empirical data analysis

All items pertaining to the same function were submitted to an exploratory factor analysis. Along with Homburg (2000) the limit of the average variance of a factor is .50, which means the factor determines on average 50% of the variance of its indicators. For the factor loadings of the indicators a minimum of .50 is required (Helfert 1998, p. 113). The minimum of the item-to-total correlation[32] was defined at .30 (Kumar et al. 1993, p. 12). All three criteria together suggest a sufficient validity.

To pass the reliability check the Cronbach's Alpha[33] has to be above .60.[34]

The following table gives a summary of the used criteria.

Criteria	≥
Explained variance	50%
Factor loading per item	.50
Item-to-total correlation per item	.30
Cronbach's Alpha	.60

Figure 6.13 Summary validity and reliability criteria in use

---

[32] The item-to-total correlation describes the correlation between an indicator and the sum of all indicators related to the factor. See Homburg (2000, p. 89).

[33] Refer to Homburg (2000, p. 89.)

[34] McAllister (1995, p. 36).

After the reliability and validity analysis of the constructs the links between the theoretical constructs are in focus of analysis. First a correlation analysis[35] has been computed. Then a regression analysis[36] was computed for identifying the relationships between the dependent and independent variables. For testing the interaction effect a hierarchical regression analysis[37] and a 2-factor variance analysis[38] have been computed. The results have been further examined by mean comparisons.

---

[35] A correlation analysis enables an interpretation of intensity and direction of linear correlations between two variables; therefore it is a tool to characterize the correlation between two parameters. The value of the correlation coefficient r values between '-1' and '1'. '0' means no correlation, whereas '1' or '-1' represents a perfect positive or negative correlation. For further details refer to Backhaus et al. (2000, p. 262).

[36] With the regression analysis the linear correlation of one dependent variable and several independent variables can be identified. It is possible to determine the impact of several independent variables on one dependent variable. These results have been tested regarding their significance. Refer to Backhaus (2000, p. 1).

[37] Cortina (1993), Lovelace et al. (2001).

[38] Elsbach (1994), Moussa (1996), Backhaus et al. (2000).

7   Operationalization of the constructs

In this chapter the operationalization of the theoretical constructs and the theoretical framework, which have been developed in the theoretical part of this work, are evaluated and documented. In chapter 7.1 the constructs of model 1 are in focus relating to the purchase situation, the B2B E-marketplace and to the relationship success. Then in chapter 7.2 the project organization is operationalized (model 2).

The proposed measures have been purified by assessing their reliability and validity. The validity and reliability measurements have been computed as described in chapter 6.5. First, all items pertaining to the same construct were submitted to an exploratory factor analysis. After eliminating items with factor loadings below the defined criteria, item-to-total correlations have been computed. Items with not significant correlations have been dropped. Then the Cronbach's Alpha has been computed. Similar to the mentioned approach above in case of an Alpha below the limit, the item with the smallest item-to-total correlation has been eliminated.

For all questions the respondent was asked to state his agreement or disagreement on a 7-point Likert scale (1=disagreement, 7=agreement).

7.1   Operationalization of the constructs of model 1

Model 1 consists of four constructs: purchase situation, B2B E-marketplace and the two functions indirect and direct value functions, describing the relationship success. The questions, that address these four constructs in the questionnaire, are discussed in the following chapters.

7.1.1   Operationalization of the purchase situation

To evaluate the purchase situation all three dimensions of the cube developed in chapter 2 have been assessed: buyer business impact, supplier market competitiveness and the relationship attractiveness. The dimensions buyer business impact and relationship attractiveness are further detailed by various factors. The following figure gives an overview of the structure of the construct purchase situation.

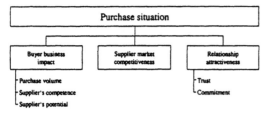

Figure 7.1 Structure of the construct purchase situation

Starting with the first dimension, the buyer business impact: To reduce complexity the author has picked the most important criteria out of the selection of various characteristics detailed in chapter 2 for characterizing the buyer business impact. Therefore three factors have been built: purchase volume, supplier's competences and supplier's potential.

The factor purchase volume comprises two items. The selected items proof the typical characteristics of a commodity product. Although the supply is a cheap product, a high business impact is caused by this supply due to its high number of transactions. In the following table the corresponding questions of the questionnaire are displayed with the item-to-total correlations, the factor loadings, the explained variance and the Cronbach's Alpha.

Factor Purchase volume	Item-to-total correlation	Factor loading
This is a supply with an extremely high number of transactions.	.51	.87
This supply has relatively low product value per unit.	.51	.87
Cronbach's Alpha	.68	
Explained variance	75.66 %	

Table 7.1 Factor purchase volume

The second factor measuring the buyer business impact is describing the supplier's competence. The selected items evaluate the buyer's dependency on the supplier by questioning, if the supply can become a bottleneck for production.

Factor Supplier's competence	Item-to-total correlation	Factor loading
The supplier's reliability concerning product quality and punctuality of delivery is key for us.	.71	.93
The supplier's service offering (payment scheme, next day delivery etc.) is beneficial to us.	.71	.93
Cronbach's Alpha	.83	
Explained variance	85.72 %	

Table 7.2   Factor supplier's competence

The third factor of the buyer business impact dimension refers to the supplier's potential.

Factor Supplier's potential	Item-to-total correlation	Factor loading
The supplier's innovation competence is important to us.	.58	.83
The supplier's business partner network is beneficial to us since it opens new opportunities for our company.	.54	.79
This supplier has a large development potential concerning production processes and supporting processes.	.57	.81
Cronbach's Alpha	.74	
Explained variance	65.59 %	

Table 7.3   Factor supplier's potential

The assessments of the three factors of the dimension buyer business impact passed the reliability and validity checks without exception. For further analysis the indicators of the three factors have been aggregated by calculating the arithmetic average to find out how suitable these three factors are to measure the dimension buyer business impact. The results of the reliability and validity measurements are displayed in the following table.

Dimension Buyer business impact	Item-to-total correlation	Factor loading
Factor purchase volume	.32	.65
Factor supplier's potential	.49	.82
Factor supplier's competence	.42	.78
Cronbach's Alpha	.61	
Explained variance	56.23 %	

Table 7.4   Dimension buyer business impact

The first dimension of the purchase situation cube has passed all quality checks with respect to reliability and validity.

The second dimension of the purchase situation, the supplier market competitiveness, is operationalized as documented in table 7.5. The dimension describes the high need of relationship support for the buyer at markets with low or no supplier market competitiveness. In a monopoly, the buyer is really dependent on the relationship to the supplier to get optimum conditions. To characterize this dependency one item has been inverted.

Dimension Supplier market competitiveness	Item-to-total correlation	Factor loading
We cannot easily replace this supplier.	.44	.85
The market can be characterized by high competition between many suppliers. (This item has been inverted.)	.44	.85
Cronbach's Alpha	.62	
Explained variance	72.18 %	

Table 7.5   Dimension supplier market competitiveness[39]

The third dimension evaluates the relationship attractiveness of the procurement environment. Therefore two factors have been examined: the buyer's trust in the supplier and the existing commitment to the supplier.

The factor trust covers two facets used in relationship marketing research, motivational or intentional trust aspects (Morgan & Hunt 1994, Wilson 1995, Helfert & Gemünden 1998) and the satisfaction aspects, which enforce the development of trust (Walter et al. 2000).

---

[39] Items with the notice (This item has been inverted.) are formulated opposite to the original question, therefore their values have been calculated by applying the formula '8-x' (x= original rating on a 7-point Likert scale).

Factor Trust	Item-to-total correlation	Factor loading
When we have an important requirement, we can depend on the supplier's support.	.55	.74
We can count on the supplier's promises made to our firm.	.61	.79
Overall we are very satisfied with this supplier.	.62	.79
Compared with our expectations, we are not satisfied with this supplier. (This item has been inverted.)	.67	.83
Cronbach's Alpha	.80	
Explained variance	62.18 %	

Table 7.6   Factor trust[40]

With the commitment factor also two facets are evaluated. On the one hand the affective and instrumental commitment is measured as defined by Walter et al. (2000), which is describing the positive attitude towards the future existence of the relationship and some form of investment in the relationship. However, in the context of this study the management aspect is also included in the commitment factor. This facet measures, if the buyer is showing special commitment to the relationship to the supplier by investing in personnel, who is supporting and managing a smooth supplier relationship and assuring continuous supply without any bottleneck for production.

---

[40] Items with the notice (This item has been inverted.) are formulated opposite to the original question, therefore their values have been calculated by applying the formula '8-x' (x= original rating on a 7-point Likert scale).

Factor Commitment	Item-to-total correlation	Factor loading
We focus on long-term goals in this relationship.	.67	.83
We are willing to invest time and other resources into the relationship with this supplier.	.57	.77
Our procurement employees are in close contact with corresponding employees of this supplier.	.67	.84
We have an intermediator who manages a stable and successful relationship with this supplier.	.37	.51
The supplier has an intermediator who manages a stable and successful relationship with us.	.64	.78
Cronbach's Alpha	.80	
Explained variance	57.00 %	

Table 7.7   Factor commitment

Based on the two factors of relationship attractiveness, arithmetic averages have been calculated for each factor. The positive results with respect to reliability and validity analysis are documented in the following table.

Dimension Relationship attractiveness	Item-to-total correlation	Factor loading
Factor commitment	.44	.85
Factor trust	.44	.85
Cronbach's Alpha	.62	
Explained variance	72.20 %	

Table 7.8   Dimension relationship attractiveness

For the purpose of future calculations the arithmetic averages of the factors of each of the three dimensions of the purchase situation have been calculated and are analyzed with respect to their measurement quality. The results are shown in below table.

Construct Purchase situation	Item-to-total correlation	Factor loading
Dimension buyer business impact	.66	.89
Dimension supplier market competitiveness	.43	.74
Dimension relationship attractiveness	.36	.70
Cronbach's Alpha	.67	
Explained variance	60.74 %	

Table 7.9   Construct purchase situation

Overall the proposed measures of the purchase situation meet the defined criteria with respect to reliability and validity.

7.1.2   Operationalization of the B2B electronic marketplace

The operationalization of the B2B electronic marketplace follows the theoretically derived portfolio of chapter 3. Two dimensions have been operationalized: The product specifics and the marketplace openness, since those two dimensions characterize the impact of B2B E-marketplaces on inter-organizational relationships. The following figure gives an overview of the structure of the construct B2B E-marketplace.

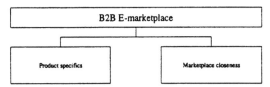

Figure 7.2   Structure of the construct B2B E-marketplace

First, the dimension product specifics is documented. The respondent was asked to answer the relevant questions by focusing only on B2B E-marketplaces. Referring to the impact on inter-organizational relationships the dimension product specifics summarizes different aspects of standardization of the products traded on B2B E-marketplaces. With increasing product complexity the need of relationship support increases. The first question addressed the product type, i.e. it was asked, if the product is a commodity, which can be differentiated by price. Then, the product value was measured, i.e. if it is a low value product with relatively high transaction costs. Finally, the life cycle of the product was in focus, since for those products with short life cycle leading to a high extent of obsolete products, the B2B E-marketplace opens a new sourcing opportunity. The following table shows the outcome of the reliability and validity analyses.

Dimension Product specifics	Item-to-total correlation	Factor loading
Product specifics of this supply do not need to be negotiated, only price is decisive. (This item has been inverted.)	.34	.59
This supply has relatively high transaction cost (transportation cost etc.) compared to its purchase volume. (This item has been inverted.)	.44	.72
This is a supply with an extremely high purchase spent per order.	.51	.77
A short life cycle is typical of this supply.	.45	.73
Cronbach's Alpha	.65	
Explained variance	49.26 %	

Table 7.10 Dimension product specifics[41]

The dimension product specifics can be seen as valid and reliable, although the explained variance is close at the border of the defined limit of 50%, but all other analyses as the total-to-item correlations, the Cronbach's Alpha and the factor loadings fulfill the requirements.

The second dimension describing the B2B E-marketplace in a relational sense is the marketplace openness. With decreasing marketplace openness the need of relationship support increases. Highly open marketplaces, as for example auctions, do not need special interpersonal contacts, they prosper with increasing number of transactions. Therefore, the author has renamed the dimension in marketplace closeness, since with increasing closeness the needed relationship support increases. Based on the pretest and intense expert interviews the most important items describing the B2B E-marketplace have been selected covering the business model, the order processing mechanism and the revenue model. The mechanism of a flat rate, meaning a subscription fee, which is paid in advance for a certain period, does not require any relationship support, since the marketplace facilitator has received the payment in

---

[41] Items with the notice (This item has been inverted.) are formulated opposite to the original question, therefore their values have been calculated by applying the formula '8-x' (x= original rating on a 7-point Likert scale).

advance, independent of the number of transactions to be processed on the B2B E-marketplace. Therefore, this item had to be inverted to be aligned with the dimension marketplace closeness. In the following table the results of the reliability and validity analyses are summarized:

Dimension Marketplace closeness	Item-to-total correlation	Factor loading
For this sourcing group our firm is purchasing from a neutral marketplace owned by a software provider. (This item has been inverted.)	.43	.62
This E-marketplace is run by catalogs.	.63	.81
This E-marketplace is run by auction, where different bids are submitted in a limited time frame and the highest bid is successful. (This item has been inverted.)	.49	.68
This E-marketplace is run by exchange, similar to the stock exchange. (This item has been inverted.)	.53	.73
Revenue generation of this E-marketplace is run by flat rate like subscription or license fee. (This item has been inverted.)	.53	.70
Cronbach's Alpha	.76	
Explained variance	50.88 %	

Table 7.11 Dimension marketplace closeness[42]

Finally, the two dimensions product specifics and marketplace closeness have been aggregated to the construct B2B E-marketplace.

Construct B2B E-marketplace	Item-to-total correlation	Factor loading
Dimension product specifics	.37	.83
Dimension marketplace closeness	.37	.83
Cronbach's Alpha	.54	
Explained variance	68.69 %	

Table 7.12 Construct B2B E-marketplace

Although the Cronbach's Alpha is below .60 the two dimensions product specifics and marketplace closeness have been aggregated to the construct B2B E-marketplace. The low Cronbach's Alpha can be explained by the two different dimensions of product characteristics referring to the degree of standardization and attributes describing the B2B E-marketplace

---

[42] Items with the notice (This item has been inverted.) are formulated opposite to the original question, therefore their values have been calculated by applying the formula '8-x' (x= original rating on a 7-point Likert scale).

mechanism. However, for the purpose of measuring the increasing need of relationship support on B2B E-marketplaces these two dimensions need to be aggregated, which is supported by the factor loadings, the explained variance and the total-to-item correlations.

7.1.3   Operationalization of the relationship success

Since the relationship success can be measured by two absolutely different aspects (Walter et al. 2001) the author has operationalized two separate constructs. One dimension is measuring the indirect value functions, which are the soft facts impacting the success of the supplier relationship and one dimension is measuring the hard facts, which are the cost savings referring to the supplier relationship.

7.1.3.1   Operationalization of the indirect value functions

Along with the definition of indirect values two dimensions have been built: innovation functions and access and market functions. The following figure gives an overview of the structure of this construct.

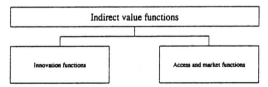

Figure 7.3 Structure of the construct indirect value functions

The selected items go along with the definition of Walter et al. (2001), but have been adapted to the buyer's perspective referring to his suppliers. The following two tables show the positive results of the validity and reliability analyses.

Dimension Innovation functions	Item-to-total correlation	Factor loading
With this supplier we have reduced cycle time.	.45	.60
Due to supply adaptations we have improved our production output reliability.	.56	.72
This supplier assists us to realize product/service innovation improvements.	.70	.85
This supplier assists us to realize product and process quality improvements.	.72	.86
Due to the cooperation with this supplier we have improved our image.	.51	.69
Cronbach's Alpha	.80	
Explained variance	56.52 %	

Table 7.13 Dimension innovation functions

Dimension Access and market functions	Item-to-total correlation	Factor loading
This supplier has introduced valuable suppliers to us.	.71	.90
This supplier has provided information about potential new suppliers.	.70	.91
This supplier assists us to increase market penetration.	.46	.70
Cronbach's Alpha	.79	
Explained variance	70.61 %	

Table 7.14 Dimension access and market functions

Along with the defined criteria the described constructs are reliable and valid. For further analysis the indicators of the constructs have been aggregated to one factor by calculating the arithmetic average. Then, the quality of the aggregation to the two dimensions of the construct indirect value functions has been analyzed.

Construct Indirect value functions	Item-to-total correlation	Factor loading
Dimension innovation functions	.53	.87
Dimension access and market functions	.53	.87
Cronbach's Alpha	.69	
Explained variance	76.36 %	

Table 7.15 Construct indirect value functions

The construct indirect value functions can be seen as reliable and valid.

7.1.3.2   Operationalization of the direct value functions

Measuring the relationship success of a supplier relationship cost savings are the main lever for success. Therefore the direct values are operationalized with items measuring the realized cost savings. On the one hand material cost reductions are beneficial, but on the other hand transaction costs also need to be optimized. The third component of interest relating to cost savings in procurement is inventory reduction, which has a direct impact on the balance sheet and cashflow. The following table documents the positive results of the reliability and validity analyses.

Construct Direct value functions	Item-to-total correlation	Factor loading
The material cost of this supply could be significantly reduced.	.35	.68
Transaction costs (all cost, which are not production related) have been reduced.	.51	.82
We could realize an inventory reduction.	.41	.75
Cronbach's Alpha	.61	
Explained variance	56.42 %	

Table 7.16 Construct direct value functions

The construct direct value functions can be seen as reliable and valid, since it passed all earlier defined criteria.

7.2   Operationalization of the constructs of model 2

Besides the constructs for measuring the appropriate fit between purchase situation and B2B
E-marketplace the constructs referring to the project organization have to be operationalized.
These operationalizations are documented in this paragraph.

7.2.1   Operationalization of procurement strategy

The operationalization of procurement strategy focuses only on the business environment of
the procurement organization. There are many more aspects of a successful strategy, but in
the content of this study only the procurement focus is relevant. Two dimensions have been
developed covering the used purchasing approach and questioning the IT focus in
procurement. Both dimensions are referring to the relational focus of this study. They are
emphasizing the need of relationship development with the supplier. The following figure
documents the structure of the construct procurement strategy.

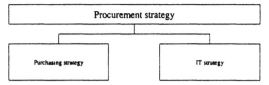

Figure 7.4 Structure of the construct procurement strategy

The items referring to the purchasing approach analyze, if monetary aspects are in focus of
the supplier relationship development or qualitative, more process-related aspects are in focus
or both. The following table shows the positive results of the validity and reliability analyses.

Dimension Purchasing strategy	Item-to-total correlation	Factor loading
For this sourcing group we focus on establishing deep relationships with suppliers to reduce overall purchase cost (material and transaction cost).	.65	.91
For this sourcing group we focus on establishing deep relationship with suppliers to optimize joint processes to reduce cycle time.	.65	.91
Cronbach's Alpha	.79	
Explained variance	82.29 %	

Table 7.17 Dimension purchasing strategy

With the dimension IT strategy the realization potential of the IT systems in procurement is analyzed, which should enable transparency within the procurement processes.

Dimension IT strategy	Item-to-total correlation	Factor loading
Supplier assessment is key for implementing IT solutions in purchasing.	.47	.86
Insights and support of our processes (e.g. inventory management, order processing) is key for implementing IT solutions in purchasing.	.47	.86
Cronbach's Alpha	.64	
Explained variance	73.48 %	

Table 7.18 Dimension IT strategy

The items of the two dimensions have been aggregated to two factors. Then the validity and reliability measures have been computed.

Construct Procurement strategy	Item-to-total correlation	Factor loading
Dimension purchasing strategy	.79	.95
Dimension IT strategy	.79	.95
Cronbach's Alpha	.88	
Explained variance	89.61 %	

Table 7.19 Construct procurement strategy

The construct procurement strategy can be seen as valid and reliable since all criteria are fulfilled.

7.2.2   Operationalization of the procurement competence

Besides the procurement strategy the procurement competence has also been assessed for characterizing the preconditions of the project organization. Similar to the procurement strategy two dimensions have been computed. The structure of the construct is displayed in the following figure.

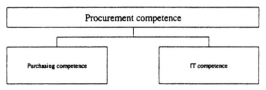

Figure 7.5 Structure of the construct procurement competence

The first dimension is focusing on specific purchasing know-how, support tools and the quality of the current process.

Dimension Purchasing competence	Item-to-total correlation	Factor loading
We invest in sufficient training for our procurement personnel.	.69	.87
We invest in support tools and procurement systems.	.70	.88
Our procurement process is best practice.	.53	.76
Cronbach's Alpha	.79	
Explained variance	70.26 %	

Table 7.20 Dimension purchasing competence

All relevant validity and reliability criteria are fulfilled.

Then the IT know-how is examined. Aspects as the current ERP system or the current classification system are analyzed. Also the data transparency is included in the IT competence measure, since it is a key lever for optimizing the procurement processes.

Dimension IT competence	Item-to-total correlation	Factor loading
We are experienced in tracking procurement performance (e.g. total purchase cost, logistics cost, inventory level, quality of product/service).	.58	.81
We have an ERP system implemented (e.g. SAP R/2, R/3, Oracle).	.50	.75
Our ERP software is compatible to marketplace software (e.g. Ariba, CommerceOne).	.56	.81
We have one uniform classification system for all our suppliers (e.g. eCl@ss, UNSPSC).	.33	.54
Cronbach's Alpha	.71	
Explained variance	54.22 %	

Table 7.21 Dimension IT competence

The operationalization of the dimension IT competence can be accepted as reliable and valid. All defined criteria are fulfilled.

Then the two dimensions have been aggregated to the construct procurement competence, supported by positive results of validity and reliability analyses.

Construct Procurement competence	Item-to-total correlation	Factor loading
Dimension purchasing competence	.44	.85
Dimension IT competence	.44	.85
Cronbach's Alpha	.61	
Explained variance	72.03 %	

Table 7.22 Construct procurement competence

7.2.3   Operationalization of the project management

The project management is analyzed by three aspects: top management support, team competence and project planning and steering. The constructs go along with the operationalization of Lechler (1997) and Gemünden et al. (1999). In some aspects they have been adapted to the B2B E-marketplace concept. The following figure shows the structure of this construct.

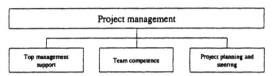

Figure 7.6 Structure of the construct project management

In the following table the results of the operationalization of the dimension top management support is displayed.

Dimension Top management support	Item-to-total correlation	Factor loading
In difficult situations the project team was fully supported by upper management to secure project success.	.81	.95
Additional resources were granted by upper management, if needed by the project.	.81	.95
Cronbach's Alpha	.89	
Explained variance	90.37 %	

Table 7.23 Dimension top management support

The dimension team competence summarizes all relevant requirements for implementing a B2B E-marketplace project. First, items as know-how and training are questioned. The project leaders competence concerning the objective decision process is also included in this measure. Besides the individual competences of the project team and the project leader the overall team competence of using support tools for project management is measured. Additionally to the appropriate know-how and technical abilities, the right communication strategy ensures a successful project management. Therefore, several items characterizing the project communication have been included in the team competence dimension.

Dimension Team competence	Item-to-total correlation	Factor loading
The project team had the appropriate qualifications.	.69	.77
The project leader and his team were sufficiently trained.	.72	.79
The project leader had considerable influence on the definition of project objectives.	.77	.84
Methods, procedures and tools for project control and supervision worked well.	.74	.81
Everybody in the project team knew exactly where help was available when difficulties arose.	.78	.85
The communication channels in the project team were predefined.	.73	.81
All project team members were always sufficiently informed about their work on the project.	.74	.82
Many personal and informal meetings have taken place.	.46	.55
Cronbach's Alpha	.91	
Explained variance	61.42 %	

Table 7.24 Dimension team competence

The results of the validity and reliability measurements are satisfying, all defined criteria are fulfilled.

Besides the top management support and the appropriate team competence the project steering and planning process is key to a successful project execution. Various aspects have been included in the project planning and steering dimension.

Dimension Project planning and steering	Item-to-total correlation	Factor loading
All essential aspects of the project execution were monitored and controlled (budget, time schedule, resources, performance progress).	.65	.91
During the project, planning data were reviewed and adapted if necessary.	.65	.91
Cronbach's Alpha	.79	
Explained variance	82.44 %	

Table 7.25 Dimension project planning and steering

For further analysis the items of the three dimensions have been aggregated to the construct project management. The following table shows the results of the quality measurements.

Construct Project management	Item-to-total correlation	Factor loading
Dimension top management support	.54	.79
Dimension team competence	.56	.81
Dimension project planning and steering	.60	.84
Cronbach's Alpha	.74	
Explained variance	66.05 %	

Table 7.26 Construct project management

The assessment of the construct project management can be seen as reliable and valid, since all criteria are met.

7.2.4   Operationalization of the project success

According to the operationalization of the project success of Lechler (1997, p. 164) the author has assessed project success. However, she has adapted Lechler's (1997) concept by including a third dimension relating to the B2B E-marketplace introduction, which is called B2B E-marketplace acceptance. The success of the B2B E-marketplace project is mainly determined by the acceptance and usage of the new E-tools. Therefore, the author has operationalized three dimensions: project efficiency, project effectiveness and the B2B E-marketplace acceptance. The dimension B2B E-marketplace acceptance is further detailed by three factors. The following figure shows the structure of the construct project success.

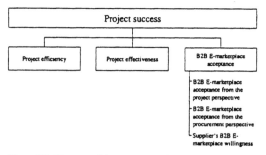

Figure 7.7 Structure of the construct project success

The following table shows the positive results of the reliability and validity analyses of the project efficiency.

Dimension Project efficiency	Item-to-total correlation	Factor loading
The targeted project end could be reached within time.	.58	.89
The project did not run over budget.	.58	.89
Cronbach's Alpha	.73	
Explained variance	78.98 %	

Table 7.27 Dimension project efficiency

Cronbach's Alpha, the item-to-total correlations and the factor loadings exceed the defined reliability and validity criteria.

For measuring the project effectiveness the pretest and expert interviews have led to the selected items. Based on the expert interviews and the results of the pretest a combination of items has been chosen representing the objectives, which have been communicated by the relevant responsibilities in the chemical industry. In the pretest phase aspects, such as process transparency, improved supplier interaction and satisfying marketplace utilization, have been underlined as key levers for an effective project besides the main objective of cost optimization. These items have been incorporated in the effectiveness measure.

Dimension Project effectiveness	Item-to-total correlation	Factor loading
We achieved the target process cost reduction.	.73	.81
We achieved the target material cost reduction.	.60	.70
We achieved the target inventory reduction.	.62	.72
We achieved the comparability of products, prices and suppliers.	.59	.68
We have improved our existent supplier relationship.	.52	.62
We have reduced the number of suppliers by half.	.65	.75
The number of transactions on the e-marketplaces is satisfying.	.62	.72
Our suppliers benefit from this project.	.82	.88
Cronbach's Alpha	.88	
Explained variance	54.59 %	

Table 7.28 Dimension project effectiveness

The selected items can be seen as valid and reliable to describe the dimension project effectiveness, all criteria are passed.

As said before, the efficiency and effectiveness alone are not sufficient for a successful execution of a B2B E-marketplace project. The new E-tool needs to be accepted by the procurement professionals and continuously used. Therefore, the author puts a high emphasis on the B2B E-marketplace acceptance measure and has developed three factors characterizing various facets of the acceptance as detailed in chapter 4. The operationalization goes along with Martin (1993), but the author has adapted the constructs to the B2B E-marketplace concept.

First, the project team was asked to evaluate the changes in the procurement environment. Various aspects, such as process improvements, transparency and reduced operative workload have been questioned. The following table documents the incorporated items. The operationalization of the factor B2B E-marketplace acceptance from the project perspective can be seen as reliable and valid.

Factor B2B E-marketplace acceptance from the project perspective	Item-to-total correlation	Factor loading
Our purchasing personnel has less operative work load.	.41	.63
Redundant purchasing processes have been eliminated.	.53	.75
Usage of B2B E-marketplaces has created more process transparency in procurement.	.67	.85
The establishment of B2B E-marketplaces has increased the work quality in procurement.	.57	.78
Cronbach's Alpha	.75	
Explained variance	57.32 %	

Table 7.29 Factor B2B E-marketplace acceptance form the project perspective

Especially the changes in the procurement environment seemed to be levers of the B2B E-marketplace acceptance. Therefore, the author addressed the same questions also to the procurement professionals measuring not only the project perspective but also the procurement perspective. Items characterizing changes in the physical transaction of the supply have also been incorporated.

Factor B2B E-marketplace acceptance from the procurement perspective	Item-to-total correlation	Factor loading
The E-marketplace has simplified the coordination of the purchase transactions.	.76	.84
The E-marketplace has simplified the exchange of supplies and services.	.76	.85
We have less operative work load.	.74	.83
Redundant purchasing processes have been eliminated.	.74	.82
Usage of B2B E-marketplaces has created more process transparency in procurement.	.76	.84
The establishment of B2B E-marketplaces has increased our work quality in procurement.	.60	.71
Cronbach's Alpha	.90	
Explained variance	66.51 %	

Table 7.30 Factor B2B E-marketplace acceptance from the procurement perspective

The third factor of the acceptance measure refers to the supplier. The acceptance within the buyer organization is not enough; the supplier also needs to be willing to utilize the new procurement environment. Therefore the procurement professionals have been asked to give a judgment on the supplier's willingness.

Factor Supplier's B2B E-marketplace willingness	Item-to-total correlation	Factor loading
All our business with this supplier is handled via the new B2B E-marketplace.	.51	.79
For qualifying as our supplier the supplier must participate on the B2B E-marketplace.	.56	.83
Our supplier is willing to invest in E-procurement solutions.	.41	.70
Cronbach's Alpha	.67	
Explained variance	60.53 %	

Table 7.31 Factor supplier's B2B E-marketplace willingness

Then the indicators of the three factors have been aggregated into one factor each by computing the arithmetic average. The measurements concerning their quality are documented in the following table.

Dimension B2B E-marketplace acceptance	Item-to-total correlation	Factor loading
Factor B2B E-marketplace acceptance from the project perspective	.56	.80
Factor B2B E-marketplace acceptance from the procurement perspective	.65	.86
Factor supplier's B2B E-marketplace willingness	.62	.84
Cronbach's Alpha	.77	
Explained variance	68.76 %	

Table 7.32 Dimension B2B E-marketplace acceptance

All criteria have been confirmed and the operationalization of the dimension B2B E-marketplace acceptance can be seen as reliable and valid.

Finally, the indicators of the three dimensions of the project success have been summarized in three factors by building the arithmetic averages. The following table documents the positive results of the reliability and validity analyses.

Construct Project success	Item-to-total correlation	Factor loading
Dimension project efficiency	.32	.62
Dimension project effectiveness	.69	.92
Dimension B2B E-marketplace acceptance	.35	.74
Cronbach's Alpha	.64	
Explained variance	59.33 %	

Table 7.33 Construct project success

Overall the operationalization of the construct project success can be seen as reliable and valid, since all earlier defined criteria have been confirmed.

Based on the constructs defined in this chapter the hypotheses of the theoretical framework are tested in the following chapter.

8   Empirical analysis of the theoretical model

Based on the operationalized constructs the hypotheses, derived in chapter 5, have to be tested. Regression analysis and correlation analysis[43] have been computed to analyze the theoretical framework.

In chapter 8.1 the hypotheses concerning the *first model*, the impact of the relationship fit between purchase situation and B2B E-marketplace on the relationship success are tested. Then in chapter 8.2 the *second model* is in focus with its various hypotheses concerning the project organization. Chapter 8.3 discusses the results of the *third model*, which focuses on the impact between model 1 and 2, which means the impact of the project organization on the fit between purchase situation and B2B E-marketplace and on the relationship success. Finally, chapter 8.4 gives an overview of the overall theoretical framework and the empirical results.

8.1   Hypothesis tests of model 1: Fit between purchase situation and B2B E-marketplace

The main model of this work analyzes the appropriate fit between purchase situation and B2B E-marketplace. This fit is depending on the relationship support, which is required by the purchase situation and which needs to be enabled by the B2B E-marketplace concept. The following propositions have been tested:

- The higher the fit between purchase situation and B2B E-marketplace characteristics is, the higher is the outcome of the direct value functions (proposition 1a).
- The higher the fit between purchase situation and B2B E-marketplace characteristics is, the higher is the outcome of the indirect value functions (proposition 1b).

The following table documents the results of the correlation analysis of the purchase situation, B2B E-marketplace concept, the fit construct and the indirect and direct value functions. For measuring the fit, the interaction term is built by the product of the construct purchase situation and B2B E-marketplace (Birnbaum 1973, p. 239).

---

[43]   Since all hypotheses of the derived theoretical framework are formulated in one specific direction, all tests are calculated one-sided.

Correlations	Indirect value functions	Direct value functions
Purchase situation	.19**	.19***
B2B E-marketplace	.27***	.26***
Fit (Purchase situation x B2B E-marketplace)	.30***	.25***

*** : 1% significance level (1-sided)
** : 5% significance level (1-sided)
* : 10% significance level (1-sided)

Table 8.1   Correlation analysis to proposition 1a and 1b

All correlation coefficients are highly significant, which is a first indication for the assumption, that the right fit between purchase situation and B2B E-marketplace causes the optimum relationship success.

For further analysis of this assumption the interaction effect has been tested with a hierarchical regression analysis along the method explained by Cortina (1993) and Lovelace et al. (2001).[44] First, all preconditions (Keller 2001, p. 551) have been tested with positive results. The independent and interaction variables are significantly correlated (p=.00), the independent and dependent variables are significantly correlated and the interaction term and the dependent variables are significantly correlated (table 8.1). Then, in a first step the independent variables purchase situation and B2B E-marketplace have been included in the regression. In a second step the interaction term, which is the product of the purchase situation and the B2B E-marketplace, has been added. The interaction effect is confirmed, if the addition of the interaction term causes a significant increase of the explained variance (R^2) of the dependent variable.

The results of this hierarchical regression analysis are documented in the following table.

---

[44] For more details on the interaction effect refer also to Stewart & Barrick (2000) and Keller (2001).

Regression analysis/ Interaction effect	Indirect value functions		Direct value functions	
	R^2	ΔR^2	R^2	ΔR^2
Purchase situation, B2B E-marketplace	.082***	.082***	.078***	.078***
Purchase situation x B2B E-marketplace	.091**	.009	.117***	.039**

*** : 1% significance level (1-sided)
** : 5% significance level (1-sided)
* : 10% significance level (1-sided)

Table 8.2 Hierarchical regression analysis concerning the interaction effect to proposition 1a and 1b

Concerning the direct value functions the interaction effect could be supported. The increase of the explained variance (R^2) is significant ($p<.05$). For the indirect values the interaction effect test shows no significant results. The increase of the explained variance (R^2) is not significant.

These results support the assumption, that the main lever of optimization due to the implementation of a B2B E-marketplace concept is the generation of direct value functions, which means cost savings. All areas of cost improvements can be covered by the appropriate B2B E-marketplace, material cost savings and process cost reductions as well as inventory reductions. For realizing the optimum direct value functions the appropriate fit between the given purchase situation and the developed B2B E-marketplace concept is key. The B2B E-marketplace concept must be adapted to the relational requirements determined by the purchase situation. Only a B2B E-marketplace, which enables the required interpersonal interaction with the supplier, can guarantee the most cost savings.

The realization potential of indirect value functions on B2B E-marketplaces is only limited. Thus the appropriate fit is not as important. The B2B E-marketplace can generate indirect values such as cycle time reduction or access to new suppliers. This assumption can be supported by the highly significant correlation coefficient between B2B E-marketplace and the indirect value functions, but the appropriate adaptation of the E-system to the purchase situation is not as important as for the direct value functions optimization. A positive tendency can be assumed by the highly significant correlation coefficient between the fit and the indirect value functions, although the interaction effect could not be supported.

For undermining the existence of the interaction effect between the appropriate fit between purchase situation and B2B E-marketplace a 2-factor variance analysis has been computed.

Since for the variance analysis the independent variables have to be nominal (Elsbach 1994, Moussa 1996, Backhaus et al. 2000, p. 80), the construct purchase situation and B2B E-marketplace have been grouped in three equal sized groups for classifying the extent of relationship support and requirement. The results are displayed in the following table.

Variance analysis	Indirect value functions	Direct value functions
	F	F
Purchase situation	0.65	3.00*
B2B E-marketplace	3.10**	3.22**
Purchase situation x B2B E-marketplace	1.91	2.40*
R²	.141	.164

The groups are built by generating groups with equal number of cases.
*** : 1% significance level (1-sided)
** : 5% significance level (1-sided)
*   : 10% significance level (1-sided)

Table 8.3   2-factor variance analysis concerning the interaction effect to proposition 1a and 1b

The results of the 2-factor variance analysis support the results of the hierarchical regression analysis. The existence of the interaction effect has been supported concerning the direct value functions, but not for the indirect value functions.

Furthermore, for testing the best fit between purchase situation and B2B E-marketplace concerning the indirect and direct value generation a mean comparison has been computed. The constructs purchase situation and B2B E-marketplace have been classified into two classes by the average plus standard deviation method, to generate one group with the above-average cases and another group with all other cases. Then, three groups have been built. Group one summarizes all cases with low extent of relationship requirement concerning the purchase situation and low extent of relationship support concerning the B2B E-marketplace. In group three all cases with high extent of relationship requirement concerning the purchase situation and high extent of relationship support concerning the B2B E-marketplace have been grouped. Group two comprises all other cases. The results of the mean comparison are displayed in the following table. The significance of the different averages has been tested by the Scheffé test[45].

---

[45] The Scheffé test enables a multiple comparison between more than two groups of different size (Bosch (1993, p. 508)).

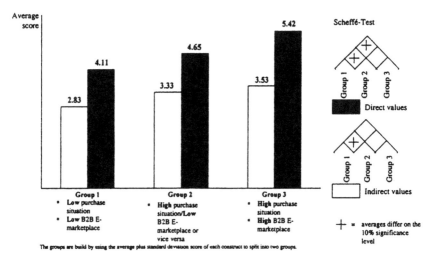

Figure 8.1 Mean comparison concerning proposition 1a and 1b

The results support the assumption that the best fit between purchase situation and B2B E-marketplace is, if the extent of relationship requirement concerning the purchase situation is high and the extent of potential relationship support of the B2B E-marketplace is also high. In this situation the cost savings generation (score 5.42) and the indirect value functions (score 3.53) have the highest scores (measured on a 7-point Likert scale) compared to the other groups. The scores for the indirect value functions are clearly below the scores of the direct value functions, which supports the weaker dependence between the appropriate fit and the indirect value functions.

For getting a more detailed understanding of which dimensions of the construct purchase situation and B2B E-marketplace concepts have the most impact on the value generation of indirect and direct functions, the mean comparison has been computed on a dimension level. The results are displayed in the following table.

Mean comparison on dimension level	Group 1 (low/low)		Group 2 (low/high, high/low)		Group 3 (high/high)	
	Indirect values	Direct values	Indirect values	Direct values	Indirect values	Direct values
Buyer business impact/ Product specifics	2.80	4.16	3.16***	4.41**	4.14***	4.69***
Supplier market competitive-ness/ Product specifics	2.85	4.15	3.03*	4.27	3.69***	4.91***
Relationship attractiveness/ Product specifics	2.85	4.21	3.23***	4.38	3.48***	5.33***
Buyer business impact/ Marketplace closeness	2.85	4.09	3.05**	4.37**	3.94***	4.89***
Supplier market competitive-ness/ Marketplace closeness	2.89	4.14	2.93	4.59***	3.54***	4.67***
Relationship attractiveness/ Marketplace closeness	2.67	4.20	2.89	4.26	3.23***	5.60***
Purchase situation/ B2B E-marketplace	2.83	4.11	3.33***	4.65***	3.53***	5.42***

*** : 1% significance level (1-sided)
** : 5% significance level (1-sided)
* : 10% significance level (1-sided)

Table 8.4   Mean comparison on a dimension level[46]

Looking at group one, where the purchase situation dimension requires low relationship support and the B2B E-marketplace dimension fosters only low relationship support, the impact on the direct and indirect values is almost equal for any combination of the dimensions. In group three, where the purchase situation dimension requires high relationship support and the B2B E-marketplace dimension enables high relationship support, optimizing the product specifics by adaptation to the buyer business impact leads to maximum indirect value generation. This means that it is key for products, which are very important to the buyer, to adapt the B2B E-marketplace concept concerning the product specifics dimension to generate the most outcome of indirect values. Customized products, which have a dominant role in the supply chain of the buyer, have a higher potential of indirect value creation. Process or product innovations can cause major improvements. For those products the supplier market is limited to only few suppliers, but the B2B E-marketplace can open new sources. On the other hand the direct values are highest, if the dimensions product specifics or/and marketplace closeness of the B2B E-marketplace are optimized according to the requirements caused by the relationship attractiveness dimension. The better the relationship

---

[46] The significance has been tested by comparing the group one with the two other group means by applying a T-test. The stars mark the level of significance. For more details of the T-test see Schnell et al. (1999, p. 415).

is supported by the B2B E-marketplace characteristics, the higher are the potential cost savings.

Overall, it can be summarized that the appropriate fit between purchase situation and B2B E-marketplace leads to optimized direct values. The impact of the right fit on the soft values or indirect values can only tendentiously be confirmed.

8.2   Hypothesis tests of model 2: Successful project organization of the B2B E-marketplace introduction project

In this chapter the hypothesis tests of all five propositions relating to the project organization are discussed.

First, the assumptions concerning the impact on the project success are detailed, which are the following three:

■ The more clearly the procurement strategy is defined, the higher is the project success (proposition 2).

■ The more competent the procurement professionals are, the higher is the project success (proposition 3).

■ The better the project is managed, the higher is the project success (proposition 6).

In the following table the results of the correlation analysis are displayed.

Correlations	Project success
Procurement strategy	.30***
Procurement competence	.31***
Project management	.45***

*** : 1% significance level (1-sided)
** : 5% significance level (1-sided)
* : 10% significance level (1-sided)

Table 8.5   Correlation analysis to proposition 2, 3 and 6[47]

All correlation coefficients are highly significant. As assumed the procurement strategy has a positive impact on the project success. A strategic focus enables a smooth project work for the

---
[47]   Results on the dimension level are displayed in the appendix B.

project team, with clear directions right from the project start. The project team does not loose any time and effort for developing various approaches. The team members are clear, what to do and which deliverables they need to show at the project end. Due to a clear purchasing and IT strategy the project team has enough arguments to convince the procurement professionals about the urgency and need to implement the B2B E-marketplace. The team members are supported by the overall strategy of the firm, which enables them to approve the advantages and optimization potential of the new procurement environment so that the acceptance and usage is guaranteed.

Looking at the procurement competence, its positive impact on the project success can be confirmed. With the appropriate purchasing competence the team is able to clearly understand the purpose of the project. The team members are highly qualified to successfully solve the given objectives. For keeping the time and budget limitations of the project especially the IT competence is advantageous, since the project team is qualified in diverse management tools for controlling the project constraints. Both the purchasing and IT competence are supportive for a smooth implementation of the new E-tools. The team has the right qualification to motivate the procurement personnel to accept the B2B E-marketplace. The team members are able to explain the new system, so that the procurement professionals have no or few resistance due to misunderstanding or any complications.

Besides the procurement strategy and the availability of the appropriate know-how the project management of the B2B E-marketplace introduction project is highly correlated with the project success. The team qualifications are key, not only technical know-how, but change management competence and project management experience are necessary for a successful project. The appropriate team competence enables a project end on time and within the budget by delivering the requested objectives. Top management support helps also to keep the project efficiency and effectiveness. Any delays can be compensated in an early stadium, so that they do not cause major conflicts. The top management support seems to be especially helpful concerning the B2B E-marketplace acceptance. The procurement professionals accept that they do not have any alternative than to adopt the new system. All project success factors are positively correlated with the project planning and steering component. A straight forward project controlling enables to anticipate any problem very early, so that real problems concerning time, cost or content can be prevented.

The strong correlations between procurement strategy, project management and the project success can also be supported by the significant results of the regression analysis. However, the regression coefficient for the procurement competence was not significant, which might suggest that the procurement competence is an operative measure, which needs to be utilized by the project team in the right way before a success occurs.

The relating regression coefficients, the significance levels (1-sided) and the explained variance are shown in the following table.

Regression analysis	Project success	
	Std Beta	Sig. level
Procurement strategy	.22	.008
Procurement competence	.10	.275
Project management	.37	.000
R^2	.262	
F	13.581	.000

Bold values are significant.

Table 8.6   Regression analysis to proposition 2, 3 and 6[48]

For further analyzing the different dependencies between procurement strategy, procurement competence, project management and the project success the impact of procurement strategy and procurement competence on project management is tested in a next step:

■ The more clearly the procurement strategy is defined, the better the project can be managed (proposition 4).

■ The higher the available procurement competence is, the better the project can be managed (proposition 5).

In table 8.7 the results of the correlation analysis between procurement strategy, procurement competence and the project management are displayed. The procurement strategy and the project management are only correlated on the 10% significance level compared to the highly significant correlation of the procurement competence and the project management.

---

[48]   Results on the dimension level are displayed in appendix B.

Correlations	Project management
Procurement strategy	.14*
Procurement competence	.43***

*** : 1% significance level (1-sided)
** : 5% significance level (1-sided)
* : 10% significance level (1-sided)

Table 8.7   Correlation analysis to proposition 4 and 5[49]

The main driver for a successful project management seems to be the appropriate procurement competence. The highly significant correlation coefficient between procurement competence and project management seems to support the above assumption, that the procurement competence has to be utilized by the project management before any success can be measured. Competence is necessary in all project aspects and on all levels including the project leader, the team members and the top management. For the project team especially the purchasing knowledge is helpful. The team members have to decide, which products to select as pilots, which concept to choose and how to redesign the new processes. Threats and potential risks have to be identified beforehand. Action plans to compensate and reduce these dangers have to be developed. Therefore, broad purchasing know-how is necessary. The project team needs to be appropriately qualified to understand the situation in the supplier market, in the competitive environment but also within the own organization. For being able to use project management tools to apply a transparent project controlling the appropriate knowledge is mandatory. On the one hand technical qualifications in purchasing and IT are needed, on the other hand project experience is also necessary. The project planning and steering process needs to be consequently adapted to the given circumstances.

The dominant impact of the procurement competence on project management compared to the strategy is also supported by the results of the regression analysis, which are shown in the following table. However, the regression coefficient of the procurement strategy is not significant. The procurement strategy influences the underlying message and direction of the project, but not really the active process of executing the project.

---

[49]   Results on the dimension level are displayed in appendix B.

Regression analysis	Project management	
	Std Beta	Sig. level
Procurement strategy	.04	.638
Procurement competence	.42	.000
R²	.187	
F	13.353	.000

Bold values are significant.

Table 8.8   Regression analysis to proposition 4 and 5[50]

Summarizing the above results proposition 5 was supported by the correlation and regression analyses, whereas proposition 4 could only be supported to some extent by the correlation analysis. It seems, that the procurement competence has a strong impact on the project management, whereas the project management supports the project success. But the direct impact of procurement competence on the project success is not significant in the regression analysis. Competence is fine, but it needs to be utilized. Only if the project team is able to apply the available know-how and experience, project success can be guaranteed.

Controversial to the procurement competence, the strategy has only a slight impact on the project execution or management, but strong impact on the project success. Reasoning behind this can be that in this study procurement strategy is limited to the procurement approach with special focus on supplier relationship development. The project management does not explicitly refer to aspects related to supplier relationship development; project management summarizes the quality of the project execution.

8.3   Hypothesis tests of model 3: Impact of a successful project organization on the fit between purchase situation and B2B E-marketplace

In model 3 the interactions between the project organization and the fit between purchase situation and B2B E-marketplace have been tested.

First, the results of the analyses concerning the impact of the project success on the relationship success are discussed. To assess this link the following two propositions have been formulated:

---

[50]   Results on the dimension level are displayed in appendix B.

- The higher the project success is, the higher is the generation of indirect value functions (proposition 7a).
- The higher the project success is, the higher is the generation of direct value functions (proposition 7b).

The following highly significant correlation coefficients support the strong influence of project success on the long-term value generation even after the project end. Concerning this correlation analysis it has to be underlined, that the project success has been evaluated by the project leaders, whereas the long-term success concerning the indirect and direct value functions has been analyzed by the procurement professionals, therefore, a common source bias can be excluded.[51]

Correlations	Indirect value functions	Direct value functions
Project success	.38***	.32***

*** : 1% significance level (1-sided)
** : 5% significance level (1-sided)
* : 10% significance level (1-sided)

Table 8.9 Correlation analysis to proposition 7a and 7b

For a more detailed understanding of the different areas of impact within the project success the following table with the results of the regression analysis provides insight.

Regression analysis	Indirect value functions		Direct value functions	
	Std Beta	Sig. level	Std Beta	Sig. level
Project efficiency	- .05	.610	- .12	.693
Project effectiveness	.41	.001	.23	.008
B2B E-marketplace acceptance	.09	.386	.32	.000
R²	.205		.225	
F	9.891	.000	11.154	.000

Bold values are significant.

Table 8.10 Regression analysis to proposition 7a and 7b

---

[51] The common source bias refers to situations, where the same respondents have to evaluate different variables for testing causal relations. Then it can happen, that the respondents try to answer in a consistent manner, which leads to a confirmation of the causal relation although it does not exist (see Campion et al. (1993, p. 836)).

One very interesting outcome is, that the project efficiency does not seem to be important for a long-term value generation. Keeping time and cost constraints does not support any value generation, neither soft values as innovation functions or access and market functions nor hard values as cost savings.

Project effectiveness seems to be the main value driver. The results suggest, that the project team should focus on quality. Team members should take their time to develop and implement perfect quality work, even if it takes more time and is more cost intense. Delivering the expected results can compensate for delays or additional costs. The project effectiveness is highly significantly correlated with both facets of the value generation, with the soft and with the hard facts. Most E-procurement projects have the realization of cost savings in focus. If the project is effectively managed, the project team is able to realize these expected cost savings. On the other hand an effective project team has the ability to build the right basis for the generation of indirect values. The team can define the new concept with respect to potential improvements concerning the quality or the processes. The cycle time from product request until delivery to production can be minimized. New market segments can be penetrated. An effective project execution has the potential to optimize all aspects of long-term relationship success.

The highly significant regression coefficient concerning the B2B E-marketplace acceptance and the direct value functions supports the assumption that the new E-tools focus on cost savings. If appropriately implemented firms can realize real cost reductions in various areas. On the one hand the purchase prices can be reduced, but on the other hand and even more important is the process cost reduction. Redundant work can be eliminated. Although idle time for quality checks becomes obsolete, the work quality increases, since the orders are automatically processed in the ERP systems. Paper work with the risk of mistakes gets replaced by automatic order confirmation. Due to the higher level of automation an inventory reduction can be the result of a proper implementation of a B2B E-marketplace concept. Safety stocks can be reduced due to a lower risk of delays in product replenishment. Order lot sizes can be reduced due to a new reliable supply source. The not significant regression coefficient concerning the indirect value functions undermines the proposition, that personal interaction, contacts, existing relationships or small-talk are more important for generating indirect values. The B2B E-marketplace is not able to replace the personal interaction between the procurement organization and the supplier.

Overall proposition 7a and 7b are supported by the results of the correlation and regression analyses.

Another area of interference between model 1 and 2 is the impact of the project organization on the fit between purchase situation and B2B E-marketplace. Therefore the following hypotheses have been tested:

■ The higher the project success is, the better is the fit between purchase situation and B2B E-marketplace (proposition 8).

■ The better the quality of the project management is, the better is the fit between purchase situation and B2B E-marketplace (proposition 9).

■ The clearer the procurement strategy is understood, the better is the fit between purchase situation and B2B E-marketplace (proposition 10).

■ The higher the competence in the procurement organization is, the better is the fit between purchase situation and B2B E-marketplace (proposition 11).

First, the results of the correlation analysis between procurement strategy, procurement competence, project management, project success and the fit construct are displayed.

Correlations	Fit (Purchase situation x B2B E-marketplace
Procurement strategy	.38***
Procurement competence	- .07
Project management	.18**
Project success	.45***

*** : 1% significance level (1-sided)
** : 5% significance level (1-sided)
* : 10% significance level (1-sided)

Table 8.11 Correlation analysis to proposition 8, 9, 10 and 11

The assumption concerning the impact of the procurement strategy on the appropriate fit has been supported by the highly significant correlation coefficient. A clear procurement strategy, with its two components purchasing and IT, predefines the requirements, which the new procurement environment needs to fulfill. Especially in the sense, how purchasing strategy is understood in this work, i.e. focusing on supplier relationship development, the purchasing strategy determines the needed relationship support, which the B2B E-marketplace should be able to provide. Besides the purchasing strategy also the IT strategy has a major impact on the appropriate fit. The IT strategy determines the objectives of the new E-system. Depending on the individual emphasis the E-system needs to deliver process transparency, high degree of automation or reduction of redundant work. For the appropriate fit the B2B E-marketplace concept needs to be aligned with the purchasing and IT strategy.

The procurement competence has no significant correlation to the fit. As tested in proposition 3 and 5 the procurement competence seems to have only direct impact on the project management. It seems, that the procurement competence has also no direct impact on the fit. Concerning the right fit, the benefit of the appropriate know-how seems to exist via the project management, which is significantly correlated with the fit. Backed by the top management the project team can systematically develop the appropriate concept adapted to the given circumstances. In case of trouble or resistance the top management support enables the project team to implement the right concept although the resistance may attract the team to implement only a compromise solution, which could be easier implemented.

Another lever for the right fit between purchase situation and B2B E-marketplace is a well-planned project. A detailed project plan, continuously controlling the project steps and the punctuality of the achievement of the defined milestones enables an early recognition of any delays or problems. In an early stadium, the project team, backed by the top management is able to close any gap or delay. Additional resources can be added to the team or the objectives can be adapted to the new circumstances. If any weaknesses of the planned concepts can be identified in an early stadium the project team can proof the concept and eventually change the plan. With a detailed project planning the project can be smoothly managed. Only a limited number of surprises or unexpected problems should occur.

The highly significant correlation coefficient between project success and the fit supported the assumption, that the project success plays a major role. As a first step to the new procurement environment the project success gives evidence of positive effects and results of the new E-tools. How can the project be successful, if the concept of the B2B E-marketplace would not fit to the given purchase situation? The project success confirms the right fit and motivates the procurement professionals to deliver even more savings and to realize even more optimization potential. The on-time project execution within the given budget was only possible, since the project objectives have been realistic. But the objectives have not only been realistic, they defined the appropriate fit. Last but not least the B2B E-marketplace acceptance plays a major role for the appropriate fit. The procurement professionals would not accept a new environment, which is much more complicated and uncomfortable. They can only be convinced to use the new system, if it is a real improvement of their work environment.

For further supporting the highly significant results of the correlation analysis concerning the impact of procurement strategy and project success on the fit between purchase situation and B2B E-marketplace a regression analysis has been computed.

Regression analysis	Fit (Purchase situation x B2B E-marketplace)	
	Std Beta	Sig. level
Procurement strategy	.27	.001
Project success	.37	.000
R^2	.274	
F	21.840	.000

Bold values are significant.

Table 8.12 Regression analysis to proposition 8 and 10

The positive impact of the procurement strategy on the appropriate fit between the purchase situation and the B2B E-marketplace can be supported. The same situation is represented for the project success with a highly significant regression coefficient.

Overall the propositions 8 and 10 have been supported by the correlation and regression analyses. Proposition 9 has been supported by the correlation analysis, whereas the procurement competence seems to have no significant direct impact on the fit between purchase situation and B2B E-marketplace (proposition 11).

8.4   Summary

Overall the results of the hypotheses tests are very satisfying. The main assumptions behind the three different theoretical models could be supported. Also the proposition concerning the needed fit between purchase situation and B2B E-marketplace could be supported. The hypotheses concerning the impact of the project organization on the project success have been tested with positive results. Finally, the link between the two models, meaning the impact of the project organization on the appropriate fit between purchase situation and B2B E-marketplace and the relationship success could also be supported. The following table gives a more detailed overview on a single hypothesis level. The most hypotheses have been positively tested and could be supported based on significant test results. Those hypotheses are marked with bold crosses in the following overview table. For some hypotheses the test results tendentiously supported the derived assumption, although the test results have only been partially significant. These hypotheses are market with light crosses. Only for two hypotheses the test results did not deliver positive results (cross in parentheses).

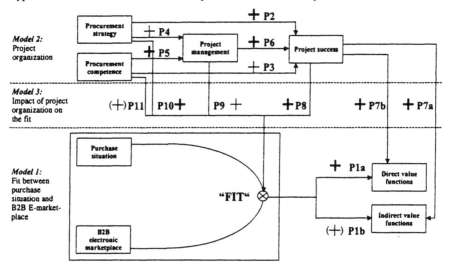

Table 8.13 Overview of the test results of the hypotheses

9   Summary and outlook

In this chapter the theoretical framework and the empirical results are summarized (chapter 9.1). Based on the results managerial implications are derived in chapter 9.2. Finally, future research areas are identified (chapter 9.3).

9.1   Summary of the study

"The revolution yet to happen" as Bell and Gray predicted in 1998. Various forecasts predicted tremendous growth rates for business-to-business E-commerce (Vijayan 2000, p. 81). "If companies don't act, somebody will step between you and your customer and turn you into a commodity-based supplier ", said McCutchean, director of E-business technology of DuPont (2000) about the supplier perspective.

But the key question is how to act. Therefore this study analyzes the levers for a successful introduction of a B2B E-marketplace. After developing a classification model of the purchase situation, the author has clustered the different B2B E-marketplace concepts from a relationship perspective. Based on this theoretical background the need of the appropriate fit between the purchase situation and B2B E-marketplace has been derived in order to optimize the supplier relationship success. The theoretical framework has been empirically validated by a study in the chemical industry in Germany.

The predicted E-hype cannot truly be confirmed by the results of this study. The vast majority of the chemical companies in Germany have been contacted. But only about half of all contacted parties could be identified as potential participants, since the others have neither implemented nor started to implement any E-procurement solution. The predicted optimization potential, which could be realized by implementing E-procurement tools, is still largely untapped. The questionable pressure of the E-hype has been highly overestimated, at least in the majority of the chemical industry in Germany it is not recognized as such.

Regarding the companies engaging in E-procurement activities and having participated in this study, nearly one fifth of all product categories are processed via B2B E-marketplaces. The firms, which have activities in the new procurement environment, have recognized the pressure of losing optimization potentials by being late adopters. All respondents are buying highly standardized products, 60% buy raw materials the others buy indirect materials. Estimates on savings of material costs vary between 2 and 4%.[52]

The theoretical framework of this study can be divided into three models: The first model covers the main assumption of this study: In order to realize the best relationship success, an appropriate fit between purchase situation and B2B E-marketplace concept needs to be generated. The purchase situation summarizes the circumstances in the procurement environment, which are characterized by several aspects: First, the buyer business impact is important. Depending on the product the lever for the buyer is different. Second, the supplier market competitiveness has a major influence on the purchase situation. In a highly competitive market with dominant buying power, for example, the buyer has to manage procurement activities in a different way than in a supplier market with one single supplier. The third component of interest concerning the purchase situation is the relationship attractiveness. Supplier relationships to highly reliable suppliers should be treated differently than those to suppliers, who are easily replaceable without any loss. It is key to the buyer to recognize and understand his purchase situation.

As stated above, the B2B E-marketplace concept needs to be adapted to the respective purchase situation. In situations with one single supplier for a highly customized product, the B2B E-marketplace concept is not the right solution, whereas commodities are suitable products to be traded on B2B E-marketplaces. Yet, the B2B E-marketplace concept must be adapted to the buyer business impact and the relationship attractiveness of the given purchase situation. In a purchase situation with the need of intense relationship support, the B2B E-marketplace concept must enable this support. Based on the appropriate fit between purchase situation and B2B E-marketplace especially the cost savings can be optimized. The potential of indirect value generation due to the introduction of a B2B E-marketplace is only limited.

The second model analyzes the project management of such a B2B E-marketplace introduction project. Based on the given business environment (i.e. procurement strategy and procurement competence), a balanced and well-structured project management enhances the project success. Backed by the top management the team needs to provide cross-functional competences to be able to cope with all relevant threats and issues.

---

[52] Most respondents rejected to complete corresponding questions.

The third model deals with the links between the project organization and the fit model. The empirical results revealed that a successful project execution has a positive impact on the appropriate fit between purchase situation and B2B E-marketplace concept.

With these three models key success factors for an efficient and effective introduction of a B2B E-marketplace have been derived.

9.2   Managerial implications

The majority of companies underestimate the strategic value of evaluating the fit between purchase situation and B2B E-marketplace. In recent years electronic marketplaces have been introduced – and many of them disappeared fairly soon due to a lack of functionality and reliability. As supported by the empirical results one key element has been neglected. It is important, that the E-marketplace supports a given purchase situation. This has implications for both, marketers and buyers. Marketers are urged to understand what situation the buyer is in before implementing a B2B E-marketplace. Additionally, marketers have to think about the value, they create for their customers and how this can be exchanged. If this value is mainly direct, i.e. cost savings, then an appropriate platform should be developed. The central message is that "one size fits all" is not the way forward.

This study has examined the impact of the implementation of E-procurement tools on value creation. Specifically the direct values (i.e. cost savings) can be optimized, but the realization of these benefits is highly difficult. Only if the appropriate fit between purchase situation and B2B E-marketplace concept is identified, optimum cost savings can be realized. Companies have to recognize the high importance of a detailed analysis of the purchase situation. A clear understanding about the given circumstances in the purchasing environment is necessary for both, buyers and sellers, to be able to identify the appropriate E-procurement concept for optimizing the direct value functions. Based on the purchase situation firms have to select and adapt the suitable B2B E-marketplace concept for optimizing their market position.

E-procurement starts with people possessing the right profiles. Commercial skills and bargaining strengths are requested, as well as knowledge about the various E-tools in procurement. Continuous training on the job and about the new conceptual trends is necessary, since the potential access to the state-of-the-art knowledge has to be guaranteed. In addition to qualified personnel the selection and introduction of appropriate computer systems and application software are important management decisions to prepare the environment for successful E-procurement concepts.

The project management is key. Savings can be realized, but only with a successful introduction project of the new E-procurement environment. Top management support is necessary. The executive management gives the primary directions and is able to take the appropriate decision in case of an emergency. The team qualification must cover all new disciplines. The team members need to have project management experience and be able to cope with aspects of change management. From technical perspective know-how about the organization, the procurement procedures and the different opportunities with the new E-tools is necessary. Also know-how about the suppliers and about the interfaces with production should not be forgotten.

The application of E-tools is especially concentrated on commodity products. The purchase of specialties and more customized products via E-systems lacks behind the commodities. Only the big players of the industry have the critical mass to invest and to loose in the beginning until severe start-up problems are solved. They are able to invest in the development of adapted B2B E-marketplace models with different objectives than for the trading process of commodities.

E-procurement solutions create new opportunities for business benefits. New interconnections along the value chain can be defined and important new suppliers can be integrated into the company's value chain. The online exchange of planning information can be used to transfer the responsibility for materials scheduling and inventories management to the suppliers. There is a significant opportunity of generating value by reducing the working capital employed.

Within multi-sites or multi-subsidiaries companies the setup of E-procurement platforms with corresponding data and organizational networks between different sites or subsidiaries opens an easy online access to all required results of the E-procurement activities, like supply schedules, best price structures, inventories or supplier audit profiles.

E-procurement projects offer opportunities of strategic alliances within the globalized business world. Strategic alliances between independent companies in the field of E-procurement provide benefits of local regional advantages in contractually defined areas of B2B E-marketplaces. The partners have benefits as gaining purchasing power, economies of scale and minimizing inventory cost or transportation costs, generally speaking logistics costs.

For a successful introduction of a B2B E-marketplace concept the following seven-step approach is recommended:

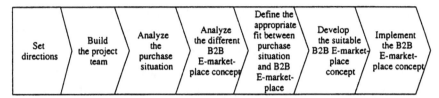

Figure 9.1 Guidelines for a successful implementation of the appropriate B2B E-marketplace concept

In the beginning the overall directions and objectives need to be defined by the top management. These directions should be aligned with the procurement strategy and the strategy of the company. Then the project team members can be identified. They should provide the appropriate profile concerning project experience, purchasing and IT know-how. Additionally they need to be excellent communicators. For a smooth and effective project execution the full backing of the top management is required. A sufficient project planning and steering tool assures an efficient project execution. Then the project team has to analyze the purchase situation with all its facets as buyer business impact, supplier market and the supplier relationship. Based on a broad market research they have to identify the potential supplier with whom they want to start the B2B E-marketplace. In a next step the various B2B E-marketplace concepts have to be analyzed. Based on this knowledge the appropriate fit between the given purchase situation and the B2B E-marketplace can be defined. Then the appropriate concept can be developed and finally be implemented. This approach gives guidance for a successful introduction of a B2B E-marketplace.

9.3   Future research areas

Even though the study has contributed to a more successful implementation of B2B E-marketplaces, there are some limitations to the study, which at the same time open the need of further research.

The study has been executed with focus on Germany. All chemical companies listed as VCI members have been contacted. However, in order to validate the results on a broader basis, this research should be rolled-out to other European countries. By doing so, the status of the usage of E-procurement tools could be compared between the different countries. In a next step the chemical market in U.S. could be included in the study. This research would enable the validation of the assumption that Europe lacks behind the U.S concerning the internet age. The finding, that only half of the contacted firms have implemented or started implementing any E-procurement tools, highlights the need to repeat this study in one or two years. Thus, the forecasts of future transformation of further product categories can be tested and savings potentials can be better validated. By then the companies would have enough time to realize savings. They would also have more experience and know-how and not be struggling with implementation problems of a completely new system.

This study has focused on the process industry with special emphasis on the chemical industry. In the chemical industry many companies have already had EDI interfaces with their suppliers. Therefore, data transfer between the business partners was business as usual. This progressive industry standard leads to the assumption, that the chemical industry will become a fast mover concerning the new E-procurement tools. Based on these arguments the chemical industry has been selected. However, interesting research areas would also be other industries outside the process industry, such as the automotive industry. This would allow for comparisons and help to find out, if the E-procurement activities in the automotive industry are further progressed than in the process industry or if the product categories purchased via B2B E-marketplaces are also limited to commodities.

In addition to the conceptual extensions some extensions to the model are suggested:

In this study the project management and the procurement environment have been found to be levers of impact on the fit between purchase situation and B2B E-marketplace concept. This also raises the question, if there are other levers impacting this fit, which have not been considered in this research. Maybe more industry driven aspects have an impact on the fit, e.g the degree of technology or the age of the industry (e.g. biochemicals, mobile commerce).

Another area of interest requiring further research is the organizational setup of the procurement organization. The appropriate organizational structure of purchasing is a key preposition for a successful implementation of the new E-procurement concepts. Job descriptions and definitions of responsibilities should consider the potential adding value to be contributed by procurement. Procurement management should be seen as value driver and therefore be positioned on the right leadership and managerial level.

To get a complete picture and a broad understanding on the benefits and advantages of the new E-procurement tools, it is not enough to analyze just the perspective of the buyer. The supplier perspective also needs to be analyzed in detail to be able to fully understand the potential of B2B E-marketplaces. The levers, organizational background and the objectives of suppliers implementing the new E-tools might be quite different from the results of this study. Further research should be investigated in an extended supplier relationship. Not only the transaction process between buyer and supplier can be redesigned due to the new E-tools, the whole supply chain of the buyer and supplier could be connected. In this context further network partners such as logistic partners or research organizations could participate on the enlarged B2B E-marketplace. Further effort should be spent to understand wider network effects. Which interdependences do exist between the different partners and which impact do they have?

The E-procurement tools open new opportunities. Further research could focus on possibilities of combined usage of conservative procurement tools and new E-tools. The question needs to be answered, which new approaches of interaction with the supplier would enable further values. Which multi-channel strategy would be the best in a given purchase situation?

Although this study has covered a broad research area concerning B2B E-marketplaces in procurement there is still need for further research to examine these new concepts entirely. B2B E-marketplaces are still in their early days and an anticipated rapid future development should offer various cornerstones for further research areas.

10   References

Abmeier, H.-L., Herold, L. (1998): Die Rolle von Beschaffung und Logistik im Wettbewerb um die Zeit, in: Koppelmann, U.: Time to market: mögliche Beiträge von Einkauf und Logistik, Schäffer Poeschel, Stuttgart, 85-110

Alaniz, S., Roberts, R. (1999): E-procurement-A Guide to Buy-Side Applications, Stephens Research, Arkansas

Al-Tabtabai, H., Alex, A. P., Abou-Alfotouh, A. (2001): Conflict resolution using cognitive analysis approach, in: Project Management Journal, 32(2), 4-16

Anderson, E., Chu, W., Weitz, B. (1987): Industrial Purchasing: An Empirical Exploration of the Buyclass Framework, in: Journal of Marketing, 51(7), 71-88

Anderson, J. C., Hakansson, H., Johanson, J. (1994): Dyadic Business Relationships Within a Business Network Context, in: Journal of Marketing, 58(10), 1-15

Anderson, J. C., Jain, D. C., Chintagunta, P. K. (1993): Customer value assessment in business markets: A state-of-practice study, in: Journal of Business-to-Business Marketing, 1(1), 3-29

Anklesaria, J., Burt, D. N. (1988): Personal Factors In The Purchasing/Engineering Interface, in: Journal of Purchasing and Materials Management, Winter, 9-18

Ansoff, H. I., Leontiades, J. (1976): Strategic Portfolio Management, in: Journal of Management, 4

Araujo, L., Dubois, A., Gadde, L.-E. (1999): Managing Interfaces with Suppliers, in: Industrial Marketing Management, 28 (5), 497-506

Arnold, U. (1998): Erfolg durch Einkaufskooperationen, Gabler, Wiesbaden

Atteslander, P. (1995): Methoden der empirischen Sozialforschung, de Gruyter Verlag, Berlin

Avery, S. (2000): E-procurement: A wealth of information for buyers, in: Purchasing, September 21, 111

Baccarini, D. (1999): The logical framework method for defining project success, in: Project Management Journal, 30(4), 25-32

Bacheldor, B. (2000): Bills For The 21st Century, in: Informationweek, (01/05), 22-24

Backhaus, K. (1999): Industriegütermarketing, Vahlen, München

Backhaus, K., Aufderheide, D., Späth, G.-M. (1994): Marketing für System-Technologien, Schäffer Poeschel, Stuttgart

Backhaus, K., Erichson, B., Plinke, W., Weiber, R. (2000): Multivariate Analysemethoden, Springer, Berlin

Bagozzi, R. P., Fornell, C. (1982): Theoretical Concepts, Measurement and Meanings, in: Fornell, C.: A Second Generation of Multivariate Analysis, Praeger, New York, 24-38

Baguley, P. (1999): Optimales Projektmanagement, Falken Verlag, Niedernhausen

Baker, H. (2000): E-Sourcing: 21st Century Purchasing, in: Scheer, A.-W.: E-Business. Wer geht? Wer bleibt? Wer kommt?, Physica-Verlag, Heidelberg, 101-114

Bakos, J. Y. (1991a): A Strategic Analysis of Electronic Marketplaces, in: MIS Quarterly, 9, 295-310

Bakos, J. Y. (1991b): Information Links and Electronic Marketplaces: The Role of Interorganizational Information Systems in Vertical Markets, in: Journal of Management Information Systems, 8 (2), 31-52

Bakos, Y. (1998): The Emerging Role of Electronic Marketplaces on the Internet, in: Communications of the ACM, 41(8), 35-42

Balderjahn, I. (1988): Die Kreuzvalidierung von Kausalmodellen, in: Marketing – Zeitschrift für Forschung und Praxis, 1, 61-73

Baron, J. P. Shaw, M. J., Bailey, A. D. Jr. (2000): Electronic Catalogs in the Web-Based Business-to-Business Procurement Process, in: Shaw, M., Blanning, R., Strader, T., Whinston, A.: Handbook on Electronic Commerce, Springer, Berlin, 385-410

Baumgarten, H., von Bodelschwingh, K. (1996): Kostenreduzierung durch gestraffte Abläufe, in: Beschaffung aktuell, 2, 35-38

Baumgarten, H., Wolff, S. (1999): Versorgungsmanagement – Erfolge durch Integration von Beschaffung und Logistik, in: Hahn, D., Kaufmann, L.: Handbuch Industrielles Beschaffungsmanagement, Gabler, Wiesbaden, 321-342

Beckmann, M., Kräkel, M., Schauenberg, B. (1997): Der deutsche Auktionsmarkt: Ergebnisse einer empirischen Studie, in: Zeitschrift für Betriebswirtschaft, 67 (1), 41-65

Bell, G., Gray, J. N. (1998): The Revolution Yet to Happen, in: Denning, P. J., Metcalfe, R. M.: Beyond Calculation – The Next Fifty Years of Computing, New York, 5-32

Bellmann, K. (1999): Produktion und Beschaffung – Management einer innerbetrieblichen Schnittstelle, in: Hahn, D., Kaufmann, L.: Handbuch Industrielles Beschaffungsmanagement, Gabler, Wiesbaden, 277-294

Benjamin, R., Wigand, R. (1995): Electronic Markets and Virtual Value Chains on the Information Superhighway, in: Sloan Management Review, (Winter), 62-72

Bensaou, M. (1999): Portfolios of Buyer-Supplier Relationships, in: Sloan Management Review, Summer, 35-44

Bensaou, M., Venkatraman, N. (1995): Configurations of Interorganizational Relationships: A Comparison Between U.S. and Japanese Automakers, in: Management Science, 41(9), 1471-1492

Berryman, K., Harrington, L. F., Layton-Rodin, D., Rerolle, V. (1998): Electronic commerce: Three emerging strategies, in: McKinsey Quarterly, 1, 129-136

Beßlich, J., Lumbe, H. J. (1994a): Der Success-Lieferantentag, in: Beschaffung aktuell, (12), 14-18

Beßlich, J., Lumbe, H. J. (1994b): Erster Schritt: Bestandsaufnahme der Material- und Lieferantenstruktur, in: Beschaffung aktuell, (10), 22-25

Beßlich, J., Lumbe, H. J. (1994c): Workshop gegen innerbetriebliche Barrieren, in: Beschaffung aktuell, (11), 14-18

Beßlich, J., Lumbe, H. J. (1995): Eine Gemeinschaft für mehr Wettbewerbsfähigkeit, in: Beschaffung aktuell, (1), 44-47

Bichler, M., Beam, C., Segev, A. (1998): Services of a Broker in Electronic Commerce Transactions, in: EM, 8 (1), 27-31

Bieberbach, F., Hermann, M, (1999): Die Substitution von Dienstleistungen durch Informationsprodukte auf elektronischen Märkten, Electronic Business Engineering, 4th Internationale Tagung Wirtschaftsinformatik, 67-82

Birnbaum, M. H. (1973): The Devil rides Again: Correlation as an Index of Fit, in: Psychological Bulletin, 79(4), 239-242

Bloch, P. H., Richins, M. L. (1983): A Theoretical Model for the Study of Product Importance Perceptions, in: Journal of Marketing, 47, 69-81

Blömer, F., Günther, H.-O., Kaminiarz, B. (2000): Simulation-aided material flow control and strategic cost analysis of a processing plant, in: Chemical Engineering and Technology, 23, 401- 405

Bogaschewsky, R. (1999a): Electronic Procurement – Neue Wege der Beschaffung, in: Bogaschewsky, R.: Elektronischer Einkauf. Erfolgspotentiale, Praxisanwendungen, Sicherheits- und Rechtsfragen, Deutscher Betriebswirte-Verlag, Gernsbach, 13-40

Bogaschewsky, R. (1999b): Elektronischer Einkauf. Erfoglspotentiale, Praxisanwendungen, Sicherheits- und Rechtsfragen, Deutscher Betriebswirte-Verlag, Gernsbach

Bogaschewsky, R., Rollberg, R. (1999): Produktionssynchrone Zulieferungskonzepte, in: Hahn, D., Kaufmann, L.: Handbuch Industrielles Beschaffungsmanagement, Gabler, Wiesbaden, 231-250

Booker, E. (2000): On the Internet, marketing matters more than ever, in: B to B, 85(4), 10-11

Bosch, K. (1993): Statistik-Taschenbuch, Oldenbourg Verlag, München

Bouchard, V. (1998): The Supplier Selection Process: Theory versus Practice, 14th IMP Conference, Turku

Bourantas, D. (1989): Avoiding Dependence on Suppliers and Distributors, in: Long Range Planning, 22(3), 140-149

Bozdogan, K., Deyst, J., Hoult, D., Lucas, M. (1998): Architectural innovation in product development through early supplier integration, in: R&D Management, 28 (3), 163-173

Brandes, H. (1994): Strategic changes in purchasing, in: European Journal of Purchasing and Supply Management, 1(2), 77-87

Brannick, M. T., Prince, A., Prince, C., Salas, E. (1995): The measurement of team process, in: Human Factors 37(3), 641-651

Brege, E.-M. (1998): Meeting Purchasing Strategies in the Corrugated Board Industry, 14th IMP Conference, Turku

Brennan, R., Turnbull, P. W. (1995): Adaptations in Buyer-Supplier Relationships, in: Nauru, P. , Turnbull, P. W. (1998): International Marketing, Pergamon, 26-41

Brennan, R., Turnbull, P. W. (1999): Adaptive Behavior in Buyer-Supplier Relationships, in: Industrial Marketing Management, 28 (5), 481-495

Brooks, F. P. (1975): The Mythical Man – Month, Essays on Software Engineering, Addison-Wesley Publishing Company, London

Brown, S. L., Eisenhardt, K. M. (1995): Product Development: Past Research, Present Findings, and Future Directions, in: Academy of Management Review, 20(2), 343-378

Buchholz, W., Bach, N. (2001): The Evolution of Netsourcing Business Models. Learning from the Past and Exploiting Future Opportunities,Working Paper, Justus-Liebig-Universität Giessen, Fachbereich Wirtschaftswissenschaften

Bullinger, H.-J., Wasserloos, G. (1990): Reduzierung der Produktentwicklungszeiten durch Simultaneous Engineering, in: CIM, 6(6), 4-30

Burt, D. N. (1989a): Managing Product Quality through Strategic Purchasing, in: Sloan Management Review, Spring, 39-48

Burt, D. N. (1989b): Managing Suppliers Up to Speed, in: Harvard Business Review, July-August, 127-135

Burt, D. N., Pinkerton, R. L. (1996): A Purchasing Manager's Guide to Strategic Proactive Procurement, Amacom, New York

Butler, J. K. Jr. (1991): Toward Understanding and Measuring Conditions of Trust: Evolution of a Conditions of Trust Inventory, in: Journal of Marketing, 17 (3), 643-663

Butscher, S. A., Krohn, F. (2001): Auf das richtige Pferd setzen. Eine Systematik zur Bewertung von Internet-Marktplätzen, in: FAZ, 6, 25

Cammish, R., Keough, M. (1991): A Strategic Role for Purchasing, in: The McKinsey Quarterly, 3, 22-39

Campbell, N. C. G. (2000): An Interaction Approach to Organizational Buying Behavior, in: Ford, D.: Understanding Business Markets, Thomson Learning, London, 385-399

Campbell, N. C. G., Cunningham, M. T. (1982): Customer Analysis for Strategy Development in Industrial Markets, in: Strategic Management Journal, 4, 369-380

Campion, M. A., Medsker, G. J., Higgs, A. C. (1993): Relations between work group characteristics and effectiveness: Implications for designing effective work groups, in: Personnel Psychology, 46(4), 823-850

Cannon, J. P., Homburg, C., Willauer, B. (1998): International Supplier Relationships and Organizational Learning, 14th IMP Conference, Turku

Cannon, J. P., Narayandas, N. (2000): Relationship Marketing and Key Account Management, in: Sheth, J. N., Parvatiyar, A. (2000): Handbook of Relationship Marketing, Sage Publications, Thousand Oaks, 407-429

Cannon, J. P. , Perreault, W. D. Jr. (1999): Buyer-Seller Relationships in Business Markets, in: Journal of Marketing Research, Vol. 36 (11), 439-460

Carter, J. R., Narasimhan, R. (1990): Purchasing in the International Marketplace: Implications for Operations, in: Journal of Purchasing and Materials Management, Summer, 2-11

Carter, J. R., Narasimhan, R. (1994): The Role of Purchasing and Materials Management in Total Quality Management and Customer Satisfaction, in: International Journal of Purchasing and Materials Management, Summer, 3-13

Carter, J. R., Narasimhan, R. (1996a): A Comparison of North American and European Future purchasing Trends, in: International Journal of Purchasing and Materials Management, Spring, 12-22

Carter, J. R., Narasimhan, R. (1996b): Is Purchasing Really Strategic?, in: International Journal of Purchasing and Materials Management, Winter, 20-28

Chang, J. (2000): Chemical Makers Plan Internet Service, in: Chemical Market Reporter, March 27, 5

Chemical Market Reporter (2001): E-Business in Chemicals, 26/03/01, 1-3

Chen, H.-Y., Wilson, D. T. (2000): Online Auctions: Are Relationships Doomed?, 16th IMP conference, Bath

Choudhury, V., Hartzel, K. S., Konsynski, B. R. (1998): Uses and Consequences of Electronic Markets: An Empirical Investigation in the Aircraft Parts Industry, in: MIS Quarterly, 12, 471-507

Christopher, M. (1998): Logistics and Supply Chain Management, Financial Times Prentice Hall, Essex

Clark, K. B. (1989): Project Scope and Project Performance: The Effect of Parts Strategy and Supplier Involvement on Product Development, in: Management Science, 35 (10), 1247-1263

Cooper, M. C., Ellram, L. M., Gardner, J. T., Hanks, A. M. (1997): Meshing Multiple Alliances, in: Journal of Business Logistics, 18(1), 67-89

Copeland, M. T. (1924): Principles of Merchandising, Chicago

Corsten, H. (1996): Beschaffung, p. 682, in: Corsten, H., Reiß, M.: Betriebswirtschaftslehre, München, 609-736

Corsten, H. (2000): Projektmanagement, Oldenbourg Verlag, München

Cortina, J. M. (1993): Interaction, Nonlinearity, and Multicollinearity: Implications for Multiple Regression, in: Journal of Management, 19(4), 915-922

Cousins, P. (1992): Choosing the Right Partner, in: Purchasing and Supply Management Journal, March, Institute of Purchasing and Supply, Stamford

Cousins, P. D., Spekman, R. (2000): Strategic Supply and the Management of Inter and Intra Organizational Relationships, 16th IMP Conference, Bath

Cox, A. (1997): On power, appropriateness and procurement competence, in: SupplyManagement, 10/02, 24-27

Cox, A., Harris, L. (1997): Strength in numbers, in: Supply Management, (16/01/1997), 33-52

Cunningham, M. H., Varadarajan, P .R. (1995): Strategic Alliances: A Synthesis of Conceptual Foundations, in: Journal of the Academy of Marketing Science, 23 (4), 282-296

Cunningham, M. J. (2001): B2B. How to Build a Profitable E-commerce Strategy, Perseus Publishing, Cambridge

Cusumano, M. A., Takeishi, A. (1991): Supplier Relations and Management: A Survey of Japanese, Japanese-Transplant, and U.S. Auto Plants, in: Strategic Management Journal, 12, 563-588

Daniel, E., Klimis, G. M. (1999): The Impact of Electronic Commerce on Market Structure: An Evaluation of the Electronic Market Hypothesis, in: European Management Journal, Vol. 17 (3), 318-325

Daum, A. (1993): Erfolgs- und Misserfolgsfaktoren im Büro-Projektmanagement, Rainer Hampp Verlag, München

Davenport, T. H., Short, J. E. (1990): The new industrial engineering: information technology and business process redesign, in: Sloan Management Review, 31(4), 11-27

Davenport, T. H., Stoddard, D. B. (1994): Reengineering: Business change of mythic propositions? In: MIS Quarterly, 18(2), 121-127

David, St., Günther, H.-O., Lochmann, M. (1998): Vermittlung von Produktionsaufträgen im Internet, in: Industrie-Management, 14, 1, 42-45

Denning, P. J., Metcalfe, R. M. (1998): Beyond Calculation – The Next Fifty Years of Computing, New York

Dey, P. K., Ogunlana, S. O. (2001): Project time risk analysis through simulation, in: Cost Engineering, 43(7), 24-28

Dobler, D. W., Burt, D. N. (1996): Purchasing and Supply Management. Text and cases, McGraw-Hill, Singapore

Donada, C. (1999): Vertical Partnerships: Do they pay off for the supplier?, 15th IMP Conference, Dublin

Doney, P. M., Cannon, J. P. (1997): An Examination of the Nature of Trust in Buyer-Seller Relationships, in: Journal of Marketing, 61(4), 35-51

Doney, P. M., Cannon, J. P. , Mullen, M. R. (1998): Understanding the Influence of National Culture on the Development of Trust, in: Academy of Management Review, 23(3), 601-620

Droege, W. P. J. (1998): Gewinne einkaufen, Gabler, Wiesbaden

Dröge, C., Jayaram, J., Vickery, S. K. (2000): The Ability to Minimize the Timing of New Product Development and Introduction: An Examination of Antecedent Factors in the North American Automobile Supplier Industry, in: Journal of Product Innovation Management, 17, 24-40

Du Pont, B. (2001): WWW – Weltweites Wissen. Marktplatz für Technologietransfer im Internet, in: FAZ (15.05.01), B2

Dubinsky, A. J., Ingram T. N. (1984): A Portfolio Approach to Account Profitability, in: Industrial Marketing Management, 13, 33-41

Dubois, A. (1994): Organizing industrial activities, Dissertation, Chalmers University, Göteborg

Dunn, S. C. (2001): Motivation by project and functional managers in matrix organizations, in: Engineering Management Journal, 13(2), 3-9

Dwyer, F. R., Oh, S. (1987): Output Sector Munificence Effects on the Internal Political Economy of Marketing Channels, in: Journal of Marketing Research, 24(11), 347-358

Dwyer, F. R., Schurr, P. H., Oh, S. (1987): Developing Buyer-Seller Relationships, in: Journal of Marketing, 51, 11-27

Dyer, J. H. (1994): Dedicated-Assets: Japan's Manufacturing Edge, in: Harvard Business Review, November-December, 174-178

Dyer, J. H., Cho, D. S., Chu, W. (1998): Strategic Supplier Segmentation: The Next "Best Practice" in Supply Chain Management, in: California Management Review, 40 (2), 57-77

Dyer, J. H., Chu, W. (2000): The Determinants of Trust in Supplier-Automaker Relationships in the US, Japan and Korea, in: Journal of International Business Studies, 31(2), 259

Eastwood, M., Clover, R., Seyfried, A. (2000): B2B – An E-xciting Development, Morgan Stanley Dean Witter Equity Research, London

Eisenhardt, K. M., Sull, D. N. (2001): Strategy as Simple Rules, in: Harvard Business Review, January-February, 107-116

Elliott, G., Glynn, W. (1998): Segmenting Financial Services Markets for Customer Relationships: A Portfolio-Based Approach, in: Service Industries Journal, 18(3), 38-54

Elliott, G., Glynn, W. (2000): Segmenting Industrial Buyers by Loyalty and Value, 16th IMP Conference, Bath

Ellram, L. (1993): Total Cost of Ownership: Elements and Implementation, in: International Journal of Purchasing and Materials Management, Fall, 3-11

Ellram, L. M. (1990): The Supplier Selection Decision in Strategic Partnerships, in: Journal of Purchasing and Materials Management, Fall, 8-14

Ellram, L. M. (1991): A Managerial Guideline for the Development and Implementation of Purchasing Partnerships, in: International Journal of Purchasing and Materials Management, Summer, 2-8

Elofson, G., Robinson, W. N. (1998): Creating a Custom Mass-Production Channel on the Internet, in: Communications of the ACM, 41(3), 56-62

Elsbach, K. D. (1994): Managing Organizational Legitimacy in the California Cattle Industry: The Construction and Effectiveness of Verbal Accounts, in: Administrative Science Quarterly, 39, 57-88

Engelhardt, W. H., Backhaus, K., Günter, B. (1977): Investitionsgüter-Marketing – Eine kritische Analyse und Ansatzpunkte zur Weiterentwicklung, in: Zeitschrift für Betriebswirtschaft, 47, 153-166

Engelhardt, W. H., Günter, B. (1980): Investitionsgüter-Marketing, Verlag Kohlhammer, Stuttgart

Evans, J. R., Berman, B. (2001): Conceptualizing and Operationalizing the Business-to-Business Value Chain, in: Industrial Marketing Management, 30, 135-148

Evans, P. , Wurster, T. (1998): Die Internet-Revolution: Alte Geschäfte vergehen, neue entstehen, in: Harvard Business Manager, 2, 51-62

Evans, P. , Wurster, T. (1999): Getting Real About Virtual Commerce, in: Harvard Business Review, (Nov-Dec), 84-94

Evans, P. , Wurster, T. (2000): E-Commerce: Jetzt geht es ums Geld verdienen, in: Harvard Business Manager, 3, 82-94

Faber, A. (1998): Global Sourcing, Peter Lang, Frankfurt

Farr, C. M., Fischer, W. A. (1992): Managing International High Technology Cooperative Projects, in: R&D Management, 22(1), 55-67

Fingar, P., Kumar, H., Sharma, T. (2000): Enterprise E-Commerce. The Software Component Breakthrough for Business-to-Business Commerce, Meghan-Kiffer Press, Tampa

Fiocca, R. (1982): Account Portfolio Analysis for Strategy Development, in: Industrial Marketing Management, 11, 53-62

Fisher, L. (1969): Industrial Marketing, London

Ford, D. (1980): The Development of Buyer-Seller Relationships in Industrial Markets, in: European Journal of Markteing, 14 (5/6), 339-354

Ford, D. (1997): Understanding Business Markets, Thomson Learning, London

Ford, D., Gadde, L.-E., Hakansson, H., Lundgren, A., Snehota, I., Turnbull, P., Wilson, D. (1999): Managing Business Relationships, John Wiley & Sons, Chichester

Ford, D., Lamming, R., Thomas, R. (1992): Relationship strategy, development and purchasing practice, 8th IMP conference, Lyon

Freiling, J. (1995): Die Abhängigkeit der Zulieferer. Ein strategisches Problem, Gabler, Wiesbaden

Freudenberg, T., Klenk, U. (1996): Strategie-Check für Zulieferer, in: Automobil-Produktion Jubiläum, 52-58

Friedag, H. R., Schmidt, W. (2001): Balanced Scorecard, Haufe Verlag, Freiburg

Fröhlich-Glantschnig, E. (1997): Der Entscheidungsprozeß wird transparent, in: Beschaffung aktuell, (6), 32-34

Fröhling, O. (1999): Portfolios für die Beschaffung, in: Hahn, D., Kaufmann, L.: Handbuch Industrielles Beschaffungsmanagement, Gabler, Wiesbaden, 475-488

Fulkerson, B., Shank, M. (2000): The New Econcomy Electronic Commerce, and the Rise of Mass Customization, in: Shaw, M., Blanning, R., Strader, T., Whinston, A.: Handbook on Electronic Commerce, Springer, Berlin, 411-430

Gadde, L. E., Mattsson, L. G. (1987): Stability and Change in Network Relationships, in: International Journal of Research in Marketing, 4(1), 29-41

Gadde, L.-E., Snehota, I. (1999): Developing Effective Supply Strategy – Is Outsourcing, Single Sourcing and Partnering with Suppliers the only Solution?, 15th IMP Conference, Dublin

Gadde, L.-E., Snehota, I. (2000): Making the Most of Supplier Relationships, in: Industrial Marketing Management, 29 (4), 305-316

Ganesan, S. (1994): Determinants of Long-Term Orientation in Buyer-Seller Relationships, in: Journal of Marketing, 58(4), 1-19

Geck, H. M., Petry, G. (1983): Nachfragermacht gegenüber Zulieferern, Carl Heymanns Verlag, Köln

Gemünden, H. G. (1981): Investitionsgütermarketing. Interaktionsbeziehungen zwischen Hersteller und Verwender innovativer Investitionsgüter, Mohr, Tübingen

Gemünden, H. G. (1990a): Erfolgsfaktoren des Projektmanagements – eine kritische Bestandsaufnahme der empirischen Untersuchungen, in: Projekt Management, 1&2, 4-15

Gemünden, H. G. (1990b): Innovationen in Geschäftsbeziehungen und Netzwerken. Arbeitspapier des Institutes für Angewandte Betriebswirtschaftslehre und Unternehmensführung der Universität Karlsruhe (TH), Karlsruhe

Gemünden, H. G. (1993): Zeit – Strategischer Erfolgsfaktor in Innovationsprozessen, in: Domsch, M., Sabisch, H., Siemers, S.: F&E Management, Schäffer Poeschel, Stuttgart, 67-118

Gemünden, H. G. (1994): Zeit – Strategischer Wettbewerbsfaktor in Innovationsprozessen, in: Projekt Management, 1, 3-14

Gemünden, H.-G. (1985): Perceived risk and information search. A systematic meta-analysis of the empirical evidence, in: International Journal of Research in Marketing, 2, 79-100

Gemünden, H.-G., Högl, M., Lechler, T. und Saad, A. (1999): Starting Conditions of Successful European R&D-Consortia, in: K. Brockhoff, A. Chacrabarti und J. Hauschildt: The Dynamics of Innovation. Strategic and Managerial Implications, Springer, Berlin, 237-275

Gerpott, T. J., Wittkemper, G. (1991): Verkürzung von Produktentwicklungszeiten: Vorgehensweise und Ansatzpunkte zum Erreichen technologischer Sprintfähigkeit, in: Booz, Allen & Hamilton: Integriertes Technologie- und Innovationsmanagement, E. Schmidt, Berlin, 117-145

Gerstenfeld, A. (1976): A Study of Successful Projects, Unsuccessful Projects and Projects in Process in West Germany, in: IEEE Transactions on Engineering Management, 5, 116-123

Ghosh, S. (1998): Rein ins Internet – aber wie?, in: Harvard Business Manager, (5), 86-95

Gierke, L. (1999): Instrumentarium zur Planung und Umsetzung von Zulieferer-Hersteller-Netzwerken, Peter Lang, Frankfurt

Gillies, C., Jayarajan, J., Jenkins, G., Koort, R., Herrmann, L. (2000): e-commerce and chemicals, Deutsche Bank Chemical Research Team, London

Glass, R. L. (1999): Evolving a new theory of project success, in: Communications of the ACM, 42(11), 17-19

Goldman Sachs (1999): B2B e-markets. Internal Report, New York, citation in: Ordanini, A., Pol, A. (2001): Infomediation and Competitive Advantage in B2b Digital Marketplaces, in: European Management Journal, 19(3), 276-285

Göltenboth, M. (1998): Global Sourcing und Kooperationen als Alternativen zur vertikalen Integration, Peter Lang, Frankfurt

Granovetter, M. (1985):Economic Action and Social Structure: The Problem of Embeddedness, in: American Journal of Sociology, 91 (3), p. 481-510

Grant, B., Gadde, L. E. (1984): Auto component supply strategies, CIM Report Paper, Chalmers

Gruen, T. W. (2000): Membership Customers and Relationship Marketing, in: Sheth, J. N., Parvatiyar, A. (2000): Handbook of Relationship Marketing, Sage Publications, Thousand Oaks, 355-380

Guay, D., Ettwein, J. (1998): Internet Commerce Basics, in: Electronic Markets, 8(1), 12-15

Günther, H.-O., Tempelmeier, H. (2000): Produktion und Logistik, Springer, Berlin

Gules, H. K., Burgess, T. F. (1996): Manufacturing technology and the supply chain. Linking buyer-supplier relationships and advanced manufacturing technology, in: European Journal of Purchasing & Supply Management, 2(1), 31-38

Gulley, M. R., McCarthy, K., Chin, H. (2000): Coverage initiated of B2B Chemicals Vertical, Banc of America Securities Research, New York

Gummesson, E. (2000): Total Relationship Marketing. Rethinking Marketing Management: From 4Ps to30Rs, Butterworth-Heinemann, Oxford

Gupta, M., Zhender, D. (1994): Outsourcing and Its Impact on Operations Strategy, in: Production and Inventory Management Journal, (3rd Quart.), 70-76

Habermehl, H. (1996): Feuer am Dach..., in: Logistik Heute, 9, 46-53

Hagel III, J., Rayport, J. F. (1997): The Coming Battle for Customer Information, in: Harvard Business Review, (Jan-Feb), 53-65

Hahn, C. K., Watts, C. A., Kim, K. Y. (1990): The Supplier Development Program: A Conceptual Model, in: Journal of Purchasing and Materials Management, Spring, 2-7

Hahn, D., Kaufmann, L. (1999): Handbuch Industrielles Beschaffungsmanagement, Gabler, Wiesbaden

Hakansson, H., Eriksson, A.-K. (1993): Getting Innovations Out of Supplier Networks, in: Journal of Business-to-Business Marketing, 1(3), 3-33

Hakansson, H., Gadde, L.-E. (1992): Supplier Relations, in: Ford, D. (2000): Understanding Business Markets, Thomson Learning, London, 400-429

Hakansson, H., Lorange, P. (1989): R&D based cooperative ventures, Research Paper 88/14, revised May 1989, Institute of International Business, Stockholm School of Economics, Stockholm

Hakansson, H., Östberg, C. (1975): Industrial Marketing: An Organizational Problem?, in: Industrial Marketing Management, 4, 113

Hallén, L., Johanson, J. (1985): Industrial Marketing Strategies and Different National Environments, in: Journal of Business Research, 13, 495-509

Hallén, L., Johanson, J., Sayed-Mohamed, N. (1991): Interfirm Adaptation in Business Relationships, in: Journal of Marketing, 55, 29-37

Hammann, P., Lohrberg, W. (1986): Beschaffungsmarketing, Schäffer Poeschel, Stuttgart

Hammer, M., Champy, J. (1993): Reengineering the Corporation, Harper Business, New York

Hammer, M., Mangurian, G. E. (1987): The Changing Value of Communications Technology, in: Sloan Management Review, (Winter), 65-71

Handfield, R. B., Ragatz, G. L., Petersen, K. J., Monczka, R. M. (1999): Involving Suppliers in New Product Development, in: California Management Review, 42 (1), 59-82

Harbin, J. (2001): Top Trading Exchange Services for Industry Verticals, AMR Research, May, Boston

Harland, C. M., Lamming, R. C., Cousins, P. D. (1999): Developing the concept of supply strategy, in: International Journal of Operations & Production Management, 19(7), 650-673

Harting, M. C. (2000): Business Exchanges, KPMG, New York

Hartley, J. L., Meredith, J. R., McCutcheon, D., Kamath, R. R. (1997): Suppliers' Contributions to Product Development: An Exploratory Study, in: IEEE Transactions on Engineering Management, 44(3), 258-267

Hartmann, E., Ritter, T., Gemünden, H. G. (2001): Determining the Purchase Situation: Cornerstone of Supplier Relationship Management, 17th IMP conference, Oslo

Hartmann, H. (1992): Lieferantenbewertung - aber wie?, Deutscher Betriebswirte-Verlag, Gernsbach

Hauschildt, J., Chakrabati, A. K. (1988): Arbeitsteilung im Innovationsmanagement, in: Zeitschrift Führung + Organisation, 57, 378-388

Hauschildt, J., Gemünden, H. G. (1999): Promotoren. Champions der Innovation, Gabler, Wiesbaden

Hauschildt, J., Keim, G. (1999): Projektleiter als Prozesspromotor, in: Hauschildt, J., Gemünden, H. G.: Promotoren. Champions der Innovation, Gabler, Wiesbaden, 211-232

Hauschildt, J., Pulcinsky, J. (1992): Rigidität oder Flexibilität der Zielbildung in Innovationsprozessen?, in: zfo, 2, 74-81

Heege, F. (1987): Lieferantenportfolio, VWP Verlag, Nürnberg

Heide, J. B. (1994): Interorganizational Governance in Marketing Channels, in: Journal of Marketing, 58 (1), 71-85

Heide, J. B., John, G. (1988): The Role of Dependence Balancing in Safeguarding Transaction-Specific Assets in Conventional Channels, in: Journal of Marketing, 52(1), 20-35

Heide, J. B., John, G. (1990): Alliances in Industrial Purchasing: The Determinants of Joint Action in Buyer-Supplier Relationships, in: Journal of Marketing Research, 27(2), 24-36

Helfert, G. (1998): Teams im Relationship Marketing. Design effektiver Kundenbeziehungsteams, Gabler, Wiesbaden

Helfert, G., Gemünden, H. G. (1998): Relationship Marketing Team Design: A Powerful Predictor for Relationship Effectiveness, in: ISBM Report # 6-1998, Institute for the Study of Business Markets, Pennsylvania State University, University Park, PA, USA

Hendrix, J. (2001): Seven keys to successful systems-integration projects, in: Heating, Piping, Air Conditioning Engineering, 5, 122-127

Herbig, P. , Shao, A. T. (1993): American Keiretsu: Fad or Future, in: Journal of Business-to-Business Marketing, 1(4), 3-30

Herkommer, F., Pitz, R., Schellmoser, F., Schneck, M., Woller, K. (2001): IT-Services/ERP-Unternehmen, HypoVereinsbank Equity Research, München

Hesse, B. (2001): Kundenbindungsmanagement im Internet. Kritische Erfolgsfaktoren für E-CRM-Projekte, in: FAZ, (15.05.01), B16

Heydebreck, P. (1995): Technologische Verflechtung. Ein Instrument zum Erreichen von Produkt- und Prozessinnovationserfolg, Peter Lang, Frankfurt

Hilbig, W. (1984): Akzeptanzforschung neuer Bürotechnologien. Ergebnisse einer empirischen Fallstudie, in: Office Management, 4, 320-323

Hildebrandt, H., Koppelmann, U. (2000): Beziehungsmanagement mit Lieferanten, Schäffer Poeschel, Stuttgart

Hofer, C. W., Schendel, D. (1978): Strategy Formulation: Analytical Concepts, West Publishing, St. Paul

Högl, M. (1998): Teamarbeit in innovativen Projekten. Einflußgrößen und Wirkungen, Gabler, Wiesbaden

Högl, M., Gemünden, H. G. (2000): Determinanten und Wirkungen der Teamarbeit in innovativen Projekten. Eine theoretische und empirische Analyse, in: Gemünden,, H. G., Högl, M.: Management von Teams. Theoretische Konzepte und empirische Befunde, Gabler, Wiesbaden, 33-66

Homburg, C. (1995): Single Sourcing, Double Sourcing, Multiple Sourcing...?, in: ZfB, 5 (8), 813-834

Homburg, C. (1999): Bestimmung der optimalen Lieferantenzahl für Beschaffungsobjekte. Konzeptionelle Überlegungen und empirische Befunde, in: Hahn, D., Kaufmann, L.: Handbuch Industrielles Beschaffungsmanagement, Gabler, Wiesbaden, 149-167

Homburg, C. (2000): Kundennähe von Industriegüterunternehmen – Konzeptualisierung, organisationale Determinanten und Erfolgsauswirkungen, Gabler, Wiesbaden

Homburg, C., Giering, A. (1996): Konzeptualisierung und Operationalisierung komplexer Konstrukte, in: Marketing ZFP, 1(1), 5-24

Hosmer, L. T. (1995): Trust: The Connecting Link Between Organizational Theory and Philosophical Ethics, in: Academy of Management Journal, 20 (2), 379-403

Howard, J. A., Sheth, J. N. (1969): The Theory of Buyer Behavior, New York

Hubmann, H. E., Barth, M. (1990): Das neue Strategiebewußtsein im Einkauf, in: Beschaffung aktuell, 10, 26-32

Hutzel, J. W: (1981): Große und kleine Zulieferer, Sprint, Tübingen

Jacoby, J. H. (1978): Consumer Research – A State of the Art. Review, in: Journal of Marketing, 42(4), 87-96

Janssen, J., Laatz, W. (1999): Statistische Datenanalyse mit SPSS für Windows, Springer, Berlin

Jekewitz, U. (1992): Verschlafen die Hochschulen die Wirklichkeit?, in: Beschaffung aktuell, (5), 101

Jenkins, M., Nauman, J., Wetherbey, J. (1984): Empirical Investigation of Systems Development Practices and Results, in: Information & Management, 7, 73-82

Johanson, J., Mattsson, L. G. (1987): Interorganizational Relations in Industrial Systems: A Network Approach Compared with the Transaction-Cost Approach, in: International Studies of Management and Organization, 17(1), 34-48

John, G., Reve, T. (1982): The Reliability and Validity of Key Informant Data from Dyadic Relationships in Marketing Channels, in: Journal of Marketing Research, 19(November), 517-524

Johnson, T., Eindhoven, F. W., Zheng, J., Harland, C., Lamming, R. (1999): Networking Activities in Supply Networks, 15th IMP Conference, Dublin

Johnson, W. C., Chinuntdej, N. Weinstein, A. (1999): Creating Value Through Customer and Supplier Relationships, 15th IMP Conference, Dublin

Joseph, J. (1990): Arbeitswissenschaftliche Aspekte der betrieblichen Einführung neuer Technologien am Beispiel von Computer Aided Design (CAD), Peter Lang Verlag, Frankfurt

Joshi, A. W., Stump, R. L. (1999): Determinants of commitment and opportunism: Integrating and extending insights from transaction cost analysis and relational exchange theory, in: Revue Canadienne des Sciences de l'Administration, Vol. 16 (4), 334-352

Kafka, S. J. (2000a): B2B Auctions Go Beyond Price, Forrester Report, Cambridge

Kafka, S. J. (2000b): eMarketplaces Boost B2B Trade, Forrester Research, Cambridge

Kajüter, H., Ruland, D. (2000): Getting the Most Out of eB2B-Bilateral e-Trade vs. e-Markteplaces, in: Scheer, A.-W. (2000): E-Business – Wer geht?, Wer bleibt?, Wer kommt?, Physica-Verlag, Heidelberg, 237-254

Kalbfuß, W. (1998): Einkaufsstrategien, in: Strub, M.: Das große Handbuch Einkaufs- und Beschaffungsmanagement, Verlag Moderne Industrie, Landsberg, 19-38

Kalwani, M. U., Narayandas, N. (1995): Long-Term Manufacturer-Supplier Relationships: Do They Pay Off for Supplier Firms?, in: Journal of Marketing, 59 (1), 1-16

Kamath, R. R., Liker, J. K. (1990): Supplier dependence and innovation: A contingency model of suppliers' innovative activities, in: Journal of Engineering and Technology Management, 7, 111-127

Kamath, R. R., Liker, J. K. (1995): A Second Look at Japanese Product Development, in: Harvard Business Review, November-December, 155-170

Kanter, E. M. (2001): Evolve! Succeeding in the Digital Culture of Tomorrow, Harvard Business School Press, Boston

Kaplan, S., Sawhney, M. (2000a): E-Hubs: The New B2B Marketplaces, in: Harvard Business Review, May/June, 97-103

Kaplan, S., Sawhney, M. (2000b): Revolution im Einkauf - die neuen elektronischen Marktplätze, in: Harvard Business Manager, (6), 56-63

Kapoor, V., Gupta, A. (1997): Aggressive Sourcing: A Free-Market Approach, in: Sloan Management Review, Fall, 21-31

Kaufmann, L. (1995): Strategisches Sourcing, in: zfbf, 47(3), 275-296

Keller, R. T. (2001): Cross-Functional Project Groups in Research and New Product Development: Diversity, Communications, Job Stress, and Outcomes, in: Academy of Management Journal, 44(3), 547-555

Keplinger, W. (1991): Merkmale erfolgreichen Projekt-Managements, dbv-Verlag, Graz

Kern, E., Knauth, P. (2000): Ein System zur Lenkung von teilautonomen Gruppen,. Betriebswirtschaftliche und sozialwissenschaftliche Auswirkungen in der betrieblichen Praxis, in: Gemünden, H. G., Högl, M.: Management von Teams. Theoretische Konzepte und empirische Befunde, Gabler, Wiesbaden, 97-128

Kerrigan, R., Roegner, E. V., Swinford, D. D., Zawada, C. C. (2001): B2Basics, in: McKinsey Quarterly, (1), 1-4

Kiedaisch, I. (1997): Internationale Kunden-Lieferanten-Beziehungen, Gabler, Wiesbaden

Kirsch, W., Kutschker, M. (1978): Das Marketing von Investitionsgütern. Theoretische und empirische Perspektiven eines Interaktionsansatzes, Gabler, Wiesbaden

Kirsch, W., Kutschker, M., Lutschewitz, H. (1980): Ansätze und Entwicklungstendenzen im Investitionsgütermarketing, Schäffer Poeschel, Stuttgart

Klein, L. R., Quelch, J. A. (1997): Business-to-business market making on the Internet, in: International Marketing Review, 14 (5), 345-361

Kleinaltenkamp, M., (1997): Business-to-Business-Marketing, in: Gabler Wirtschafts-Lexikon, Gabler, Wiesbaden

Kleinaltenkamp, M., Fließ, S., Jacob, F. (1996): Customer integration, Gabler, Wiesbaden

Köglmayr, H.-G., Strub, M. F. (1998): Einkaufsorganisation, in: Strub, M. (1998): Das große Handbuch Einkaufs- und Beschaffungsmanagement, Verlag Moderne Industrie, Landsberg/Lech

Körbs, H.-T. (2000): Lernen durch Projekte, in: FB/IE. Zeitschrift für Unternehmensentwicklung und Industrial Engineering, 49(4), 168-174

Kollmann, T. (1999): Wie der virtuelle Marktplatz funktionieren kann, in: Harvard Business Manager, 21 (4), 27-34

Kollmann, T. (2000): Elektronische Marktplätze – Die Notwendigkeit eines bilateralen One-to-one-Marketingansatzes, in: Bliemel, F., Fassott, G., Theobald, A.: Electronic Commerce, Gabler, Wiesbaden, 123-144

Koppelmann, U. (1997): Beschaffungsmarketing für die Praxis, Springer, Berlin

Korper, S., Ellis, J. (2000): The E-Commerce Book. Building the E-Empire, Academic Press, San Diego

Kotabe, M. (1999): Global Sourcing Strategy and Sustainability of Core Competencies. Fundamental Differences between U.S. and Japanese Companies, in: Hahn, D., Kaufmann, L.: Handbuch Industrielles Beschaffungsmanagement, Gabler, Wiesbaden, 187-210

Krähenmann, N. (1994): Ökonomische Gestaltungsanforderungen für die Entwicklung elektronischer Märkte, Difo-Druck, Bamberg

Kraljic, P. (1983): Purchasing must become supply management, in: Harvard Business Review, September-October, 109-117

Krapfel, R. E., Salmond, D., Spekman, R. (1991): A Strategic Approach to Managing Buyer-Seller Relationships, in: European Journal of Marketing, 25(9), 22-37

Kueng, P. (1997): Verbesserung von Geschäftsprozessen durch Prozessmonitoring, in: io Management, 12, 47-55

Kumar, N., Scheer, L. K., Steenkamp, J.-B. (1993): Powerful Suppliers, Vulnerable Resellers, and the Effects of Supplier Fairness: A Cross-National Study, Working paper, Institute for the Study of Business Markets, Pennsylvania State University, State College

Kurz, E., Ortwein, E. (1999): Integrierte Unternehmensstrategien für Electronic Commerce im Business-to-Business-Bereich – Bedeutung, Konzeption und Fallbeispiele von Business Networks, in: Hermann, A., Sauter, M.: Management-Handbuch Electronic Commerce, Verlag Vahlen, München, 129-139

Kusterer, F. (2000): Services in E-Hubs, in: Scheer, A.-W. (2000): E-Business – Wer geht?, Wer bleibt?, Wer kommt?, Physica-Verlag, Heidelberg, 215-235

Kutschker, M., Kirsch, W. (1979): Industriegütermarketing und Einkauf in Europa – Deutschlandstudie, Planungs- und Organisationswissenschaftliche Schriften, München

Lamming, R. (1989): The International Automotive Components Supply Industry: The Next "Best Practice" for Suppliers, MIT, Cambridge

Lamming, R. (1996): Beyond Partnership: Strategies for Innovation and Lean Supply, Prentice Hall, Hempstead

Lamming, R. C., Caldwell, N., Harrison, D. (2000): Developing the concept and practice of transparency in inter-organizational relationships, North American Academy of Management Meeting, Toronto Ontario

Lamming, R. C., Cousins, P. D., Notman, D. M. (1996): Beyond vendor assessment, in: European Journal of Purchasing & Supply Management, 2(4), 173-181

Landeros, R., Reck, R., Plank, R. E. (1995): Maintaining Buyer-Supplier Partnerships, in: International Journal of Purchasing and Materials Management, Summer, 3-11

Larson, E., Gobeli, D. (1989): Significance of Project Management Structure on Development Success, in: IEEE Transactions on Engineering Management, 2, 119-125

Lechler, T. (1997): Erfolgsfaktoren des Projektmanagements, Peter Lang, Frankfurt

Lee, E. C., Whittle, M., Austrian, B. (2000): B2B e-Markets & Trading Hub Primer, Bank of America Securities, San Francisco

Lee, H. G. (1998): Do Electronic Marketplaces Lower the Price of Goods?, in: Communications of the ACM, 41(1), 73-80

Lee, H. G., Clark, T. H. (1997): Market Process Reengineering through Electronic Market Systems: Opportunities and Challenges, in: Journal of Management Information Systems, 13 (3), 113-136

Leek, S., Turnbull, P. W., Naudé, P. (2000): Is the Interaction Approach of Any Relevance in an IT/e-commerce Driven World?, 16th IMP Conference, Bath

Leenders, M. R., Blenkhorn, D. L. (1988): Reverse Marketing, The Free Press, New York

Leifer, R., McDermott, C. M., O'Connor, G. C., Peters, L. S., Rice, M., Veryzer, R. W. (2000): Radical Innovation. How mature companies can outsmart upstarts, Harvard Business School Press, Boston

Levine, J. M., Moreland, R. L. (1990): Progress in small group research, in: Annual Review of Psochology, 41, 585-634

Levitt, T. (1980): Marketing Success Through Differentiation - of Anything, in: Harvard Business Review, 58 (January-February), 83-91

Lief, V. (1999): Net Marketplaces Grow Up, Forrester Research, Cambridge

Lientz, B. P., Rea, K. P. (2001): Project Management for the 21st Century, Academic Press, London

Lingenfelder, M., Lauer, A., Groh, S. (2000): Kundenzufriedenheit im Business-to-Business-Marketing, in: Strauss, B., Bruhn, M.: Jahrbuch für Dienstleistungsmanagement, Gabler, Wiesbaden, 159-195

Liker, J. K., Kamath, R., Wasti, N., Nagamachi, M. (1996): Supplier Involvement in Automotive Component Design: Are there really large US Japan differences?, in: Research Policy, 25(1), 59-89

Liliecreutz, J. (1998): Orchestrating resource base, role, and position: a supplier's strategy in buyer-dominated relationships, in: European Journal of Purchasing & Supply Management, 4, 73-85

Lincoln, J. R., Ahmadjian, C. L., Mason, E. (1998): Organizational Learning and Purchase-Supply Relations in Japan: Hitachi, Matsushita, and Toyota compared, in: California Management Review, 40(3), 241-264

Litke, H.-D. (1995): Projektmanagement, Hanser Verlag, Wien

Littler, D., Leverick, F., Bruce, M. (1995): Factors Affecting the Process of Collaborative Product Development: A Study of UK Manufacturers of Information and Communications Technology Products, in. Journal of Product Innovation Management, 12 (1), 16-23

Lock, D. (1997): Projektmanagement, Wirtschaftsverlag Carl Ueberreuter, Wien

Lovelace, K., Shapiro, D. L., Weingart, L. R. (2001): Maximizing Cross-Functional New Product Teams' Innovativeness and Constraint Adherence: A Conflict Communications Perspective, in: Academy of Management Journal, 44(4), 779-793

Lyons, T. F., Kranchenberg, A. R., Henke, J. W. Jr. (1990): Mixed Motive Marriages: What's Next for Buyer-Supplier Relations?, in: Sloan Management Review, Spring, 29-36

MacLeod, M. (2000): Join the hub, in: SupplyManagement, 03/23, 26-30

MacNeil, I. R. (1980): The New Social Contract, Yale University Press, New Haven

Madauss, B. J. (2000): Handbuch Projektmanagement, Schäffer Poeschel, Stuttgart

Malone, T., Yates, J., Benjamin, R. I. (1987): Electronic markets and electronic hierarchies, in: Communications of the ACM (30), 484-497

Markowitz, H. (1952): Portfolio Selection, in: Journal of Finance, 7, 77-91

Maron, B., Brückner, J. (1998): Aktives Lieferantenmanagement, in: OZ, 43(6), 718-720

Marrian, J. (1968): Marketing Characteristics of Industrial Goods and Buyers, in: Wilson, A.: The Marketing of Industrial Products, London, 10-23

Martin, R. (1993): Einflussfaktoren auf Akzeptanz und Einführungsumfang von Produktionsplanung und –steuerung (PPS). Eine Untersuchung der mittelständischen Industrie, Peter Lang, Frankfurt

Martin, R. (1997): Tools erleichtern die Administration, in: PC Magazin, 10(3), 48-49

Martino, R. L. (1964): Project management and Control. Finding the Critical path, New York

Matthyssens, P. , Van den Bulte, C. (1994): Getting Closer and Nicer: Partnerships in the Supply Chain, in: Longe Range Planning, 27 (1), 72-83

McAllister, D. J. (1995): Affect- and cognition-based trust as foundations for interpersonal cooperation in organizations, in: Academy of Management Journal, 38, 24-59

McCoy, E. A. (1986): Measuring success: Establishing and maintaining a baseline, PMI Annual Seminar & Symposium, Montreal

McCutchean, S. (2000), citation in: Vijayan, J.: B-to-B Portals worry industry, in: Computerworld, 34(8), 80-81

McMillan, J. (1990): Managing Suppliers: Incentive Systems in Japanese and U.S. Industry, in: California Management Review, Summer, 38-55

McQuinston, D. H. (2001): A Conceptual Model for Building and Maintaining Relationships between Manufacturers' Representatives and Their Principals, in: Industrial Marketing Management, 30, 165-181

Merz, M. (1999): Electronic Commerce. Marktmodelle, Anwendungen und Technologien, dpunkt-Verlag, Heidelberg

Metcalf, L. E., Frear, C. R. (1993): The Role of Perceived Product Importance in Organizational Buyer-Seller Relationships, in: Journal of Business-to-Business Marketing, Vol. 1 (3), 63-85

Might, R., Fischer, W. (1985): The Role of Structural Factors in Determining Project Management Success, in: IEEE Transactions on Engineering Management, 2, 71-77

Mirani, R., Moore, D., Weber, J. A. (2001): Emerging Technologies for Enhancing Supplier-Reseller Partnerships, in: Industrial Marketing Management, 30, 101-114

Mische, J., Buchholz, W. (1999): Hoechst Procurement International (HPI). Neuausrichtung der strategischen Beschaffung bei Hoechst, in: Hahn, D., Kaufmann, L.: Handbuch Industrielles Beschaffungsmanagement, Gabler, Wiesbaden, 639-656

Mittner, K. A. (1991): Differenzierte Lieferantenpolitik, in: Beschaffung aktuell, 4, 21-23

Moller, K. K., Halinen, A. (1999): Business Relationships and Networks. Managerial Challenge of Network Era, in: Industrial Marketing Management, 28 (5), 413-427

Möller, K., Törrönen, P. (2000): Business Suppliers' Value Creation Potential: A Conceptual Analysis, 16th IMP Conference, Bath

Monczka, R., Trent, R., Handfield, R. (1998): Purchasing and Supply Chain Management, South-Western College Publishing, Cincinnati

Moorman, C., Zaltman, G., Deshpandé, R. (1992): Relationships Between Providers and Users of Market Research: The Dynamics of Trust Within and Between Organizations, in: Journal of Marketing Research, 29(8), 314-328

Morgan, R. M., Hunt, S. D. (1994): The Commitment-Trust Theory of Relationship Marketing, in: Journal of Marketing, 58 (7), 20-38

Moussa, F. M. (1996): Determinants and Process of the Choice of Goal Difficulty, in: Group & Organization Management, 21(4), 414-438

Müller, E. W. (1990): Gemeinsam Spitzenleistungen erreichen, in: Beschaffung aktuell, 4, 51-53

Müller, E., Preissner, A. (2000): Ihre Chancen im Cyberspace, in: Manager Magazin, 2, p. 141-180

Müller-Böling, D. , Müller, M. (1986): Akzeptanzfaktoren der Bürokommunikation, Oldenbourg Verlag, München

Müller-Merbach, H., Koenig, J., Schulz, S. (2001): Elektronische Marktplätze, in: zfo, 70(4), 249-252

Murphy, D., Baker, N., Fisher, D. (1974): Determinants of Project Success, Boston College, National Aeronautics and Space Administration, Boston

Nachtweh, K.-P. (1998): Prozess- und zielorientierte Lieferantenauswahl, in: Beschaffung aktuell, 2, 41-43

Narasimhan, R., Carter, J. R. (1998): Linking Business Unit and Material Sourcing Strategies, in: Journal of Business Logistics, 19(2), 155-171

Neef, D. (2001): e-Procurement. From Strategy to Implementation, Prentice Hall International, London

Newell, F. (2000): loyalty.com. Customer Relationship Management in the New Era of Internet Marketing, McGraw-Hill, New York

Nokkentved, C. (2000): Collaborative Processes in supply Networks, 16th IMP conference, Bath

Norris, D. G., McNeilly, K. M. (1995): The Impact of Environmental Uncertainty and Asset Specificity on the Degree of Buyer-Seller Commitment, in: Journal of Business-to-Business Marketing, Vol. 2(2), 59-85

Nunnally, J. C. (1978): Psychometric Theory, McGraw Hill, New York

Österle, H., Fleisch, E., Alt, R. (2000): Business Networking. Shaping Enterprise Relationships on the Internet, Springer, Berlin

O'Leary, D. E. (2000): Supply Chain Processes and Relationships for Electronic Commerce, in: Shaw, M., Blanning, R., Strader, T., Whinston, A.: Handbook on Electronic Commerce, Springer, Berlin, 431-444

Olsen, F., Ellram, L. M. (1997): A Portfolio Approach to Supplier Relationships, in: Industrial Marketing Management, 26 (2), 101-113

Ordanini, A., Pol, A. (2001): Infomediation and Competitive Advantage in B2b Digital Marketplaces, in: European Management Journal, 19(3), 276-285

Orths, H. (1999): Neue Abwicklungssysteme für Kleinbestellungen am Beispiel VISA Purchasing Card, in: Hahn, D., Kaufmann, L.: Handbuch Industrielles Beschaffungsmanagement, Gabler, Wiesbaden, 609-621

Palmer, J. W., Johnston, J. S. (1991): Business-to-Business Connectivity on the Internet: EDI, Intermediaries, and Interorganizational Dimensions, in: EM, 6 (2), 3-6

Patel, J. (1999): E-Market Models Matter, in: Informationweek, August 16, 102

Pearson, J. N., Ellram, L. M. (1995): Supplier Selection and Evaluation in Small versus Large Electronic Firms, in: Journal of Small Business Management, (October), 53-65

Pfeffer, J., Salancik, G. (1978): The External Control of Organizations. A resource Dependences Perspective, Harper & Row, citation in: Bourantas, D. (1989): Avoiding Dependence on Suppliers and Distributors, in: Long Range Planning, 22(3), 141

Pfeiffer, W., Tomkins, A. (2000): E-Business in the Chemicals Industry: Success for Those Who Experiment and Learn, Arthur D. Little, London

Phillips, C., Meeker, M. (2000): The B2B Internet Report-Collaborative Commerce, Morgan Stanley Dean Witter, New York

Phillips, L. W. (1981): Assessing Measurement Error in Key Informant Reports: A Methodological Note on Organizational Analysis in Marketing, in: Journal of Marketing Research, 18(November), 395-415

Picot, A., Reichwald, R., Wigand, R. T. (2001): Die grenzenlose Unternehmung-Information, Organisation und Management, Gabler, Wiesbaden

Pinto, M. B., Pinto, J. K., Prescott, J. E. (1993): Antecedents and consequences of project team cross-functional cooperation, in: Management Science, 39(10), 1281-1297

Piontek, J. (1997): Global Sourcing, Oldenbourgh Verlag, München

Platz, J., Schmelzer, H. (1986): Projektmanagement in der industriellen Forschung und Entwicklung, Springer Verlag, Heidelberg

Ploss, T., Johnson, E. (2000): E-Marketplaces in Chemicals, PriceWaterhouseCoopers, London

Porter, A. M. (2000a): A purchasing manager's guide to the E-procurement galaxy, in: Purchasing, (21/09), S72-S88

Porter, A. M. (2000b): E-Auction model morphs to meet buyers' needs, in: Purchasing, (15/06), S31-S46

Porter, M. E. (1996): Wettbewerbsvorteile, Campus, Frankfurt

Portum (2000): Reaping profits with purchasing auctions, in: Frick, H. M.: E-procurement in der Praxis, ZfU Zentrum für Unternehmensführung, Konferenz 18.-19. September, Thalwil

Prahalad, Hamel (1995): Wettlauf um die Zukunft, Ueberreuter, Wien

Provan, K. G. (1993): Embeddedness, Interdependence, and Opportunism in Organizational Supplier- Buyer Networks, in: Journal of Management, 19 (4), 841-856

Pugh, D. S., Hickson, D. J., Hinings, C. R., Macdonald, K. M., Turner, C., Lupton, T. (1963): A Conceptual Scheme for Organizational Analysis, in: Administrative Science Quarterly, 8, 289

Quayle, M. (1995): Changing a supplier – How do they do that?, in: Purchasing & Supply Management, January, 26-32

Quelch, J. A., Klein, L. R. (1996): The Internet and International Marketing, in: Sloan Management Review, Spring, 60-75

Quinn, J. B. (1999): Core-Competency-with-Outsourcing Strategies in Innovative Companies, in: Hahn, D., Kaufmann, L.: Handbuch Industrielles Beschaffungsmanagement, Gabler, Wiesbaden, 33-52

Raisch, W. D. (2001): The E-Marketplace Strategies for Success in B2B E-Commerce, McGraw-Hill, New York

Ravitz, L., Lee, R. (2000): Diversified Chemicals: E-nough!, in: B2Basic Materials. The Supply Chain Moves Online, Equity Research Morgan Stanley Dean Witter, New York, 26-35

Rebstock, M. (1998): Electronic Commerce, in: DBW, 58 (2), 265-267

Reck, R. F., Long, B. G. (1988): Purchasing: A Competitive Weapon, in: Journal of Purchasing and Materials Management, Fall, 2-8

Reichheld, F. F., Schefter, P. (2001): Warum Kundentreue auch im Internet zählt, in: Harvard Business manager, 1, 70-81

Reid, D. A., Plank, R. E. (2000): Organizational Buying, in: Journal of Business-to-Business Marketing, 7 (2/3), 36-127

Reim, F. (1997): WWW ändert Verhältnis von Kunden zu Lieferant, in: Office Management, (4), 19-22

Rexha, N. (2000): Integrating Relationship Marketing Activities with Offering Quality in the Supplier's Relational Marketing Program, in: Journal of Business-to-Business Marketing, 7(1), 1-17

Riebel, P. (1965): Typen der Markt- und Kundenproduktion in produktions- und absatzwirtschaftlicher Sicht, in: Zeitschrift für betriebswirtschaftliche Forschung, 17, 633-685

Rinza, P. (1985): Projekmanagement, Planung, Überwachung und Steuerung von technischen und nichttechnischen Vorhaben, VDI Verlag, Düsseldorf

Ritter, T. (1998): Innovationserfolg durch Netzwerkkompetenz, Gabler, Wiesbaden

Roberts, B., Mackay, M. (1998): IT supporting supplier relationships: The role of electronic commerce, in: European Journal of Purchasing and Supply Management, 4, 175-184

Robinson, P. J., Faris, C. W., Wind, Y. (1967): Industrial Buying and Creative Marketing, Boston

Rodin, R., Hartmann, C. (1999): Free, Perfect, and Now. Connecting to the Three Insatiable Customer Demands: A CEO's True Story, Simon & Schuster, New York

Rohrmann, B. (1978): Empirische Studien zur Entwicklung von Antwortskalen für die sozialwissenschaftliche Forschung, in: Zeitschrift für Sozialpsychologie, 9, 222-245

Rosson, P. (2000): Electronic Trading Hubs: Review and Research Questions, 16th IMP conference, Bath

Rothman, S. (2000): Industry can learn from past project failures, in: Oil & Gas Journal, 98(17), 37-40

Ruekert, R. W., Churchill, G. A. Jr. (1984): Reliability and Validity of Alternative Measures of Channel Member Satisfaction, in: Journal of Marketing Research, 21(5), 226-233

Ryssel, R., Ritter, T., Gemünden, H. G. (2000): Trust, Commitment and Value-Creation in Inter-Organizational Customer-Supplier Relationships, 16th IMP Conference, Bath

Saad, A. (1998): Anbahnung und Erfolg von europäischen kooperativen F&E-Projekten, Peter Lang, Frankfurt

Sakakibara, K. (1993): R&D cooperation among competitors: A case study of the VLSI Semiconductor Research Project in Japan, in: Journal of Engineering and Technology Management, 10, 393-407

Sander, J., Behlke, J. (2001): Leitfaden Internetmarktplätze. Investitionsgüterindustrie, VDMA Verlag, Frankfurt

Saunders, M. (1997): Strategic Purchasing & Supply Chain Management, 2nd Edition, Prentice Hall, Essex

Sauter, M. (1999): Chancen, Risiken und strategische Herausforderungen des Electronic Commerce, in: Hermanns, A., Sauter, M.: Management-Handbuch Electronic Commerce, Verlag Vahlen, München, 101-117

Sawhney, M., Kaplan, S. (1999): The Emerging Landscape of Business to Business E-Commerce, to appear in Business 2.0 Magazine September 1999

Scheer, A.-W.: E-Business. Wer geht? Wer bleibt? Wer kommt?, Physica-Verlag, Heidelberg

Schlueter-Langdon, C. (2001): Elektronische Märkte und Netze ändern Industriestrukturen, in: FAZ, (11/91), 23

Schmelzer, H. (1986): Aufbauorganisation, in: Platz, J., Schmelzer, H.: Projektmanagement in der industriellen Forschung und Entwicklung, Springer Verlag, Heidelberg

Schmelzer, H. (1992): Organisation und Controlling von Produktentwicklungen. Praxis des wettbewerbsorientierten Entwicklungsmanagement, Schäffer Poeschel, Stuttgart

Schmid, B. (1991): Elektronische Märkte, in: EM, 9 (1), 1-6

Schmid, B. (1993): Electronic Markets, in: EM, 9-10 (10), 3-4

Schneider, D., Schnetkamp, G. (2000): E-Markets. B2B-Strategien im Electronic Commerce, Galber, Wiesbaden

Schnell, R., Hill, P., Esser, E. (1999): Methoden der empirischen Sozialforschung, Oldenbourg Verlag, München

Scholz, C. (1992): Effektivität und Effizienz, in: Frese, E.: Handwörterbuch der Organisation, C.E. Poeschel Verlag, Stuttgart

Schönecker, H. (1985): Kommunikationstechnik und Bedienerakzeptanz, CW-Publikationen, München

Schuh, G., Müller, M., Tockenbürger, L. (1998): Controlling von Change-Management Projekten. Konzeptionelles Vorgehen erleichtert Überwindung mentaler Barrieren bei Change-Projekten, in: IO Management, 7/8, 26-30

Schwartz, R. J., Gremmels, D., Brosseau, D. (1999): Business-To-Business E-Commerce – Here Come The Online Intermediaries, SG Cowen, New York

Scott-Morton, M. S. (1991): The Cooperation of the 1990s: Information Technology and Organisational Transformation, Oxford University Press, New York

Sculley, A. B., Woods, W. W. A. (1999): B2B Exchanges. The Killer Applications in the Business-to-Business Internet Revolution, ISI Publications, New York

Seggewiß, K.-H. (1985): Die Organisation der Materialwirtschaft in Großunternehmungen, Peter Lang, Frankfurt

Sebastian, K.-H., Niederdrenk, R.(1999): Beschaffung und Verkauf – Von der Konfrontation zur Kooperation, in: Hahn, D., Kaufmann, L.: Handbuch Industrielles Beschaffungsmanagement, Gabler, Wiesbaden, 381-398

Seely, M. A., Duong, Q. P. (2001): The dynamic baseline model for project management, in: Project Management Journal, 32(2), 25-36

Seybold, P. B. (1998): customers.com. How to create a profitable business strategy for the internet and beyond, Times Business Random House, New York

Shapiro, B. P., Rangan, V. K., Moriarty, R. T., Ross, E. B. (1987): Manage Customers for Profits, in: Harvard Business Review, September-October, 101-108

Shaw, M. (2000): Electronic Commerce: State of the Art, in: Shaw, M., Blanning, R., Strader, T., Whinston, A.: Handbook on Electronic Commerce, Springer, Berlin, 3-24

Shaw, M., Blanning, R., Strader, T., Whinston, A. (2000): Handbook on Electronic Commerce, Springer, Berlin

Sheth, J. N., Sharma, A. (1997): Supplier Relationships: Emerging Issues and Challenges, in: Industrial Marketing Management, 26 (2), 91-100

Sheth, J., Parvatiyar, A. (2000): Relationship Marketing, Sage Publications, Thousand Oaks

Siguaw, J. A., Simpson, R. M., Baker, T. L. (1998): Effects of Supplier Market Orientation on Distributor Market Orientation and the Channel Relationship: The Distributor Perspective, in: Journal of Marketing, 62(7), 99-111

Simon, H. (1989): Die Zeit als strategischer Erfolgsfaktor, in: ZfB, 59 (1), 70-93

Simpson, J. (2001): The measure of success, in: Intelligent Enterprise, 4(10), 22-23

Singh, A., Vlatas, D. A. (1991): Using conflict management for better decision making, in: Journal of Management in Engineering, 7(1), 70-82

Skarmeas, D. A, Katsikeas, C. S. (2001): Drivers of Superior Importer Performance in Cross-Cultural Supplier-Reseller Relationships, in: Industrial Marketing Management, 30, 227-241

Skinner, S. (2000): Business to Business e-Commerce-Investment Perspective, Durlacher Research, London

Skulmoski, G. (2001): Project maturity and competence interface, in: Cost Engineering, 43(6), 11-18

Smeltzer, L. R. (1997): The Meaning and Origin of Trust in Buyer-Supplier Relationships, in: International Journal of Purchasing and Materials Management, Winter, 40-48

Soellner, F. N., Mackrodt, C. (1999): Leadership Practices in Procurement Management, in: Hahn, D., Kaufmann, L.: Handbuch Industrielles Beschaffungsmanagement, Gabler, Wiesbaden, 75-99

Sotiriou, D., Wittmer, D. (2001): Influence methods of project managers: Perceptions of team members and project managers, in: Project Management Journal, 32(3), 12-20

Standifird, S. S. (2001): Reputation and e-commerce: eBay auctions and the asymmetrical impact of positive and negative ratings, in: Journal of Management, 27, 279-295

Stearns Sgarioto, M. (2000): Internet-based trade exchanges, in: Manufacturing Systems, (December), http://www.manufacturingsystems.com/archives/2000/dec/ms1200f4.asp

Stern, L. W. (1988): Reflections on Channel Research, in: Journal of Retailing, 64(Spring), 1-4

Stevens, M. J., Campion, M. A. (1994): The knowledge, skill, and ability requirements for teamwork: Implications for human resource management, in: Journal of Management, 20(2), 503-530

Stewart, G. L., Barrick, M. R. (2000): Team Structure and Performance: Assessing the Mediation Role of Intrateam Process and the Moderating Role of Task Type, in: Academy of Management Journal, 43(2), 135-148

Stewart, W. E. (2001): Balanced scorecard for projects, in: Project Management Journal, 32(1), 38-53

Stier, W. (1999): Empirische Forschungsmethoden, Springer, Berlin

Stoddard, D. B., Jarvenpaa, S. L. (1995): Business process redesign: Tactics for managing radical change, in: Journal of Management Information Systems, 12(1), 81-107

Stoelzle, W. (2000): Beziehungsmanagement – Konzeptverständnis und Implikationen für die Beschaffung, in: Hildebrandt, H., Koppelmann, U.: Beziehungsmanagement mit Lieferanten, Schäffer Poeschel, Stuttgart, 1-24

Stone, M., Woodcock, N., Wilson, M. (1996): Managing the Change from Marketing Planning to Customer Relationship Management, in: Long Range Planning, 29(10), 675-683

Strader, T. J., Shaw, M. J. (2000): Electronic Markets: Impact and Implications, in: Shaw, M., Blanning, R., Strader, T., Whinston, A.: Handbook on Electronic Commerce, Springer, Berlin, 77-98

Strub, M. (1998): Das große Handbuch Einkaufs- und Beschaffungsmanagement, Verlag Moderne Industrie, Landsberg/Lech

Stuart, F. I. (1993): Supplier Partnerships: Influencing Factors and Strategic Benefits, in: International Journal of Purchasing and Materials Management, Fall, 22-28

Stuart, F. I., Mueller, P. Jr. (1994): Total Quality Management and Supplier Partnerships: A Case Study, in: International Journal of Purchasing and Materials Management, Winter, 14-20

Stump, R. L. (1995): Antecedents of Purchasing Concentration: A Transaction Cost Explanation, in: Journal of Business Research, 34, 145-157

Stump, R. L., Heide, J. B. (1996): Controlling Supplier Opportunism in Industrial Relationships, in: Journal of Marketing Research, 33(11), 431-441

Stundza, T. (1999): E-Commerce is expanding – slowly, mostly in chemicals, in: Purchasing, (21/10), S14-S29

Tan, G. W., Shaw, M. J., Fulkerson, W. (2000): Web-based Global Supply Chain Management, in: Shaw, M., Blanning, R., Strader, T., Whinston, A.: Handbook on Electronic Commerce, Springer, Berlin, 457-478

Tanner, J. F. Jr., Castleberry, S. B. (1993): The Participation Model: Factors Related to Buying Decision Participation, in: Journal of Business-to-Business Marketing, 1(3), 35-61

Tapscott, D. (1998): Blueprint to the Digital Economy. Creating Wealth in the Era of E-Business, McGraw Hill, New York

Taylor, D., Berg, T. (1995): The Business Value of Electronic Commerce, Gartner Group, September

Thomas, E. (2000): Opening bids, in: Supply Management, (21/09), 36-37

Thompson, K. N. (1991): Scaling Evaluative Criteria and Supplier Performance Estimates in Weighted Point Prepurchase Decision Models, in: International Journal of Purchasing and Materials Management, Winter, 27-36

Thorelli, H. B. (1986): Networks: Between Markets and Hierarchies, in: Strategic Management Journal, (7), 37-51

Ticoll, D., Lowy, A. (1998): Joined at the Bit. The Emergence of the E-Business Community, in: Tapscott, D.: Blueprint to the Digital Economy. Creating Wealth in the Era of E-Business, McGraw Hill, New York, 19-33

Timmers, P. (2000): Electronic Commerce. Strategies and models for business-to-business trading, John Wiley & Sons, Chichester

Turnbull, P. W. (1983): A Review of Portfolio Planning Models for Industrial Marketing and Purchasing Management, in: European Journal of Marketing, 24 (3), 7-22

Turnbull, P. W., Zolkiewski, J. (1995): Profitability in Customer Portfolio Planning, 11th IMP Conference, Manchester

Tushman, M., Katz, R. (1980): External Communication and Project Performance: An Investigation into the Role of Gatekeepers, in: Management Science, 11, 1071-1085

Tuten, T. L., Urban, D. J. (2001): An Expanded Model of Business-to-Business Partnership Formation and Success, in: Industrial Marketing Management, 30, 149-164

Utterback, J., Allen, T., Hollomon, J., Sirbu, M. (1976): The Process of Innovation in Five Industries in Europe and Japan, in: IEEE Transactions On Engineering Management, 3, 3-9

Van Doesburg, H., Rees, R., Simons, T. J. (1999): The Changing Structure of the Global Chemical industry, Andersen Consulting, London

Van Heck, E. (2000): The Cutting Edge in Auctions, in: Harvard Business Review, March-April, 18-19

Van Weele, A. J. (2000): Purchasing and Supply Chain Management. Analysis, Planning and Practice, Thomson Learning, London

Venkatesan, R. (1992): Strategic Sourcing: To Make or Not to Make, in: Harvard Business Review, November-December, 98-107

Venkatraman, N. (2000): Five Steps to a Dot-Com Strategy: How to Find Your Footing on the Web, in: Sloan Management Review, 42(2), 15-28

Vijayan, J. (2000): B-to-B Portals worry industry, in: Computerworld, 34(8), 80-81

Vollmann, T. E., Cordon, C. (1998): Building Successful Customer-Supplier Alliances, in: Long Range Planning, 31(5), 684-694

Von Hippel, E. (1988): The Sources of Innovation, Oxford University Press, New York

Voss, W. (2000): Praktische Statistik mit SPSS, Hanser Verlag, München

Walter, A. (1998): Der Beziehungspromotor. Ein personaler Gestaltungsansatz für erfolgreiches Relationship Marketing, Gabler, Wiesbaden

Walter, A., Müller, T. A., Helfert, G. (2000): The Impact of Satisfaction, Trust, and Relationship Value on Commitment: Theoretical Considerations and Empirical Results, 16th IMP Conference, Bath

Walter, A., Ritter, T., Gemünden, H. G. (1999): Value Creating Functions of Customer Relationships from a Supplier's Perspective: Theoretical Considerations and Empirical Results, 15th IMP Conference, Dublin

Walter, A., Ritter, T., Gemünden, H.-G. (2001): Value-Creation in Buyer-Seller-Relationships: Theoretical Considerations and Empirical Results from a Supplier's Perspective, in: Industrial Marketing Management, 30(4), 365-378

Wasti, S. N., Liker, J. K. (1999): Collaborating with Suppliers in Product Development: A U.S. and Japan Comparative Study, in: IEEE Transactions on Engineering Management, 46(4), 444-461

Wateridge, J. (1998): How can IT/IS projects be measured for success, in: International Journal of Project Management, 16(1), 59-63

Watts, C. A., Kim, K. Y., Hahn, C. K. (1992): Linking Purchasing to Corporate Competitive Strategy, in: International Journal of Purchasing and Materials Management, Fall, 2-8

Weber, J. A. (2001): Partnering with Resellers in Business Markets, in: Industrial Marketing Management, 30, 87-99

Webster, F. E., Wind, Y. (1972): Organizational Buying Behavior, Englewood Cliffs, New Jersey

Weiber, R., Krämer, T. (2001): Paradoxien des Electronic Business und Ansatzpunkte zur Überwindung, in: zfo, 70(4), 188-196

Wells, W. G. (1998): From the editor, in: Project Management Journal, 29(4), 4-6

Weltz, F., Ortmann, R. (1992): Das Sotware-Projekt. Projektmanagement in der Praxis, Campus Verlag, Frankfurt

Wertz, B. (2000): Management von Lieferanten-Produzenten-Beziehungen, Gabler, Wiesbaden

Westland, J. C., Clark, T. H. K. (2000): Global Electronic Commerce. Theory and Case Studies, The MIT Press, Cambridge

Wichmann, T., Weitzel, U. (1999): Virtual Intermediaries: Business-to-Business Marketplaces on the Internet, Berlecon Research, Berlin

Wildemann, H. (1996): Produktions- und Zuliefernetzwerke, Transfer-Centrum-Verlag, München

Wildemann, H. (1997): Koordination von Unternehmensnetzwerken, in: ZfB, 67 (4), 417-438

Wildemann, H. (1999): Das Konzept der Einkaufspotentialanalyse, in: Hahn, D., Kaufmann, L.: Handbuch Industrielles Beschaffungsmanagement, Gabler, Wiesbaden, 435-452

Wilkinson, I. F., Young, L. C. (1996): Business Dancing – The Nature and Role of Interfirm Relations in Business Strategy, in: Asia-Australia Marketing Journal, 2(1), 67-79

Williams, T. M. (1995): A Classified Bibliography of Recent Research Relating to Project Risk Management, in: European Journal of Operational Research, 85, 18-38

Williamson, O. E. (1975): Markets and Hierarchies: Analysis and Antitrust Implications, Free Press, New York

Williamson, O. E. (1979): Transaction cost economics: The governance of contractual relations, in: Journal of Law and Economics, 22(10), 223-261

Williamson, P. J. (1991): Supplier strategy and customer responsiveness: Managing the links, in: Business Strategy Review, Summer, 75-90

Wilson, D. T. (1995): An Integrated Model of Buyer-Seller Relationships, in: Journal of the Academy of Marketing Science, 23 (4), 335-345

Wilson, D. T., Jantrania, S. (1996): Understanding the Value of a Relationship, in: Asia-Ausralia Marketing Journal, 2 (1), 55-66

Wilson, D. T., Jantrania, S. (1996): Understanding the Value of a Relationship, in: Asia-Australia Marketing Journal, 2(1), 55-66

Wilson, E. J., Woodside, A. G. (1995): The Relative Importance of Choice Criteria in Organizational Buying: Implications for Adaptive Selling, in: Journal of Business-to-Business Marketing, 2(1), 33-57

Wind, Y., Douglas, S. (1981): International Portfolio & Strategy – The Challenge of the 80s, in: Journal of International Business Studies, Fall, 69-82

Windham, L. (1999): Dead Ahead. The Web dilemma and the new rules of business, Allworth Press, New York

Wirtz, B. W. (2000): Electronic Business, Gabler, Wiesbaden

Wirtz, B. W., Lihotzky, N. (2001): Internetökonomie, Kundenbindung und Portalstrategie, in: DBW 61(3), 285-305

Wise, R., Morrison, D. (2000): Beyond the Exchange. The Future of B2B, in: Harvard Business Review, (Nov-Dec), 86-96

Witt, F.-J. (1986): Beschaffungs-Portfolios als strategisches Instrument, in: Beschaffung aktuell, 11, 33-35

Wolff, H., Beche, G., Delpho, H., Kuhlmann, S., Kuntze, U., Stock, J. (1994): FuE-Kooperationen von kleinen und mittleren Unternehmen: Bewertung der Fördermaßnahmen des Bundesforschungsministerium, Physika-Verlag, Heidelberg

Wolters, H. (1996): Auswirkungen der Systembeschaffung für die Customer Integration aus Sicht von Zulieferunternehmen der Automobilindustrie, in: Kleinaltenkamp, M., Fließ, S., Jacob, F.: Customer Integration. Von der Kundenorientierung zur Kundenintegration, Gabler, Wiesbaden, 233-244

Wolters, P. (1999): Forward Sourcing – Entwicklungsbegleitende Lieferantenauswahl, in: Hahn, D., Kaufmann, L.: Handbuch Industrielles Beschaffungsmanagement, Gabler, Wiesbaden, 253-264

Womack, J. P. , Jones, D. T., Roos, D. (1990): The Machine That Changed the World, MacMillan Publishing Company, New York

Woodruff, R. B. (1997): Customer Value: The Next Source for Competitive Advantage, in: Journal of the Academy of Marketing Science, 25(2), 139-153

Yang, B. R. (2000): Supply Chain Management: Developing Visible Design Rules across Organizations, in: Shaw, M., Blanning, R., Strader, T., Whinston, A.: Handbook on Electronic Commerce, Springer, Berlin, 445-456

Yap, N. (2001): New eProject tools for project managers, in: Computimes Malaysia, 7, 1

Zeithaml, V. A. (1988): Consumer Perceptions of Price, Quality and Value: A Means-End Model and Synthesis of Evidence, in: Journal of Marketing, 52 (7), 2-22

Zeithaml, V. A., Bitner, M. J. (2000): Services Marketing. Integrating Customer Focus Across the Firm, McGraw Hill, Boston

Zenz, P. (1981): Die betriebswirtschaftliche Beurteilung von Forschungs- und Entwicklungsleistungen im Industriebetrieb, Dissertation, Frankfurt

Zheng, J., Johnsen, T., Harland, C. M., Lamming, R. C. (1998): Initial Conceptual Framework for creation and Operation of Supply Networks, 14th IMP Conference, Turku, 591-613

Zimmermann, H.-D. (2000): Aktuelle Entwicklungen im Kontext Elektronischer Märkte, in: NetAcademy, St. Gallen

Zogg, A. (1974): Systemorientiertes Projekt-Management, Zürich

Zwass, V. (1996): Electronic commerce: structure and issues, in: International Journal of Electronic Commerce, 1(1), 3-23

11 Appendix

Correlations	Project efficiency	Project effectiveness	B2B E-market-place acceptance	Project success
Purchasing strategy	.22***	.24***	.21***	.29***
IT strategy	.21**	.26***	.15*	.27***
Procurement strategy	.22***	.26***	.19**	.30***
Purchasing competence	.12*	.23***	.31***	.27***
IT competence	.29**	.10	.18**	.26***
Procurement competence	.24***	.19**	.28***	.31***
Top management support	.22***	.19**	.37***	.33***
Team competence	.44***	.36***	.09	.42***
Project panning/steering	.16**	.29***	.41***	.36***
Project management	.32***	.33***	.38***	.45***

*** : 1% significance level (1-sided)
** : 5% significance level (1-sided)
* : 10% significance level (1-sided)

Table 11.1 Detailed correlation analysis to proposition 2, 3 and 6

Regression analysis	Project efficiency		Project effectiveness		B2B E-market-place acceptance		Project success	
	Std Beta	Sig. level	Std Beta	Sig. level	Std Beta	Sig. level	Std Beta	Sig. level
Procurement strategy	.17	.065	.22	.016	.12	.177	.22	.008
Procurement competence	.09	.350	.01	.885	.13	.196	.10	.275
Project management	.26	.009	.30	.002	.31	.002	.37	.000
R²	.141		.158		.172		.262	
F	6.289	.001	7.184	.000	7.988	.000	13.581	.000

Bold values are significant.

Table 11.2 Detailed regression analysis to proposition 2, 3 and 6

Correlations	Top management support	Team competence	Project planning and steering	Project management
Purchasing strategy	.06	.06	.15*	.11
IT strategy	.08	.19**	.14*	.16**
Procurement strategy	.07	.13*	.15*	.14*
Purchasing competence	.59***	.29***	.20**	.46***
IT competence	.43***	.01	.18**	.28***
Procurement competence	.60***	.17**	.22***	.43***

*** : 1% significance level (1-sided)
** : 5% significance level (1-sided)
* : 10% significance level (1-sided)

Table 11.3 Detailed correlation analysis to proposition 4 and 5

Regression analysis	Top management support		Team competence		Project planning and steering		Project management	
	Std Beta	Sig. level	Std Beta	Sig. level	Std Beta	Sig. level	Std Beta	Sig. level
Procurement strategy	- .07	.341	.09	.325	.10	.266	.04	.638
Procurement competence	**.61**	**.000**	.15	.115	**.20**	**.036**	**.42**	**.000**
R²	**.360**		.037		**.059**		**.187**	
F	32.559	.000	2.250	.110	3.660	.029	13.353	.000

Bold values are significant.

Table 11.4 Detailed regression analysis to proposition 4 and 5

GPSR Compliance
The European Union's (EU) General Product Safety Regulation (GPSR) is a set
of rules that requires consumer products to be safe and our obligations to
ensure this.

If you have any concerns about our products, you can contact us on

ProductSafety@springernature.com

In case Publisher is established outside the EU, the EU authorized
representative is:

Springer Nature Customer Service Center GmbH
Europaplatz 3
69115 Heidelberg, Germany